Keto Air Fryer Cookbook for Beginners

Keto Air Fryer Cookbook for Beginners

800 Easy and Quick Keto Diet Recipes for Beginners and Advanced Users

Grant Kelly

Disclaimer Notice:

Please note the information contained within this document is for educational and entertainment purposes only. All effort has been executed to present accurate, up to date, reliable, complete information. No warranties of any kind are declared or implied. Readers acknowledge that the author is not engaged in the rendering of legal, financial, medical or professional advice. The content within this book has been derived from various sources. Please consult a licensed professional before attempting any techniques outlined in this book.

By reading this document, the reader agrees that under no circumstances is the author responsible for any losses, direct or indirect, that are incurred as a result of the use of the information contained within this document, including, but not limited to, errors, omissions, or inaccuracies.

CONTENT

Chapter 1 Is Keto Just Another Diet Craze?   1

Chapter 2 The World's Laziest Cook!   6

Chaptr 3 Breakfast   8

Chapter 4 Appetizers and Snacks   25

Chapter 5 Side Dishes 39

Chapter 6 Vegetarian Mains   51

Chapter 7 Poultry   64

Chapter 8 Beef, Pork, and Lamb   87

Chapter 9 Fish and Seafood   114

Chapter 10 Desserts   130

Chapter 11 Staples   143

Appendix 1: Measurement Conversion Chart 148

Appendix 2: Air Fryer Cooking Chart   149

Appendix 3: Recipe Index 151

Chapter 1 Is Keto Just Another Diet Craze?

A lot of diets are specially tailored to suit different types of people. They cover very different dietary needs and individual preferences. A lot of modern diets are very good. They will generally help you to lose weight and be healthier. The keto diet is, for me, better than any of the numerous others that I have tried.

Why not follow these recipes for a month? I promise, you will really enjoy amazing health benefits from following a keto diet, and you may be persuaded to continue, because it is so easy, and the keto-friendly food that you can make in your air fryer is so delicious!

Let Me Tell You about Keto

The ketogenic diet, or keto, is a very low-carb, moderate-protein, and high-fat diet that allows the body to fuel itself without the use of glucose or high levels of carbohydrates. Keto diets have been around for a long time, and it has been scientifically proven that keto is completely natural for your body. So, it's not some new fad. Ketogenic eating is an extremely effective means of losing weight quickly and keeping the weight off. Typically, a ketogenic diet restricts carbs to 0–50 grams per day.

Carbohydrates are not all bad. They do a great job, by giving you lots of energy. The downside it that they also help you pack on fat that you don't need. This is because carbs are converted into sugar once your body has processed them. A bowl of pasta (even the whole-grain stuff) simply converts to sugar! Same with fruit juice/smoothies. You may think they are doing your body good, but they are poisoning you with sugar! And we all know that sugar will cause you to gain weight.

If you take the plunge and go keto, you will have to cut out fruit juices, and those "diet" soft drinks that you think are helpful for maintaining a healthy weight. To successfully go keto, you need to start re-thinking how you eat. You need to make some lifestyle changes too.

Why Do I Eat Keto?

I was in excellent health and very fit until I turned forty. I was always health conscious, and I ate what I thought were the best foods to keep me strong and fit. I consulted a dietician and nutritionist when I began to gain weight inexplicably.

My doctor tested my blood, and found that I had quite a high level of blood sugar, and my cholesterol levels were not too impressive either. The dietician confirmed for me that my metabolism had changed–it slowed down in middle age–so I would have to adjust my diet and exercise regime if I wanted to maintain a healthy weight. For women, menopause also plays a large part in changes to metabolic rates, so see your doctor if you suspect that you may be peri-menopausal.

On the advice of my dietician, I tried a few of the popular, conventional diet plans on the market. I did lose some weight, temporarily. I found the diets both limiting and boring, and I would lapse frequently. So, as quickly as they came off, the kilos came back on again!

As with most middle-aged people, my excess fat was around my middle. My health was suffering. I felt tired all day, and I craved carbs and sugar. It just became a depressing cycle of diet-lose-weight-lapse-gain-weight.

I found a book on ketogenic eating in my local library, and I looked at the delicious-looking food. I love to eat, so that was all the inspiration that I needed to start thinking about keto! I decided to try eating keto for one month, and I promised myself that if I got a weight loss result that impressed me, I would keep going. The meals I tried out were easy and fuss-free. There were no expensive foods involved that were hard to source. By the end of my first week on the keto diet I didn't feel so good, but I had read that this was a normal reaction to my body adjusting, so I pressed on. By the end of that month, eating exclusively keto, I felt much better, so I committed myself to a six-month trial. At this stage, I figured that some further research was essential. And I also wanted to check out different ways to prepare food.

Now I'm Making Healthier Choices!

I read numerous blogs, books and websites about ketogenic diet to confirm that I could be healthy if I ate like this. I am not a particularly good cook. So, it was important for me to work out some combinations that I could use to maintain ketosis, yet not have to be thinking about what I was going to cook every hour of the day.

Keto Works in Mysterious Ways!

A ketogenic diet places your body into a new metabolic state, which is called ketosis. After you eat fewer carbs, and high amounts of protein for just three days, your body will start to take its energy from the ketones that are stored in fats. So, instead of using the sugars that are stored in the carbs you eat, the fats are what give you energy. In this state of ketosis it is much easier to lose weight. There are other health benefits too: Increased cognitive performance, enhanced mood overall, and better general mental alertness. You will feel just a little bit sharper and more on form. In the state of ketosis your appetite will usually decrease, so you will feel fuller eating less food.

For your body to successfully achieve and maintain ketosis, you need to do a little math: Your daily diet should match this intake of nutrients: 70% from fat, 25% from protein. Only 5% of your daily nutrient intake should come from carbohydrates. Is eating so much fat good for you? Fats are the most important part of the keto diet. As your body enters the state of ketosis, you start using fat as your internal source of energy, instead of sugars.

Many people think that all fats are bad, but really, fats are quite healthy. Fats contain twice as much energy and calories as proteins contain. Same with carbs. Triggering ketosis simply takes advantage of this process, so your metabolism gets a little boost of extra energy to work with.

Why should a quarter of your nutrients come from protein? It is because protein is such an important energy source. You probably already know that protein is great for building muscle mass, and it is essential for getting a more complete nutritional intake. To maintain your muscle mass, you need to focus on putting enough protein into your body while you are on the keto diet. So, it's not just about eating a lot of fat. That would be very unhealthy. The 5% carb intake rule is there to help you to increase your intake of essential nutrients in order to stay healthy. Carbs are necessary, whether we like it or not. But we have to eat the right amounts at the right times.

Many of our favourite fruits and vegetables contain carbs, and any healthy diet needs to take into account the essential vitamins and minerals in these foods. Just losing weight isn't going to be healthy unless you are taking in the right vitamins and minerals. So, you must eat lots of veggies as well as proteins. These new recipes reflect this need, and they show you how to use lots of lovely fresh vegetables in interesting ways. If you are vegetarian, or vegan, you can still do keto. But you should be careful to ensure that you are getting the balance of proteins and carbs right.

So, what exactly do you get to eat on the keto diet? While you are entering, or within, ketosis you can eat the following foods freely:

Healthy Fats

- Saturated fat (goose fat, tallow, clarified butter / ghee, coconut oil, duck fat, lard, butter, chicken fat)
- Monounsaturated (olive, macadamia and avocado oil)
- Polyunsaturated Omega-3 (seafood and fatty fish)

Non-Starchy Vegetables

- Spinach
- Endive
- Bamboo shoots
- Asparagus
- Lettuce
- Cucumber
- Kale
- Radishes
- Celery stalk
- Chives
- Zucchini

Dairy Products

- Cream cheese
- Heavy whipping cream
- Whole milk yogurt (unsweetened)

Fruits

- Avocado, berries

Nuts and Seeds

- Macadamia nuts, pine nuts, walnuts, sunflower seeds, sesame seeds, hemp seeds, pumpkin seeds, pecans, hazelnuts, and almonds

Beverages

- Water
- Unsweetened herbal tea
- Unsweetened coconut milk
- Decaf coffee
- Unsweetened almond milk
- Unsweetened soy milk
- Unsweetened herbal tea

Protein

- **Fish:** Cod, halibut, tuna, salmon, trout, flounder, mackerel, snapper, and catfish
- **Meat:** Goat, beef, lamb, and other wild game
- **Poultry:** Chicken meat, duck meat, and quail meat
- **Shellfish:** Squid, clams, scallops, lobster, mussels, crab, and oysters

- Whole eggs
- Pork products
- Sausage and bacon
- Peanut butter

There's a world of choices in the keto diet, and these exciting recipes will enable you to combine all of these crucial foods not only accurately, but creatively.

Some foods are going to come off the menu now. "No pain, no gain" used to be a popular saying. And, unfortunately, there are some foods that you will have to avoid eating. These include the following items:

- All grains, pastas, and breads
- Beans, lentils, and other legumes
- Corn
- Potatoes
- Most fresh and dried fruits
- Juice and soda
- Milk
- Pastries
- Pizza
- Maple syrup, honey, agave, and table sugar

These groups of foods are either too high in carbohydrate or they simply don't offer enough fatty content, which must have if ketosis is to happen.

Don't worry though, the keto diet is not so strict, once you are used to it. It is pretty uncompromising, that's true, but look on the bright side; keto is very, very effective. I invite you to check out these recipes. You will see just how much delicious variety there is when you eat keto. You will not feel limited at all. This book contains lots of tasty meals for you to make and enjoy eating, while they help you to maintain ketosis.

If you want to start exercising more and tone up, keto is one of the best ways to get rid of unsightly belly fat. Your body will burn off belly fat much quicker than on a conventional diet. Once your body stops relying on carbs for its energy all the time, your energy levels will really crank up, and you will feel able to exercise more vigorously, which will help you to get fitter. It may take a little while to see the best results though, so it's crucial that you stick with it. If you're doing keto the right way, and you are also exercising to optimum benefit levels, the keto diet will reward you much better than you could imagine.

My Personal Results

Yes, it was tough to make the changes I needed to make, at first. Cutting out starchy carbs, and naughty sweet things like pastries and cakes, was a pain! I got into the swing of keto after a few weeks, and then I actually started to enjoy the new food choices that I was making, without even thinking about it. Cooking keto challenged by kitchen skills. I needed to make meals that I really wanted to eat, without feeling that I was being deprived of the foods I loved. I just had to get more focussed on the different ways that I could prepare and serve my new diet. I have a

partner who is not eating Keto, so it was also a challenge to make recipes that we could both enjoy, which didn't wreck my keto meal plans.

There are Amazing Health Benefits

Results for everyone, on any diet, are entirely personal. I am in my fifties, and I am not very fit, nor particularly active, as I have a fairly sedentary job. I don't have any major health issues, though. Just as a precaution, I checked with my doctor before I started on the keto diet. So, maybe you should play it safe, and check with a medical practitioner before you get started.

What Weight Loss Can I Expect?

I lost about 12 kilos during the first six months of doing Keto, and I didn't ramp up my basic exercise regime during that time. I did start to exercise more later on, when my energy levels started to ascend. What was incredibly encouraging was that the weight I lost has stayed off. I don't want to eat carbs and sugars anymore, because my palate has changed. My body does not tolerate carbs and sugar, so I don't crave them.

I definitely lost a lot of excess fat, faster than I lost it on previous, traditional diets. I am careful to take into account my current weight, my body fat percentage, my activity levels, and my exercise output each day, so that I am consuming enough calories to keep me going.

The first few weeks into my new keto regime, was a slight disappointment: my energy levels started to fall a little. I made an appointment with my dietician, and he simply helped me to adjust my calorie intake to suit my increased activity levels. Long-term, that is the way to go.

Chapter 2 The World's Laziest Cook!

I am not an enthusiastic cook. I can make the basics, but I love to eat good food. I am always way too busy with my work, and I just don't have the time to spend on evenings and weekends, to shop, plan and cook meals in advance for the freezer. I am just not that organized! A lot of the recipe books that I used to buy were useless once I started doing keto. Too carb-heavy and not the right combinations to help me to attain ketosis. I did not want to have to keep up my new lifestyle by having to spend hours in the store and the kitchen.

I realized that I needed to find a way to prepare keto meals without making a huge mess, the fuss of shopping every day, or spending a lot of time in the kitchen, after a busy day at work.

I was reading a keto blog one day as I thought about this problem a little more, and the blogger suggested switching to an air fryer to help cut down on calories. Air fryers are a great kitchen tool for meal prep generally, but I never really thought about owning one before.

I went out and bought myself an air fryer that afternoon, and I started to cook most of my meals using the air fryer technique once I got the hang of it. A few of the recipes that I had already put together for myself that were keto worked well in the air fryer too. But a keto air fryer cookbook was what I needed!

Now that I cook this way all the time, I am combining air fryer recipes with the keto diet and it really works for me. I use my air fryer every day. So, it was a really good investment. So much so, that I have never put it back in the cupboard. It stays on the kitchen bench, ready to go when I get home!

Air Fryers, and How They Work with the Keto Diet

In a nutshell, an air fryer quickly blows hot air around a small container which holds your food, so that the food cooks efficiently, and to the perfect specification, and it doesn't use a lot of oil. Although keto is a fat-friendly way to eat, and animal fats such as butter, lard and duck fat are all excellent fats to use in keto recipes, air fryers work best with certain types of oils. Oils should have the following qualities if you want to use them in keto recipes with your air fryer:

- The oil must be able to withstand high temperatures without breaking down into toxic by-products.

- It must provide you with healthy fats and health benefits.

- It must be versatile and pair well with various types of keto meals.

Extra-virgin olive oil, coconut oil, and avocado oil are all good in this respect, and they all make the food taste delicious too!

My Air Fryer and Keto Tips

With a little experimentation, and lots of practise, I think I have got it just about right. I now have around 500 recipes that I regularly use in my daily diet plans, which are super-easy to prepare in my air fryer. Air frying is simply more convenient, cleaner to use, and it's really fast. Using the air fryer has actually altered the way that I eat.

If my friends come over, and they don't wish to eat keto meals, I can easily prepare food for them the same way in the air fryer. I just use some of the foods that I no longer eat, and I do separate batches. So, everyone gets to eat their favorites, and everyone is happy!

My Number One Tip:

There are some smaller air fryers on the market, however, the air fryer basket holds only enough for one person. I have a partner, so I cook for two. So, my suggestion is that you buy a larger fryer at the start, unless you live alone and don't entertain much.

Tip Number Two:

I always use an oil spray bottle. I usually fill it with avocado oil. I love the taste of this oil, and it handles high temperatures well without smoking. I use it to spray the air fryer basket before I preheat the air fryer, and I also often spray the coating that I use on some of the foods that you will see in the cookbook. It really makes a difference to flavour and crispness.

Tip Number Three:

Flip the food over at the halfway point of the prescribed cooking time. This will result in perfection! Flavour and texture are enhanced this way.

Tip Number Four:

Don't overcrowd your air fryer basket. Give the food room to cook evenly.

Tip Number Five:

Don't always use the highest heat setting. Some foods take a little bit longer to cook than others, and those with more delicate flavors will appreciate a little subtlety.

Tip Number Six:

ALWAYS preheating your air fryer. It vastly improves the results every time. It saves energy, too.

I hope that you are as impressed as I am about discovering a whole new way to cook and eat. I sincerely hope that you experience the amazing health benefits that will follow once you have lost excess weight and become more mobile and active.

Lastly, I am very excited for you! I genuinely hope that you enjoy the textures and flavors of these easy-to-prepare recipes. They have been specially designed to work in harmony with an air fryer. Cooking, eating and thinking healthy can't be bad, right?

Chaptr 3 Breakfast

Veggie Frittata

Prep time: 7 minutes | Cook time: 21 to 23 minutes | Serves 2

Avocado oil spray
¼ cup diced red onion
¼ cup diced red bell pepper
¼ cup finely chopped broccoli
4 large eggs
3 ounces (85 g)
shredded sharp Cheddar cheese, divided
½ teaspoon dried thyme
Sea salt and freshly ground black pepper, to taste

1. Spray a pan well with oil. Put the onion, pepper, and broccoli in the pan, place the pan in the air fryer, and set to 350ºF (177ºC). Bake for 5 minutes.
2. While the vegetables cook, beat the eggs in a medium bowl. Stir in half of the cheese, and season with the thyme, salt, and pepper.
3. Add the eggs to the pan and top with the remaining cheese. Set the air fryer to 350ºF (177ºC). Bake for 16 to 18 minutes, until cooked through.

Per Serving
calories: 325 | fat: 23g | protein: 22g
carbs: 6g | net carbs: 5g | fiber: 1g

Buffalo Egg Cups

Prep time: 10 minutes | Cook time: 15 minutes | Serves 2

4 large eggs
2 ounces (57 g) full-fat cream cheese
2 tablespoons buffalo
sauce
½ cup shredded sharp Cheddar cheese

1. Crack eggs into two ramekins.
2. In a small microwave-safe bowl, mix cream cheese, buffalo sauce, and Cheddar. Microwave for 20 seconds and then stir. Place a spoonful into each ramekin on top of the eggs.
3. Place ramekins into the air fryer basket.
4. Adjust the temperature to 320ºF (160ºC) and bake for 15 minutes.
5. Serve warm.

Per Serving
calories: 354 | fat: 22g | protein: 21g
carbs: 2g | net carbs: 2g | fiber: 0g

Sausage and Cheese Balls

Prep time: 10 minutes | Cook time: 12 minutes | Makes 16 balls

1 pound (454 g) pork breakfast sausage
½ cup shredded Cheddar cheese
1 ounce (28 g) full-fat cream cheese, softened
1 large egg

1. Mix all ingredients in a large bowl. Form into sixteen (1-inch) balls. Place the balls into the air fryer basket.
2. Adjust the temperature to 400ºF (204ºC) and air fry for 12 minutes.
3. Shake the basket two or three times during cooking. Sausage balls will be browned on the outside and have an internal temperature of at least 145ºF (63ºC) when completely cooked.
4. Serve warm.

Per Serving
calories: 424 | fat: 32g | protein: 23g
carbs: 2g | net carbs: 2g | fiber: 0g

Mexican Shakshuka

Prep time: 5 minutes | Cook time: 6 minutes | Serves 1

½ cup salsa
2 large eggs, room temperature
½ teaspoon fine sea salt
¼ teaspoon smoked paprika
⅛ teaspoon ground cumin

For Garnish:
2 tablespoons cilantro leaves

1. Preheat the air fryer to 400ºF (204ºC).
2. Place the salsa in a pie pan or a casserole dish that will fit into your air fryer. Crack the eggs into the salsa and sprinkle them with the salt, paprika, and cumin.
3. Place the pan in the air fryer and bake for 6 minutes, or until the egg whites are set and the yolks are cooked to your liking.
4. Remove from the air fryer and garnish with the cilantro before serving.
5. Best served fresh.

Per Serving
calories: 258 | fat: 17g | protein: 14g
carbs: 11g | net carbs: 7g | fiber: 4g

Jalapeño Popper Egg Cups

Prep time: 10 minutes | Cook time: 10 minutes | Serves 2

4 large eggs
¼ cup chopped pickled jalapeños
2 ounces (57 g) full-

fat cream cheese
½ cup shredded sharp Cheddar cheese

1. In a medium bowl, beat the eggs, then pour into four silicone muffin cups.
2. In a large microwave-safe bowl, place jalapeños, cream cheese, and Cheddar. Microwave for 30 seconds and stir. Take a spoonful, approximately ¼ of the mixture, and place it in the center of one of the egg cups. Repeat with remaining mixture.
3. Place egg cups into the air fryer basket.
4. Adjust the temperature to 320ºF (160ºC) and bake for 10 minutes.
5. Serve warm.

Per Serving
calories: 354 | fat: 25g | protein: 21g
carbs: 2g | net carbs: 2g | fiber: 0g

Southwestern Ham Egg Cups

Prep time: 5 minutes | Cook time: 12 minutes | Serves 2

4 (1-ounce / 28-g) slices deli ham
4 large eggs
2 tablespoons full-fat sour cream
¼ cup diced green bell pepper

2 tablespoons diced red bell pepper
2 tablespoons diced white onion
½ cup shredded medium Cheddar cheese

1. Place one slice of ham on the bottom of four baking cups.
2. In a large bowl, whisk eggs with sour cream. Stir in green pepper, red pepper, and onion.
3. Pour the egg mixture into ham-lined baking cups. Top with Cheddar. Place cups into the air fryer basket.
4. Adjust the temperature to 320ºF (160ºC) and bake for 12 minutes or until the tops are browned.
5. Serve warm.

Per Serving
calories: 328 | fat: 23g | protein: 29g
carbs: 6g | net carbs: 4g | fiber: 2g

Bacon, Cheese, and Avocado Melt

Prep time: 5 minutes | Cook time: 3 to 5 minutes | Serves 2

1 avocado
4 slices cooked bacon, chopped
2 tablespoons salsa

1 tablespoon heavy cream
¼ cup shredded Cheddar cheese

1. Preheat the air fryer to 400ºF (204ºC).
2. Slice the avocado in half lengthwise and remove the stone. To ensure the avocado halves do not roll in the basket, slice a thin piece of skin off the base.
3. In a small bowl, combine the bacon, salsa, and cream. Divide the mixture between the avocado halves and top with the cheese.
4. Place the avocado halves in the air fryer basket and air fry for 3 to 5 minutes until the cheese has melted and begins to brown. Serve warm.

Per Serving
calories: 290 | fat: 25g | protein: 11g
carbs: 7g | net carbs: 2g | fiber: 5g

Cheesy Bell Pepper Eggs

Prep time: 10 minutes | Cook time: 15 minutes | Serves 4

4 medium green bell peppers
3 ounces (85 g) cooked ham, chopped
¼ medium onion,

peeled and chopped
8 large eggs
1 cup mild Cheddar cheese

1. Cut the tops off each bell pepper. Remove the seeds and the white membranes with a small knife. Place ham and onion into each pepper.
2. Crack 2 eggs into each pepper. Top with ¼ cup cheese per pepper. Place into the air fryer basket.
3. Adjust the temperature to 390ºF (199ºC) and air fry for 15 minutes.
4. When fully cooked, peppers will be tender and eggs will be firm. Serve immediately.

Per Serving
calories: 314 | fat: 18g | protein: 25g
carbs: 6g | net carbs: 4g | fiber: 2g

Egg White Cups

Prep time: 10 minutes | Cook time: 15 minutes | Serves 4

2 cups 100% liquid egg whites
3 tablespoons salted butter, melted
¼ teaspoon salt
¼ teaspoon onion powder
½ medium Roma tomato, cored and diced
½ cup chopped fresh spinach leaves

1. In a large bowl, whisk egg whites with butter, salt, and onion powder. Stir in tomato and spinach, then pour evenly into four ramekins greased with cooking spray.
2. Place ramekins into air fryer basket. Adjust the temperature to 300ºF (149ºC) and bake for 15 minutes. Eggs will be fully cooked and firm in the center when done. Serve warm.

Per Serving
calories: 146 | fat: 8g | protein: 14g
carbs: 1g | net carbs: 1g | fiber: 0g

Jalapeño and Bacon Breakfast Pizza

Prep time: 5 minutes | Cook time: 10 minutes | Serves 2

1 cup shredded Mozzarella cheese
1 ounce (28 g) cream cheese, broken into small pieces
4 slices cooked sugar-free bacon, chopped
¼ cup chopped pickled jalapeños
1 large egg, whisked
¼ teaspoon salt

1. Place Mozzarella in a single layer on the bottom of an ungreased round nonstick baking dish. Scatter cream cheese pieces, bacon, and jalapeños over Mozzarella, then pour egg evenly around baking dish.
2. Sprinkle with salt and place into air fryer basket. Adjust the temperature to 330ºF (166ºC) and bake for 10 minutes. When cheese is brown and egg is set, pizza will be done.
3. Let cool on a large plate 5 minutes before serving.

Per Serving
calories: 361 | fat: 24g | protein: 26g
carbs: 5g | net carbs: 5g | fiber: 0g

Cheddar Soufflés

Prep time: 15 minutes | Cook time: 12 minutes | Serves 4

3 large eggs, whites and yolks separated
¼ teaspoon cream of tartar
½ cup shredded sharp Cheddar cheese
3 ounces (85 g) cream cheese, softened

1. In a large bowl, beat egg whites together with cream of tartar until soft peaks form, about 2 minutes.
2. In a separate medium bowl, beat egg yolks, Cheddar, and cream cheese together until frothy, about 1 minute. Add egg yolk mixture to whites, gently folding until combined.
3. Pour mixture evenly into four ramekins greased with cooking spray. Place ramekins into air fryer basket. Adjust the temperature to 350ºF (177ºC) and bake for 12 minutes. Eggs will be browned on the top and firm in the center when done. Serve warm.

Per Serving
calories: 183 | fat: 14g | protein: 9g
carbs: 1g | net carbs: 1g | fiber: 0g

Bacon and Cheese Quiche

Prep time: 5 minutes | Cook time: 12 minutes | Serves 2

3 large eggs
2 tablespoons heavy whipping cream
¼ teaspoon salt
4 slices cooked sugar-free bacon, crumbled
½ cup shredded mild Cheddar cheese

1. In a large bowl, whisk eggs, cream, and salt together until combined. Mix in bacon and Cheddar.
2. Pour mixture evenly into two ungreased ramekins. Place into air fryer basket. Adjust the temperature to 320ºF (160ºC) and bake for 12 minutes. Quiche will be fluffy and set in the middle when done.
3. Let quiche cool in ramekins 5 minutes. Serve warm.

Per Serving
calories: 380 | fat: 28g | protein: 24g
carbs: 2g | net carbs: 2g | fiber: 0g

Breakfast Meatballs

Prep time: 10 minutes | Cook time: 15 minutes | Makes 18 meatballs

1 pound (454 g) ground pork breakfast sausage
½ teaspoon salt
¼ teaspoon ground black pepper
½ cup shredded sharp Cheddar cheese
1 ounce (28 g) cream cheese, softened
1 large egg, whisked

1. Combine all ingredients in a large bowl. Form mixture into eighteen 1-inch meatballs.
2. Place meatballs into ungreased air fryer basket. Adjust the temperature to 400°F (204°C) and air fry for 15 minutes, shaking basket three times during cooking. Meatballs will be browned on the outside and have an internal temperature of at least 145°F (63°C) when completely cooked. Serve warm.

Per Serving (3 meatballs)
calories: 288 | fat: 24g | protein: 11g
carbs: 1g | net carbs: 1g | fiber: 0g

Pancake for Two

Prep time: 5 minutes | Cook time: 30 minutes | Serves 2

1 cup blanched finely ground almond flour
2 tablespoons granular erythritol
1 tablespoon salted butter, melted
1 large egg
$^1/_3$ cup unsweetened almond milk
½ teaspoon vanilla extract

1. In a large bowl, mix all ingredients together, then pour half the batter into an ungreased round nonstick baking dish.
2. Place dish into air fryer basket. Adjust the temperature to 320°F (160°C) and bake for 15 minutes. The pancake will be golden brown on top and firm, and a toothpick inserted in the center will come out clean when done. Repeat with remaining batter.
3. Slice in half in dish and serve warm.

Per Serving
calories: 434 | fat: 38g | protein: 15g
carbs: 11g | net carbs: 5g | fiber: 6g

Spinach Omelet

Prep time: 5 minutes | Cook time: 12 minutes | Serves 2

4 large eggs
1½ cups chopped fresh spinach leaves
2 tablespoons peeled and chopped yellow onion
2 tablespoons salted butter, melted
½ cup shredded mild Cheddar cheese
¼ teaspoon salt

1. In an ungreased round nonstick baking dish, whisk eggs. Stir in spinach, onion, butter, Cheddar, and salt.
2. Place dish into air fryer basket. Adjust the temperature to 320°F (160°C) and bake for 12 minutes. Omelet will be done when browned on the top and firm in the middle.
3. Slice in half and serve warm on two medium plates.

Per Serving
calories: 368 | fat: 28g | protein: 20g
carbs: 3g | net carbs: 2g | fiber: 1g

Pizza Eggs

Prep time: 5 minutes | Cook time: 10 minutes | Serves 2

1 cup shredded Mozzarella cheese
7 slices pepperoni, chopped
1 large egg, whisked
¼ teaspoon dried
oregano
¼ teaspoon dried parsley
¼ teaspoon garlic powder
¼ teaspoon salt

1. Place Mozzarella in a single layer on the bottom of an ungreased round nonstick baking dish. Scatter pepperoni over cheese, then pour egg evenly around baking dish.
2. Sprinkle with remaining ingredients and place into air fryer basket. Adjust the temperature to 330°F (166°C) and bake for 10 minutes. When cheese is brown and egg is set, dish will be done.
3. Let cool in dish 5 minutes before serving.

Per Serving
calories: 241 | fat: 15g | protein: 19g
carbs: 4g | net carbs: 4g | fiber: 0g

Blueberry Muffins

Prep time: 10 minutes | Cook time: 15 to 18 minutes | Serves 6

1 cup finely ground blanched almond flour
1/3 cup Swerve
1½ teaspoons baking powder
½ teaspoon baking soda
¼ teaspoon sea salt
¼ teaspoon xanthan gum
1 large egg, beaten
½ cup sour cream
2 tablespoons heavy (whipping) cream
1 teaspoon pure vanilla extract
½ cup fresh or frozen blueberries
Almond Glaze (optional)

1. In a large bowl, combine the almond flour, Swerve, baking powder, baking soda, sea salt, and xanthan gum.
2. In a medium bowl, whisk together the egg, sour cream, heavy cream, and vanilla.
3. Add the wet ingredients to the dry ingredients, and stir until just combined. Gently stir in the blueberries.
4. Divide the batter among 6 silicone muffin cups or the cups of a muffin pan that fits into your air fryer. Place in the air fryer basket and set to 300ºF (149ºC). Bake for 15 to 18 minutes, until the tops are golden brown and a toothpick inserted into the center appears clean when removed.
5. Drizzle with the almond glaze (if using) before serving.

Per Serving
calories: 194 | fat: 16g | protein: 6g
carbs: 8g | net carbs: 6g | fiber: 2g

Bacon and Spinach Egg Muffins

Prep time: 7 minutes | Cook time: 12 to 14 minutes | Serves 6

6 large eggs
¼ cup heavy (whipping) cream
½ teaspoon sea salt
¼ teaspoon freshly ground black pepper
¼ teaspoon cayenne pepper (optional)
¾ cup frozen chopped spinach, thawed and drained
4 strips cooked bacon, crumbled
2 ounces (57 g) shredded Cheddar cheese

1. In a large bowl (with a spout if you have one), whisk together the eggs, heavy cream, salt, black pepper, and cayenne pepper (if using).
2. Divide the spinach and bacon among 6 silicone muffin cups. Place the muffin cups in your air fryer basket.
3. Divide the egg mixture among the muffin cups. Top with the cheese.
4. Set the air fryer to 300ºF (149ºC). Bake for 12 to 14 minutes, until the eggs are set and cooked through.

Per Serving
calories: 180 | fat: 14g | protein: 11g
carbs: 2g | net carbs: 1g | fiber: 1g

Smoky Sausage Patties

Prep time: 10 minutes | Cook time: 9 minutes | Serves 8

1 pound (454 g) ground pork
1 tablespoon coconut aminos
2 teaspoons liquid smoke
1 teaspoon dried sage
1 teaspoon sea salt
½ teaspoon fennel seeds
½ teaspoon dried thyme
½ teaspoon freshly ground black pepper
¼ teaspoon cayenne pepper

1. In a large bowl, combine the pork, coconut aminos, liquid smoke, sage, salt, fennel seeds, thyme, black pepper, and cayenne pepper. Work the meat with your hands until the seasonings are fully incorporated.
2. Shape the mixture into 8 equal-size patties. Using your thumb, make a dent in the center of each patty. Place the patties on a plate and cover with plastic wrap. Refrigerate the patties for at least 30 minutes.
3. Working in batches if necessary, place the patties in a single layer in the air fryer, being careful not to overcrowd them.
4. Set the air fryer to 400ºF (204ºC) and air fry for 5 minutes. Flip and cook for about 4 minutes more.

Per Serving
calories: 152 | fat: 12g | protein: 10g
carbs: 1g | net carbs: 1g | fiber: 0g

Buffalo Chicken Breakfast Muffins

Prep time: 7 minutes | Cook time: 13 to 16 minutes | Serves 10

6 ounces (170 g) shredded cooked chicken
3 ounces (85 g) blue cheese, crumbled
2 tablespoons unsalted butter, melted
⅓ cup Buffalo hot sauce, such as Frank's RedHot
1 teaspoon minced garlic
6 large eggs
Sea salt and freshly ground black pepper, to taste
Avocado oil spray

1. In a large bowl, stir together the chicken, blue cheese, melted butter, hot sauce, and garlic.
2. In a medium bowl or large liquid measuring cup, beat the eggs. Season with salt and pepper.
3. Spray 10 silicone muffin cups with oil. Divide the chicken mixture among the cups, and pour the egg mixture over top.
4. Place the cups in the air fryer and set to 300ºF (149ºC). Bake for 13 to 16 minutes, until the muffins are set and cooked through. (Depending on the size of your air fryer, you may need to cook the muffins in batches.)

Per Serving
calories: 120 | fat: 8g | protein: 9g
carbs: 1g | net carbs: 1g | fiber: 0g

Meritage Eggs

Prep time: 5 minutes | Cook time: 8 minutes | Serves 2

2 teaspoons unsalted butter (or coconut oil for dairy-free), for greasing the ramekins
4 large eggs
2 teaspoons chopped fresh thyme
½ teaspoon fine sea salt
¼ teaspoon ground black pepper
2 tablespoons heavy cream (or
unsweetened, unflavored almond milk for dairy-free)
3 tablespoons finely grated Parmesan cheese (or Kite Hill brand chive cream cheese style spread, softened, for dairy-free)
Fresh thyme leaves, for garnish (optional)

1. Preheat the air fryer to 400ºF (204ºC). Grease two (4-ounce / 113-g) ramekins with the butter.
2. Crack 2 eggs into each ramekin and divide the thyme, salt, and pepper between the ramekins. Pour 1 tablespoon of the heavy cream into each ramekin. Sprinkle each ramekin with 1½ tablespoons of the Parmesan cheese.
3. Place the ramekins in the air fryer and bake for 8 minutes for soft-cooked yolks (longer if you desire a harder yolk).
4. Garnish with a sprinkle of ground black pepper and thyme leaves, if desired. Best served fresh.

Per Serving
calories: 331 | fat: 29g | protein: 16g
carbs: 2g | net carbs: 2g | fiber: 0g

Breakfast Pizza

Prep time: 5 minutes | Cook time: 8 minutes | Serves 1

2 large eggs
¼ cup unsweetened, unflavored almond milk (or unflavored hemp milk for nut-free)
¼ teaspoon fine sea salt
⅛ teaspoon ground black pepper
¼ cup diced onions
¼ cup shredded Parmesan cheese (omit for dairy-free)
6 pepperoni slices (omit for vegetarian)
¼ teaspoon dried oregano leaves
¼ cup pizza sauce, warmed, for serving

1. Preheat the air fryer to 350ºF (177ºC). Grease a cake pan.
2. In a small bowl, use a fork to whisk together the eggs, almond milk, salt, and pepper. Add the onions and stir to mix. Pour the mixture into the greased pan. Top with the cheese (if using), pepperoni slices (if using), and oregano.
3. Place the pan in the air fryer and bake for 8 minutes, or until the eggs are cooked to your liking.
4. Loosen the eggs from the sides of the pan with a spatula and place them on a serving plate. Drizzle the pizza sauce on top. Best served fresh.

Per Serving
calories: 357 | fat: 25g | protein: 24g
carbs: 9g | net carbs: 7g | fiber: 2g

Spinach and Feta Egg Bake

Prep time: 7 minutes | Cook time: 23 to 25 minutes | Serves 2

Avocado oil spray
⅓ cup diced red onion
1 cup frozen chopped spinach, thawed and drained
4 large eggs
¼ cup heavy (whipping) cream

Sea salt and freshly ground black pepper, to taste
¼ teaspoon cayenne pepper
½ cup crumbled feta cheese
¼ cup shredded Parmesan cheese

1. Spray a deep pan with oil. Put the onion in the pan, and place the pan in the air fryer basket. Set the air fryer to 350ºF (177ºC) and bake for 7 minutes.
2. Sprinkle the spinach over the onion.
3. In a medium bowl, beat the eggs, heavy cream, salt, black pepper, and cayenne. Pour this mixture over the vegetables.
4. Top with the feta and Parmesan cheese. Bake for 16 to 18 minutes, until the eggs are set and lightly brown.

Per Serving
calories: 424 | fat: 32g | protein: 26g
carbs: 11g | net carbs: 8g | fiber: 3g

Southwestern Breakfast Taco

Prep time: 10 minutes | Cook time: 9 minutes | Serves 1

1 large egg, beaten
½ cup shredded Mozzarella cheese
1 tablespoon finely ground blanched almond flour
1 tablespoon canned chopped green chiles
1 teaspoon Taco Seasoning
½ teaspoon baking powder
2 strips cooked

bacon, crumbled
¼ avocado, diced
2 tablespoons shredded Cheddar cheese
2 tablespoons sour cream
1 tablespoon salsa
Chopped fresh cilantro, for serving (optional)
Hot sauce, for serving (optional)

1. In a medium bowl, whisk together the egg, Mozzarella cheese, almond flour, chiles, taco seasoning, and baking powder.

2. Line a baking pan with parchment paper. Spread the egg-cheese mixture in an even layer in the prepared pan. Place the pan in the air fryer basket and set to 400ºF (204ºC). Bake for 9 minutes or until the mixture is set.
3. Remove from the pan and top with the bacon, avocado, Cheddar cheese, sour cream, and salsa.
4. Serve warm with cilantro and hot sauce (if using).

Per Serving
calories: 563 | fat: 42g | protein: 34g
carbs: 11g | net carbs: 6g | fiber: 5g

Lemon-Blueberry Muffins

Prep time: 5 minutes | Cook time: 20 to 25 minutes | Makes 6 muffins

1¼ cups almond flour
3 tablespoons Swerve
1 teaspoon baking powder
2 large eggs
3 tablespoons melted butter

1 tablespoon almond milk
1 tablespoon fresh lemon juice
½ cup fresh blueberries

1. Preheat the air fryer to 350ºF (177ºC). Lightly coat 6 silicone muffin cups with vegetable oil. Set aside.
2. In a large mixing bowl, combine the almond flour, Swerve, and baking soda. Set aside.
3. In a separate small bowl, whisk together the eggs, butter, milk, and lemon juice. Add the egg mixture to the flour mixture and stir until just combined. Fold in the blueberries and let the batter sit for 5 minutes.
4. Spoon the muffin batter into the muffin cups, about two-thirds full. Air fry for 20 to 25 minutes, or until a toothpick inserted into the center of a muffin comes out clean.
5. Remove the basket from the air fryer and let the muffins cool for about 5 minutes before transferring them to a wire rack to cool completely.

Per Serving
calories: 165 | fat: 11g | protein: g
carbs: 8g | net carbs: 7g | fiber: 1g

Bunless Breakfast Turkey Burgers

Prep time: 5 minutes | Cook time: 15 minutes | Serves 4

1 pound (454 g) ground turkey breakfast sausage	chopped green bell pepper
½ teaspoon salt	2 tablespoons mayonnaise
¼ teaspoon ground black pepper	1 medium avocado, peeled, pitted, and sliced
¼ cup seeded and	

1. In a large bowl, mix sausage with salt, black pepper, bell pepper, and mayonnaise. Form meat into four patties.
2. Place patties into ungreased air fryer basket. Adjust the temperature to 370ºF (188ºC) and air fry for 15 minutes, turning patties halfway through cooking. Burgers will be done when dark brown and they have an internal temperature of at least 165ºF (74ºC).
3. Serve burgers topped with avocado slices on four medium plates.

Per Serving
calories: 276 | fat: 17g | protein: 22g
carbs: 4g | net carbs: 1g | fiber: 3g

Nutty Granola

Prep time: 5 minutes | Cook time: 1 hour | Serves 4

½ cup pecans, coarsely chopped	2 tablespoons melted butter
½ cup walnuts or almonds, coarsely chopped	¼ cup Swerve
	½ teaspoon ground cinnamon
¼ cup unsweetened flaked coconut	½ teaspoon vanilla extract
¼ cup almond flour	¼ teaspoon ground nutmeg
¼ cup ground flaxseed or chia seeds	¼ teaspoon salt
2 tablespoons sunflower seeds	2 tablespoons water

1. Preheat the air fryer to 250ºF (121ºC). Cut a piece of parchment paper to fit inside the air fryer basket.
2. In a large bowl, toss the nuts, coconut, almond flour, ground flaxseed or chia seeds, sunflower seeds, butter, Swerve, cinnamon, vanilla, nutmeg, salt, and water until thoroughly combined.

3. Spread the granola on the parchment paper and flatten to an even thickness.
4. Air fry for about an hour, or until golden throughout. Remove from the air fryer and allow to fully cool. Break the granola into bite-size pieces and store in a covered container for up to a week.

Per Serving
calories: 305 | fat: 28g | protein: 8g
carbs: 10g | net carbs: 4g | fiber: 6g

Cheesy Cauliflower "Hash Browns"

Prep time: 30 minutes | Cook time: 24 minutes | Makes 6 hash browns

2 ounces (57 g) 100% cheese crisps	instructions
	1 large egg
1 (12-ounce / 340-g) steamer bag cauliflower, cooked according to package	½ cup shredded sharp Cheddar cheese
	½ teaspoon salt

1. Let cooked cauliflower cool 10 minutes.
2. Place cheese crisps into food processor and pulse on low 30 seconds until crisps are finely ground.
3. Using a kitchen towel, wring out excess moisture from cauliflower and place into food processor.
4. Add egg to food processor and sprinkle with Cheddar and salt. Pulse five times until mixture is mostly smooth.
5. Cut two pieces of parchment to fit air fryer basket. Separate mixture into six even scoops and place three on each piece of ungreased parchment, keeping at least 2 inch of space between each scoop. Press each into a hash brown shape, about ¼ inch thick.
6. Place one batch on parchment into air fryer basket. Adjust the temperature to 375ºF (191ºC) and air fry for 12 minutes, turning hash browns halfway through cooking. Hash browns will be golden brown when done. Repeat with second batch.
7. Allow 5 minutes to cool. Serve warm.

Per Serving (1 hash brown)
calories: 120 | fat: 8g | protein: 8g
carbs: 3g | net carbs: 2g | fiber: 1g

Pumpkin Spice Muffins

Prep time: 10 minutes | Cook time: 15 minutes | Serves 6

1 cup blanched finely ground almond flour
½ cup granular erythritol
½ teaspoon baking powder
¼ cup unsalted butter, softened
¼ cup pure pumpkin purée
½ teaspoon ground cinnamon
¼ teaspoon ground nutmeg
1 teaspoon vanilla extract
2 large eggs

1. In a large bowl, mix almond flour, erythritol, baking powder, butter, pumpkin purée, cinnamon, nutmeg, and vanilla.
2. Gently stir in eggs.
3. Evenly pour the batter into six silicone muffin cups. Place muffin cups into the air fryer basket, working in batches if necessary.
4. Adjust the temperature to 300ºF (149ºC) and bake for 15 minutes.
5. When completely cooked, a toothpick inserted in center will come out mostly clean. Serve warm.

Per Serving

calories: 208 | fat: 18g | protein: 6g
carbs: 17g | net carbs: 3g | fiber: 14g

Bacon, Egg, and Cheese Roll Ups

Prep time: 15 minutes | Cook time: 15 minutes | Serves 4

2 tablespoons unsalted butter
¼ cup chopped onion
½ medium green bell pepper, seeded and chopped
6 large eggs
12 slices sugar-free bacon
1 cup shredded sharp Cheddar cheese
½ cup mild salsa, for dipping

1. In a medium skillet over medium heat, melt butter. Add onion and pepper to the skillet and sauté until fragrant and onions are translucent, about 3 minutes.
2. Whisk eggs in a small bowl and pour into skillet. Scramble eggs with onions and peppers until fluffy and fully cooked, about 5 minutes. Remove from heat and set aside.

3. On work surface, place three slices of bacon side by side, overlapping about ¼ inch. Place ¼ cup scrambled eggs in a heap on the side closest to you and sprinkle ¼ cup cheese on top of the eggs.
4. Tightly roll the bacon around the eggs and secure the seam with a toothpick if necessary. Place each roll into the air fryer basket.
5. Adjust the temperature to 350ºF (177ºC) and air fry for 15 minutes. Rotate the rolls halfway through the cooking time.
6. Bacon will be brown and crispy when completely cooked. Serve immediately with salsa for dipping.

Per Serving

calories: 460 | fat: 32g | protein: 28g
carbs: 6g | net carbs: 5g | fiber: 1g

Green Eggs and Ham

Prep time: 5 minutes | Cook time: 10 minutes | Serves 2

1 large Hass avocado, halved and pitted
2 thin slices ham
2 large eggs
2 tablespoons chopped green onions, plus more for garnish
½ teaspoon fine sea salt
¼ teaspoon ground black pepper
¼ cup shredded Cheddar cheese (omit for dairy-free)

1. Preheat the air fryer to 400ºF (204ºC).
2. Place a slice of ham into the cavity of each avocado half. Crack an egg on top of the ham, then sprinkle on the green onions, salt, and pepper.
3. Place the avocado halves in the air fryer cut side up and air fry for 10 minutes, or until the egg is cooked to your desired doneness. Top with the cheese (if using) and air fry for 30 seconds more, or until the cheese is melted. Garnish with chopped green onions.
4. Best served fresh. Store extras in an airtight container in the fridge for up to 4 days. Reheat in a preheated 350ºF (177ºC) air fryer for a few minutes, until warmed through.

Per Serving

calories: 307 | fat: 24g | protein: 14g
carbs: 10g | net carbs: 3g | fiber: 7g

Broccoli-Mushroom Frittata

Prep time: 10 minutes | Cook time: 20 minutes | Serves 2

1 tablespoon olive oil
1½ cups broccoli florets, finely chopped
½ cup sliced brown mushrooms
¼ cup finely chopped onion
½ teaspoon salt
¼ teaspoon freshly ground black pepper
6 eggs
¼ cup Parmesan cheese

1. In a nonstick cake pan, combine the olive oil, broccoli, mushrooms, onion, salt, and pepper. Stir until the vegetables are thoroughly coated with oil. Place the cake pan in the air fryer basket and set the air fryer to 400°F (204°C). Air fry for 5 minutes until the vegetables soften.
2. Meanwhile, in a medium bowl, whisk the eggs and Parmesan until thoroughly combined. Pour the egg mixture into the pan and shake gently to distribute the vegetables. Air fry for another 15 minutes until the eggs are set.
3. Remove from the air fryer and let sit for 5 minutes to cool slightly. Use a silicone spatula to gently lift the frittata onto a plate before serving.

Per Serving
calories: 360 | fat: 25g | protein: 25g
carbs: 10g | net carbs: 8g | fiber: 2g

Cinnamon Rolls

Prep time: 10 minutes | Cook time: 20 minutes | Makes 12 rolls

2½ cups shredded Mozzarella cheese
2 ounces (57 g) cream cheese, softened
1 cup blanched finely ground almond flour
½ teaspoon vanilla extract
½ cup confectioners' erythritol
1 tablespoon ground cinnamon

1. In a large microwave-safe bowl, combine Mozzarella cheese, cream cheese, and flour. Microwave the mixture on high 90 seconds until cheese is melted.
2. Add vanilla extract and erythritol, and mix 2 minutes until a dough forms.
3. Once the dough is cool enough to work with your hands, about 2 minutes, spread it out into a 12 × 4-inch rectangle on ungreased parchment paper. Evenly sprinkle dough with cinnamon.
4. Starting at the long side of the dough, roll lengthwise to form a log. Slice the log into twelve even pieces.
5. Divide rolls between two ungreased round nonstick baking dishes. Place one dish into air fryer basket. Adjust the temperature to 375°F (191°C) and bake for 10 minutes.
6. Cinnamon rolls will be done when golden around the edges and mostly firm. Repeat with second dish. Allow rolls to cool in dishes 10 minutes before serving.

Per Serving (1 roll)
calories: 145 | fat: 10g | protein: 8g
carbs: 4g | net carbs: 3g | fiber: 1g

Cajun Breakfast Sausage

Prep time: 10 minutes | Cook time: 15 to 20 minutes | Serves 8

1½ pounds (680 g) 85% lean ground turkey
3 cloves garlic, finely chopped
¼ onion, grated
1 teaspoon Tabasco sauce
1 teaspoon Creole seasoning
1 teaspoon dried thyme
½ teaspoon paprika
½ teaspoon cayenne

1. Preheat the air fryer to 370°F (188°C).
2. In a large bowl, combine the turkey, garlic, onion, Tabasco, Creole seasoning, thyme, paprika, and cayenne. Mix with clean hands until thoroughly combined. Shape into 16 patties, about ½ inch thick. (Wet your hands slightly if you find the sausage too sticky to handle.)
3. Working in batches if necessary, arrange the patties in a single layer in the air fryer basket. Pausing halfway through the cooking time to flip the patties, air fry for 15 to 20 minutes until a thermometer inserted into the thickest portion registers 165°F (74°C).

Per Serving
calories: 170 | fat: 11g | protein: 16g
carbs: 1g | net carbs: 1g | fiber: 0g

Double-Dipped Mini Cinnamon Biscuits

Prep time: 15 minutes | Cook time: 13 minutes | Makes 8 biscuits

2 cups blanched almond flour
½ cup Swerve confectioners'-style sweetener or equivalent amount of liquid or powdered sweetener
1 teaspoon baking powder
½ teaspoon fine sea salt

¼ cup plus 2 tablespoons (¾ stick) very cold unsalted butter
¼ cup unsweetened, unflavored almond milk
1 large egg
1 teaspoon vanilla extract
3 teaspoons ground cinnamon

Glaze:
½ cup Swerve confectioners'-style sweetener or equivalent amount of powdered sweetener

¼ cup heavy cream or unsweetened, unflavored almond milk

1. Preheat the air fryer to 350ºF (177ºC). Line a pie pan that fits into your air fryer with parchment paper.
2. In a medium-sized bowl, mix together the almond flour, sweetener (if powdered; do not add liquid sweetener), baking powder, and salt. Cut the butter into ½-inch squares, then use a hand mixer to work the butter into the dry ingredients. When you are done, the mixture should still have chunks of butter.
3. In a small bowl, whisk together the almond milk, egg, and vanilla extract (if using liquid sweetener, add it as well) until blended. Using a fork, stir the wet ingredients into the dry ingredients until large clumps form. Add the cinnamon and use your hands to swirl it into the dough.
4. Form the dough into sixteen 1-inch balls and place them on the prepared pan, spacing them about ½ inch apart. (If you're using a smaller air fryer, work in batches if necessary.) Bake in the air fryer until golden, 10 to 13 minutes. Remove from the air fryer and let cool on the pan for at least 5 minutes.
5. While the biscuits bake, make the glaze: Place the powdered sweetener in a small bowl and slowly stir in the heavy cream with a fork.
6. When the biscuits have cooled somewhat, dip the tops into the glaze, allow it to dry a bit, and then dip again for a thick glaze.
7. Serve warm or at room temperature. Store unglazed biscuits in an airtight container in the refrigerator for up to 3 days or in the freezer for up to a month. Reheat in a preheated 350ºF (177ºC) air fryer for 5 minutes, or until warmed through, and dip in the glaze as instructed above.

Per Serving
calories: 546 | fat: 51g | protein: 14g
carbs: 13g | net carbs: 7g | fiber: 6g

Denver Omelet

Prep time: 5 minutes | Cook time: 8 minutes | Serves 1

2 large eggs
¼ cup unsweetened, unflavored almond milk
¼ teaspoon fine sea salt
⅛ teaspoon ground black pepper
¼ cup diced ham (omit for vegetarian)
¼ cup diced green and red bell peppers

2 tablespoons diced green onions, plus more for garnish
¼ cup shredded Cheddar cheese (about 1 ounce / 28 g) (omit for dairy-free)
Quartered cherry tomatoes, for serving (optional)

1. Preheat the air fryer to 350ºF (177ºC). Grease a cake pan and set aside.
2. In a small bowl, use a fork to whisk together the eggs, almond milk, salt, and pepper. Add the ham, bell peppers, and green onions. Pour the mixture into the greased pan. Add the cheese on top (if using).
3. Place the pan in the basket of the air fryer. Bake for 8 minutes, or until the eggs are cooked to your liking.
4. Loosen the omelet from the sides of the pan with a spatula and place it on a serving plate. Garnish with green onions and serve with cherry tomatoes, if desired. Best served fresh.

Per Serving
calories: 476 | fat: 32g | protein: 41g
carbs: 3g | net carbs: 2g | fiber: 1g

Breakfast Sammies

Prep time: 15 minutes | Cook time: 20 minutes | Serves 5

Biscuits:

6 large egg whites
2 cups blanched almond flour, plus more if needed
1½ teaspoons baking powder
½ teaspoon fine sea salt

¼ cup (½ stick) very cold unsalted butter (or lard for dairy-free), cut into ¼-inch pieces

Eggs:

5 large eggs
½ teaspoon fine sea salt
¼ teaspoon ground black pepper

5 (1-ounce / 28-g) slices Cheddar cheese (omit for dairy-free)
10 thin slices ham

1. Spray the air fryer basket with avocado oil. Preheat the air fryer to 350ºF (177ºC). Grease two pie pans or two baking pans that will fit inside your air fryer.
2. Make the biscuits: In a medium-sized bowl, whip the egg whites with a hand mixer until very stiff. Set aside.
3. In a separate medium-sized bowl, stir together the almond flour, baking powder, and salt until well combined. Cut in the butter. Gently fold the flour mixture into the egg whites with a rubber spatula. If the dough is too wet to form into mounds, add a few tablespoons of almond flour until the dough holds together well.
4. Using a large spoon, divide the dough into 5 equal portions and drop them about 1 inch apart on one of the greased pie pans. (If you're using a smaller air fryer, work in batches if necessary.) Place the pan in the air fryer and bake for 11 to 14 minutes, until the biscuits are golden brown. Remove from the air fryer and set aside to cool.
5. Make the eggs: Set the air fryer to 375ºF (191ºC). Crack the eggs into the remaining greased pie pan and sprinkle with the salt and pepper. Place the eggs in the air fryer to bake for 5 minutes, or until they are cooked to your liking.
6. Open the air fryer and top each egg yolk with a slice of cheese (if using). Bake for another minute, or until the cheese is melted.
7. Once the biscuits are cool, slice them in half lengthwise. Place 1 cooked egg topped with cheese and 2 slices of ham in each biscuit.
8. Store leftover biscuits, eggs, and ham in separate airtight containers in the fridge for up to 3 days. Reheat the biscuits and eggs on a baking sheet in a preheated 350ºF (177ºC) air fryer for 5 minutes, or until warmed through.

Per Serving

calories: 269 | fat: 19g | protein: 22g
carbs: 1g | net carbs: 1g | fiber: 0g

Portobello Eggs Benedict

Prep time: 10 minutes | Cook time: 10 to 14 minutes | Serves 2

1 tablespoon olive oil
2 cloves garlic, minced
¼ teaspoon dried thyme
2 portobello mushrooms, stems removed and gills scraped out
2 Roma tomatoes, halved lengthwise
Salt and freshly

ground black pepper, to taste
2 large eggs
2 tablespoons grated Pecorino Romano cheese
1 tablespoon chopped fresh parsley, for garnish
1 teaspoon truffle oil (optional)

1. Preheat the air fryer to 400ºF (204ºC).
2. In a small bowl, combine the olive oil, garlic, and thyme. Brush the mixture over the mushrooms and tomatoes until thoroughly coated. Season to taste with salt and freshly ground black pepper.
3. Arrange the vegetables, cut side up, in the air fryer basket. Crack an egg into the center of each mushroom and sprinkle with cheese. Air fry for 10 to 14 minutes until the vegetables are tender and the whites are firm. When cool enough to handle, coarsely chop the tomatoes and place on top of the eggs. Scatter parsley on top and drizzle with truffle oil, if desired, just before serving.

Per Serving

calories: 255 | fat: 20g | protein: 11g
carbs: 10g | net carbs: 7g | fiber: 3g

Gyro Breakfast Patties with Tzatziki

Prep time: 10 minutes | Cook time: 20 minutes per batch | Makes 16 patties

Patties:

2 pounds (907 g) ground lamb or beef

½ cup diced red onions

¼ cup sliced black olives

2 tablespoons tomato sauce

1 teaspoon dried oregano leaves

1 teaspoon Greek seasoning

2 cloves garlic, minced

1 teaspoon fine sea salt

Tzatziki:

1 cup full-fat sour cream

1 small cucumber, chopped

½ teaspoon fine sea salt

½ teaspoon garlic

powder, or 1 clove garlic, minced

¼ teaspoon dried dill weed, or 1 teaspoon finely chopped fresh dill

For Garnish/Serving:

½ cup crumbled feta cheese (about 2 ounces / 57 g)

Diced red onions

Sliced black olives

Sliced cucumbers

1. Preheat the air fryer to 350ºF (177ºC).
2. Place the ground lamb, onions, olives, tomato sauce, oregano, Greek seasoning, garlic, and salt in a large bowl. Mix well to combine the ingredients.
3. Using your hands, form the mixture into sixteen 3-inch patties. Place about 5 of the patties in the air fryer and air fry for 20 minutes, flipping halfway through. Remove the patties and place them on a serving platter. Repeat with the remaining patties.
4. While the patties cook, make the tzatziki: Place all the ingredients in a small bowl and stir well. Cover and store in the fridge until ready to serve. Garnish with ground black pepper before serving.
5. Serve the patties with a dollop of tzatziki, a sprinkle of crumbled feta cheese, diced red onions, sliced black olives, and sliced cucumbers.
6. Store leftovers in an airtight container in the refrigerator for up to 5 days or in the freezer for up to a month. Reheat the patties in a preheated 390ºF (199ºC) air fryer for a few minutes, until warmed through.

Per Serving

calories: 396 | fat: 31g | protein: 23g carbs: 4g | net carbs: 4g | fiber: 0g

Bacon-and-Eggs Avocado

Prep time: 5 minutes | Cook time: 17 minutes | Serves 1

1 large egg

1 avocado, halved, peeled, and pitted

2 slices bacon

Fresh parsley, for serving (optional)

Sea salt flakes, for garnish (optional)

1. Spray the air fryer basket with avocado oil. Preheat the air fryer to 320ºF (160ºC). Fill a small bowl with cool water.
2. Soft-boil the egg: Place the egg in the air fryer basket. Air fry for 6 minutes for a soft yolk or 7 minutes for a cooked yolk. Transfer the egg to the bowl of cool water and let sit for 2 minutes. Peel and set aside.
3. Use a spoon to carve out extra space in the center of the avocado halves until the cavities are big enough to fit the soft-boiled egg. Place the soft-boiled egg in the center of one half of the avocado and replace the other half of the avocado on top, so the avocado appears whole on the outside.
4. Starting at one end of the avocado, wrap the bacon around the avocado to completely cover it. Use toothpicks to hold the bacon in place.
5. Place the bacon-wrapped avocado in the air fryer basket and air fry for 5 minutes. Flip the avocado over and air fry for another 5 minutes, or until the bacon is cooked to your liking. Serve on a bed of fresh parsley, if desired, and sprinkle with salt flakes, if desired.
6. Best served fresh. Store extras in an airtight container in the fridge for up to 4 days. Reheat in a preheated 320ºF (160ºC) air fryer for 4 minutes, or until heated through.

Per Serving

calories: 536 | fat: 46g | protein: 18g carbs: 18g | net carbs: 4g | fiber: 14g

Keto Quiche

Prep time: 10 minutes | Cook time: 1 hour | Makes 1 (6-inch) quiche

Crust:

1¼ cups blanched almond flour
1¼ cups grated Parmesan or Gouda cheese
¼ teaspoon fine sea salt
1 large egg, beaten

Filling:

½ cup chicken or beef broth (or vegetable broth for vegetarian)
1 cup shredded Swiss cheese (about 4 ounces / 113 g)
4 ounces (113 g) cream cheese (½ cup)
1 tablespoon unsalted butter, melted
4 large eggs, beaten
⅓ cup minced leeks or sliced green onions
¾ teaspoon fine sea salt
⅛ teaspoon cayenne pepper
Chopped green onions, for garnish

1. Preheat the air fryer to 325°F (163°C). Grease a pie pan. Spray two large pieces of parchment paper with avocado oil and set them on the countertop.
2. Make the crust: In a medium-sized bowl, combine the flour, cheese, and salt and mix well. Add the egg and mix until the dough is well combined and stiff.
3. Place the dough in the center of one of the greased pieces of parchment. Top with the other piece of parchment. Using a rolling pin, roll out the dough into a circle about 1/16 inch thick.
4. Press the pie crust into the prepared pie pan. Place it in the air fryer and bake for 12 minutes, or until it starts to lightly brown.
5. While the crust bakes, make the filling: In a large bowl, combine the broth, Swiss cheese, cream cheese, and butter. Stir in the eggs, leeks, salt, and cayenne pepper. When the crust is ready, pour the mixture into the crust.
6. Place the quiche in the air fryer and bake for 15 minutes. Turn the heat down to 300°F (149°C) and bake for an additional 30 minutes, or until a knife inserted 1 inch from the edge comes out clean. You may have to cover the edges of the crust with foil to prevent burning.
7. Allow the quiche to cool for 10 minutes before garnishing it with chopped green onions and cutting it into wedges.
8. Store leftovers in an airtight container in the refrigerator for up to 4 days or in the freezer for up to a month. Reheat in a preheated 350°F (177°C) air fryer for a few minutes, until warmed through.

Per Serving

calories: 333 | fat: 26g | protein: 20g carbs: 6g| net carbs: 4g | fiber: 2g

Breakfast Calzone

Prep time: 15 minutes | Cook time: 15 minutes | Serves 4

1½ cups shredded Mozzarella cheese
½ cup blanched finely ground almond flour
1 ounce (28 g) full-fat cream cheese
1 large whole egg
4 large eggs, scrambled
½ pound (227 g) cooked breakfast sausage, crumbled
8 tablespoons shredded mild Cheddar cheese

1. In a large microwave-safe bowl, add Mozzarella, almond flour, and cream cheese. Microwave for 1 minute. Stir until the mixture is smooth and forms a ball. Add the egg and stir until dough forms.
2. Place dough between two sheets of parchment and roll out to ¼-inch thickness. Cut the dough into four rectangles.
3. Mix scrambled eggs and cooked sausage together in a large bowl. Divide the mixture evenly among each piece of dough, placing it on the lower half of the rectangle. Sprinkle each with 2 tablespoons Cheddar.
4. Fold over the rectangle to cover the egg and meat mixture. Pinch, roll, or use a wet fork to close the edges completely.
5. Cut a piece of parchment to fit your air fryer basket and place the calzones onto the parchment. Place parchment into the air fryer basket.
6. Adjust the temperature to 380°F (193°C) and air fry for 15 minutes.
7. Flip the calzones halfway through the cooking time. When done, calzones should be golden in color. Serve immediately.

Per Serving

calories: 560 | fat: 42g | protein: 34g carbs: 6g | net carbs: 4g | fiber: 2g

Everything Bagels

Prep time: 15 minutes | Cook time: 14 minutes | Makes 6 bagels

1¾ cups shredded Mozzarella cheese or goat cheese Mozzarella
2 tablespoons unsalted butter or coconut oil
1 large egg, beaten
1 tablespoon apple cider vinegar

1 cup blanched almond flour
1 tablespoon baking powder
⅛ teaspoon fine sea salt
1½ teaspoons everything bagel seasoning

1. Make the dough: Put the Mozzarella and butter in a large microwave-safe bowl and microwave for 1 to 2 minutes, until the cheese is entirely melted. Stir well. Add the egg and vinegar. Using a hand mixer on medium, combine well. Add the almond flour, baking powder, and salt and, using the mixer, combine well.
2. Lay a piece of parchment paper on the countertop and place the dough on it. Knead it for about 3 minutes. The dough should be a little sticky but pliable. (If the dough is too sticky, chill it in the refrigerator for an hour or overnight.)
3. Preheat the air fryer to 350°F (177°C). Spray a baking sheet or pie pan that will fit into your air fryer with avocado oil.
4. Divide the dough into 6 equal portions. Roll 1 portion into a log that is 6 inches long and about ½ inch thick. Form the log into a circle and seal the edges together, making a bagel shape. Repeat with the remaining portions of dough, making 6 bagels.
5. Place the bagels on the greased baking sheet. Spray the bagels with avocado oil and top with everything bagel seasoning, pressing the seasoning into the dough with your hands.
6. Place the bagels in the air fryer and bake for 14 minutes, or until cooked through and golden brown, flipping after 6 minutes.
7. Remove the bagels from the air fryer and allow them to cool slightly before slicing them in half and serving. Store leftovers in an airtight container in the fridge for up to 4 days or in the freezer for up to a month.

Per Serving
calories: 224 | fat: 19g | protein: 12g
carbs: 4g | net carbs: 2g | fiber: 2g

Turkey Sausage Breakfast Pizza

Prep time: 10 minutes | Cook time: 24 minutes | Serves 2

4 large eggs, divided
1 tablespoon water
½ teaspoon garlic powder
½ teaspoon onion powder
½ teaspoon dried oregano
2 tablespoons coconut flour
3 tablespoons grated

Parmesan cheese
½ cup shredded provolone cheese
1 link cooked turkey sausage, chopped (about 2 ounces / 57 g)
2 sun-dried tomatoes, finely chopped
2 scallions, thinly sliced

1. Preheat the air fryer to 400°F (204°C). Line a cake pan with parchment paper and lightly coat the paper with olive oil.
2. In a large bowl, whisk 2 of the eggs with the water, garlic powder, onion powder, and dried oregano. Add the coconut flour, breaking up any lumps with your hands as you add it to the bowl. Stir the coconut flour into the egg mixture, mixing until smooth. Stir in the Parmesan cheese. Allow the mixture to rest for a few minutes until thick and dough-like.
3. Transfer the mixture to the prepared pan. Use a spatula to spread it evenly and slightly up the sides of the pan. Air fry until the crust is set but still light in color, about 10 minutes. Top with the cheeses, sausage, and sun-dried tomatoes.
4. Break the remaining 2 eggs into a small bowl, then slide them onto the pizza. Return the pizza to the air fryer. Air fry 10 to 14 minutes until the egg whites are set and the yolks are the desired doneness. Top with the scallions and allow to rest for 5 minutes before serving.

Per Serving
calories: 345 | fat: 23g | protein: 29g
carbs: 5g | net carbs: 4g | fiber: 1g

Breakfast Cobbler

Prep time: 20 minutes | Cook time: 30 minutes | Serves 4

Filling:

10 ounces (283 g) bulk pork sausage, crumbled
¼ cup minced onions
2 cloves garlic, minced
½ teaspoon fine sea salt
½ teaspoon ground

black pepper
1 (8-ounce / 227-g) package cream cheese (or Kite Hill brand cream cheese style spread for dairy-free), softened
¾ cup beef or chicken broth

Biscuits:

3 large egg whites
¾ cup blanched almond flour
1 teaspoon baking powder
¼ teaspoon fine sea

salt
2½ tablespoons very cold unsalted butter, cut into ¼-inch pieces
Fresh thyme leaves, for garnish

1. Preheat the air fryer to 400ºF (204ºC).
2. Place the sausage, onions, and garlic in a pie pan. Using your hands, break up the sausage into small pieces and spread it evenly throughout the pie pan. Season with the salt and pepper. Place the pan in the air fryer and bake for 5 minutes.
3. While the sausage cooks, place the cream cheese and broth in a food processor or blender and purée until smooth.
4. Remove the pork from the air fryer and use a fork or metal spatula to crumble it more. Pour the cream cheese mixture into the sausage and stir to combine. Set aside.
5. Make the biscuits: Place the egg whites in a medium-sized mixing bowl or the bowl of a stand mixer and whip with a hand mixer or stand mixer until stiff peaks form.
6. In a separate medium-sized bowl, whisk together the almond flour, baking powder, and salt, then cut in the butter. When you are done, the mixture should still have chunks of butter. Gently fold the flour mixture into the egg whites with a rubber spatula.
7. Use a large spoon or ice cream scoop to scoop the dough into 4 equal-sized biscuits, making sure the butter is evenly distributed. Place the biscuits on top of the sausage and cook in the air fryer for 5 minutes, then turn the heat down to 325ºF (163ºC) and bake for another 17 to 20 minutes, until the biscuits are golden brown. Serve garnished with fresh thyme leaves.
8. Store leftovers in an airtight container in the refrigerator for up to 3 days. Reheat in a preheated 350ºF (177ºC) air fryer for 5 minutes, or until warmed through.

Per Serving
calories: 623 | fat: 55g | protein: 23g
carbs: 8g | net carbs: 5g | fiber: 3g

BLT Breakfast Wrap

Prep time: 5 minutes | Cook time: 10 minutes | Serves 4

8 ounces (227 g) reduced-sodium bacon
8 tablespoons mayonnaise
8 large romaine

lettuce leaves
4 Roma tomatoes, sliced
Salt and freshly ground black pepper, to taste

1. Arrange the bacon in a single layer in the air fryer basket. (It's OK if the bacon sits a bit on the sides.) Set the air fryer to 350ºF (177ºC) and air fry for 10 minutes. Check for crispiness and air fry for 2 to 3 minutes longer if needed. Cook in batches, if necessary, and drain the grease in between batches.
2. Spread 1 tablespoon of mayonnaise on each of the lettuce leaves and top with the tomatoes and cooked bacon. Season to taste with salt and freshly ground black pepper. Roll the lettuce leaves as you would a burrito, securing with a toothpick if desired.

Per Serving
calories: 370 | fat: 34g | protein: 11g
carbs: 7g | net carbs: 4g | fiber: 3g

Chapter 4 Appetizers and Snacks

Everything Kale Chips

Prep time: 10 minutes | Cook time: 10 to 14 minutes | Serves 8

1 bunch kale, washed, stemmed, and torn into pieces
1 tablespoon extra-virgin olive oil
2 teaspoons everything seasoning

1. Place the kale leaves in a large bowl. Toss with the olive oil and seasoning.
2. Arrange half of the kale in the air fryer basket. Set the air fryer to 325ºF (163ºC). Air fry for 5 to 7 minutes, shaking halfway through, until the kale is crispy. Repeat with the remaining kale.

Per Serving
calories: 35 | fat: 2g | protein: 1g
carbs: 3g | net carbs: 2g | fiber: 1g

Buffalo Chicken Dip

Prep time: 10 minutes | Cook time: 10 minutes | Serves 4

1 cup cooked, diced chicken breast
8 ounces (227 g) full-fat cream cheese, softened
½ cup buffalo sauce
⅓ cup full-fat ranch dressing
⅓ cup chopped pickled jalapeños
1½ cups shredded medium Cheddar cheese, divided
2 scallions, sliced on the bias

1. Place chicken into a large bowl. Add cream cheese, buffalo sauce, and ranch dressing. Stir until the sauces are well mixed and mostly smooth. Fold in jalapeños and 1 cup Cheddar.
2. Pour the mixture into a 4-cup round baking dish and place remaining Cheddar on top. Place dish into the air fryer basket.
3. Adjust the temperature to 350ºF (177ºC) and bake for 10 minutes.
4. When done, the top will be brown and the dip bubbling. Top with sliced scallions. Serve warm.

Per Serving
calories: 472 | fat: 32g | protein: 24g
carbs: 9g | net carbs: 8g | fiber: 1g

Garlic Cheese Bread

Prep time: 10 minutes | Cook time: 10 minutes | Serves 2

1 cup shredded Mozzarella cheese
¼ cup grated Parmesan cheese
1 large egg
½ teaspoon garlic powder

1. Mix all ingredients in a large bowl. Cut a piece of parchment to fit your air fryer basket. Press the mixture into a circle on the parchment and place into the air fryer basket.
2. Adjust the temperature to 350ºF (177ºC) and bake for 10 minutes.
3. Serve warm.

Per Serving
calories: 258 | fat: 16g | protein: 19g
carbs: 4g | net carbs: 4g | fiber: 0g

Bacon-Wrapped Brie

Prep time: 5 minutes | Cook time: 10 minutes | Serves 8

4 slices sugar-free bacon
1 (8-ounce / 227-g) round Brie

1. Place two slices of bacon to form an X. Place the third slice of bacon horizontally across the center of the X. Place the fourth slice of bacon vertically across the X. It should look like a plus sign (+) on top of an X. Place the Brie in the center of the bacon.
2. Wrap the bacon around the Brie, securing with a few toothpicks. Cut a piece of parchment to fit your air fryer basket and place the bacon-wrapped Brie on top. Place inside the air fryer basket.
3. Adjust the temperature to 400ºF (204ºC) and air fry for 10 minutes. Flip during cooking.
4. When cooked, bacon will be crispy and cheese will be soft and melted. To serve, cut into eight slices.

Per Serving
calories: 116 | fat: 9g | protein: 7g
carbs: 0g | net carbs: 0g | fiber: 0g

Smoky Zucchini Chips

Prep time: 15 minutes | Cook time: 8 to 10 minutes | Serves 6

2 large eggs
1 cup finely ground blanched almond flour
½ cup Parmesan cheese
1½ teaspoons sea salt
1 teaspoon garlic powder
½ teaspoon smoked paprika
¼ teaspoon freshly ground black pepper
2 zucchini, cut into ¼-inch-thick slices
Avocado oil spray

1. Beat the eggs in a shallow bowl. In another bowl, stir together the almond flour, Parmesan cheese, salt, garlic powder, smoked paprika, and black pepper.
2. Dip the zucchini slices in the egg mixture, then coat them with the almond flour mixture.
3. Set the air fryer to 400ºF (204ºC). Place the zucchini chips in a single layer in the air fryer basket, working in batches if necessary. Spray the chips with oil and air fry for 4 minutes. Flip the chips and spray them with more oil. Air fry for 4 to 6 minutes more.
4. Serve with your favorite dipping sauce.

Per Serving
calories: 181 | fat: 14g | protein: 11g
carbs: 7g | net carbs: 4g | fiber: 3g

Sweet and Spicy Pecans

Prep time: 7 minutes | Cook time: 15 minutes | Serves 8

3 tablespoons unsalted butter, melted
¼ cup Swerve
1½ teaspoons Maldon sea salt (or regular sea salt if you like)
¼ teaspoon cayenne pepper, more or less to taste
2 cups pecan halves

1. Line your air fryer basket with parchment paper or an air fryer liner.
2. Place the melted butter in a small pot and whisk in the Swerve, sea salt, and cayenne pepper. Stir until well combined.
3. Place the pecans in a medium bowl and pour the butter mixture over them. Toss to coat.

4. Set the air fryer to 275ºF (135ºC). Place the pecans in the air fryer basket in a single layer, working in batches if necessary, and air fry for 10 minutes. Stir, then air fry for 5 minutes more.
5. Transfer the pecans to a parchment paper-lined baking sheet and allow them to cool completely before serving. Store them in an airtight container at room temperature for up to 1 week.

Per Serving
calories: 225 | fat: 24g | protein: 3g
carbs: 10g | net carbs: 7g | fiber: 3g

Bacon-Wrapped Jalapeño Poppers

Prep time: 15 minutes | Cook time: 17 to 22 minutes | Serves 12

12 jalapeño peppers
8 ounces (227 g) cream cheese, at room temperature
2 tablespoons minced onion
1 teaspoon garlic powder
½ teaspoon smoked paprika
Sea salt and freshly ground black pepper, to taste
12 strips bacon

1. Slice the jalapeños in half lengthwise, then seed them and remove any remaining white membranes to make room for the filling. Set the air fryer to 400ºF (204ºC). Place the jalapeños in a single layer, cut-side down, in the air fryer basket. Air fry for 7 minutes.
2. Remove the peppers from the air fryer and place them on a paper towel, cut-side up. Allow them to rest until they are cool enough to handle.
3. While the jalapeños are cooking, in a medium bowl, stir together the cream cheese, minced onion, garlic powder, and smoked paprika. Season to taste with salt and pepper.
4. Spoon the cream cheese filling into the jalapeños.
5. Cut the bacon strips in half, and wrap 1 piece around each stuffed jalapeño half.
6. Place the bacon-wrapped jalapeños, cut-side up, in a single layer in the air fryer basket. Air fry for 10 to 15 minutes, until the bacon is crispy.

Per Serving
calories: 116 | fat: 10g | protein: 4g
carbs: 2g | net carbs: 1g | fiber: 1g

Mozzarella-Stuffed Meatballs

Prep time: 15 minutes | Cook time: 15 minutes | Makes 16 meatballs

1 pound (454 g) 80/20 ground beef
¼ cup blanched finely ground almond flour
1 teaspoon dried parsley
½ teaspoon garlic powder
¼ teaspoon onion powder

1 large egg
3 ounces (85 g) low-moisture, whole-milk Mozzarella, cubed
½ cup low-carb, no-sugar-added pasta sauce
¼ cup grated Parmesan cheese

1. In a large bowl, add ground beef, almond flour, parsley, garlic powder, onion powder, and egg. Fold ingredients together until fully combined.
2. Form the mixture into 2-inch balls and use your thumb or a spoon to create an indent in the center of each meatball. Place a cube of cheese in the center and form the ball around it.
3. Place the meatballs into the air fryer, working in batches if necessary.
4. Adjust the temperature to 350ºF (177ºC) and air fry for 15 minutes.
5. Meatballs will be slightly crispy on the outside and fully cooked when at least 180ºF (82ºC) internally.
6. When they are finished cooking, toss the meatballs in the sauce and sprinkle with grated Parmesan for serving.

Per Serving

calories: 447 | fat: 30g | protein: 30g
carbs: 5g | net carbs: 3g | fiber: 2g

Doro Wat Wings

Prep time: 5 minutes | Cook time: 32 minutes | Makes 1 dozen wings

1 dozen chicken wings or drummies
1 tablespoon coconut oil or bacon fat, melted

2 teaspoons berbere spice
1 teaspoon fine sea salt

For Serving:
2 hard-boiled eggs
½ teaspoon fine sea salt
¼ teaspoon berbere

spice
¼ teaspoon dried chives

1. Spray the air fryer basket with avocado oil. Preheat the air fryer to 380ºF (193ºC).
2. Place the chicken wings in a large bowl. Pour the oil over them and turn to coat completely. Sprinkle the berbere and salt on all sides of the chicken.
3. Place the chicken wings in the air fryer and air fry for 25 minutes, flipping after 15 minutes.
4. After 25 minutes, increase the temperature to 400ºF (204ºC) and air fry for 6 to 7 minutes more, until the skin is browned and crisp.
5. While the chicken cooks, prepare the hard-boiled eggs (if using): Peel the eggs, slice them in half, and season them with the salt, berbere, and dried chives. Serve the chicken and eggs together.
6. Store leftovers in an airtight container in the fridge for up to 4 days. Reheat the chicken in a preheated 400ºF (204ºC) air fryer for 5 minutes, or until heated through.

Per Serving

calories: 317 | fat: 24g | protein: 24g
carbs: 0g | net carbs: 0g | fiber: 0g

Ranch Roasted Almonds

Prep time: 5 minutes | Cook time: 6 minutes | Makes 2 cups

2 cups raw almonds
2 tablespoons unsalted butter, melted

½ (1-ounce / 28-g) ranch dressing mix packet

1. In a large bowl, toss almonds in butter to evenly coat. Sprinkle ranch mix over almonds and toss. Place almonds into the air fryer basket.
2. Adjust the temperature to 320ºF (160ºC) and air fry for 6 minutes.
3. Shake the basket two or three times during cooking.
4. Let cool at least 20 minutes. Almonds will be soft but become crunchier during cooling. Store in an airtight container up to 3 days.

Per Serving

calories: 190 | fat: 17g | protein: 6g
carbs: 7g | net carbs: 4g | fiber: 3g

Salt and Vinegar Pork Belly Chips

Prep time: 5 minutes | Cook time: 12 minutes | Serves 4

1 pound (454 g) slab pork belly
½ cup apple cider vinegar
Fine sea salt, to taste
For Serving (Optional):
Guacamole
Pico de gallo

1. Slice the pork belly into ⅛-inch-thick strips and place them in a shallow dish. Pour in the vinegar and stir to coat the pork belly. Place in the fridge to marinate for 30 minutes.
2. Spray the air fryer basket with avocado oil. Preheat the air fryer to 400ºF (204ºC).
3. Remove the pork belly from the vinegar and place the strips in the air fryer basket in a single layer, leaving space between them. Air fry in the air fryer for 10 to 12 minutes, until crispy, flipping after 5 minutes. Remove from the air fryer and sprinkle with salt. Serve with guacamole and pico de gallo, if desired.
4. Best served fresh. Store leftovers in an airtight container in the fridge for up to 5 days. Reheat in a preheated 400ºF (204ºC) air fryer for 5 minutes, or until heated through, flipping halfway through.

Per Serving
calories: 240 | fat: 21g | protein: 13g
carbs: 0g | net carbs: 0g | fiber: 0g

Onion Rings

Prep time: 15 minutes | Cook time: 10 minutes | Serves 6

1 large sweet onion
1 cup finely ground blanched almond flour
1 cup finely grated Parmesan cheese
1 tablespoon baking powder
1 teaspoon smoked paprika
Sea salt and freshly ground black pepper, to taste
2 large eggs
1 tablespoon heavy (whipping) cream
Avocado oil spray

1. Cut the onion crosswise into ⅓-inch-thick rings.
2. In a medium bowl, combine the almond flour, Parmesan cheese, baking powder, smoked paprika, and salt and pepper to taste.
3. In a separate medium bowl, beat the eggs and heavy cream together.
4. Dip an onion ring in the egg mixture and then into the almond flour mixture. Press the almond flour mixture into the onion. Transfer to a parchment paper-lined baking sheet (I find the parchment helps reduce sticking during prep) and repeat with the remaining onion slices.
5. Set the air fryer to 350ºF (177ºC). Arrange the onion rings in a single layer in the air fryer basket, working in batches if needed. Spray the onion rings with oil and air fry for 5 minutes.
6. Use a spatula to carefully reach under the onions and flip them. Spray the onion rings with oil again and air fry for 5 minutes more.

Per Serving
calories: 220 | fat: 14g | protein: 14g
carbs: 10g | net carbs: 7g | fiber: 3g

Spicy Cheese-Stuffed Mushrooms

Prep time: 10 minutes | Cook time: 8 minutes | Makes 20 mushrooms

4 ounces (113 g) cream cheese, softened
6 tablespoons shredded Pepper Jack cheese
2 tablespoons chopped pickled jalapeños
20 medium button mushrooms, stems removed
2 tablespoons olive oil
¼ teaspoon salt
⅛ teaspoon ground black pepper

1. In a large bowl, mix cream cheese, pepper jack, and jalapeños together.
2. Drizzle mushrooms with olive oil, then sprinkle with salt and pepper. Spoon 2 tablespoons cheese mixture into each mushroom and place in a single layer into ungreased air fryer basket. Adjust the temperature to 370ºF (188ºC) and roast for 8 minutes, checking halfway through cooking to ensure even cooking, rearranging if some are darker than others. When they're golden and cheese is bubbling, mushrooms will be done. Serve warm.

Per Serving (2 mushrooms)
calories: 87 | fat: 7g | protein: 3g
carbs: 2g | net carbs: 2g | fiber: 0g

Fried Pickles

Prep time: 20 minutes | Cook time: 10 to 12 minutes | Serves 8

16 ounces (454 g) whole dill pickles
2 large eggs, beaten
2 tablespoons heavy (whipping) cream
½ cup finely ground blanched almond flour
½ cup grated Parmesan cheese
1 teaspoon Cajun seasoning
¼ teaspoon cayenne pepper, more or less to taste
Salt and freshly ground black pepper, to taste
Avocado oil spray

1. Cut the pickles in half lengthwise and then cut each half into quarters. Alternatively, you can slice them into rounds.
2. Combine the eggs and heavy cream in a shallow bowl. In a separate bowl, combine the almond flour, Parmesan cheese, Cajun seasoning, cayenne pepper, and salt and black pepper to taste.
3. Dip the pickles in the eggs and then coat them with the almond flour mixture. Press the almond flour mixture firmly into the pickles. Place the coated pickles on a parchment paper-lined baking sheet or platter and freeze for 20 minutes.
4. Preheat the air fryer to 400ºF (204ºC). Spray the pickles with oil and arrange them in a single layer in the air fryer basket, working in batches if necessary. Air fry for 6 minutes. Flip the pickles and spray them again with oil. Air fry for 4 to 6 minutes more, until they are golden brown.
5. Serve warm with your favorite dipping sauce.

Per Serving
calories: 105 | fat: 8g | protein: 6g
carbs: 4g | net carbs: 3g | fiber: 1g

Dry Rub Chicken Wings

Prep time: 5 minutes | Cook time: 35 to 40 minutes | Serves 4

1 tablespoon paprika
1 tablespoon Swerve
½ teaspoon dried oregano
½ teaspoon garlic powder
½ teaspoon freshly ground black pepper
½ teaspoon cayenne
1 pound (454 g) chicken wings, tips removed

1. In a large bowl, combine the paprika, Swerve, oregano, garlic powder, black pepper, and cayenne. Add the chicken wings and toss until thoroughly coated. Cover and refrigerate for at least 1 hour or up to 8 hours.
2. Preheat the air fryer to 400ºF (204ºC).
3. Working in batches if necessary, arrange the wings in a single layer in the air fryer basket. Spray lightly with olive oil. Pausing halfway through the cooking time to turn the wings, air fry for 35 to 40 minutes until browned and crispy and a thermometer inserted into the thickest part registers 165ºF (74ºC).

Per Serving
calories: 290 | fat: 19g | protein: 27g
carbs: 1g | net carbs: 0g | fiber: 1g

Sweet and Spicy Beef Jerky

Prep time: 10 minutes | Cook time: 4 hours | Serves 6

1 pound (454 g) eye of round beef, fat trimmed, sliced into ¼-inch-thick strips
¼ cup coconut aminos
2 tablespoons
Sriracha hot chili sauce
½ teaspoon ground black pepper
2 tablespoons granular brown erythritol

1. Place beef in a large sealable bowl or bag. Pour coconut aminos and Sriracha into bowl or bag, then sprinkle in pepper and erythritol. Shake or stir to combine ingredients and coat steak. Cover and place in refrigerator to marinate at least 2 hours up to overnight.
2. Once marinated, remove strips from marinade and pat dry. Place into ungreased air fryer basket in a single layer, working in batches if needed. Adjust the temperature to 180ºF (82ºC) and air fry for 4 hours. Jerky will be chewy and dark brown when done. Store in airtight container in a cool, dry place up to 2 weeks.

Per Serving
calories: 99 | fat: 2g | protein: 18g
carbs: 1g | net carbs: 1g | fiber: 0g

Pepperoni Rolls

Prep time: 5 minutes | Cook time: 8 minutes | Makes 12 rolls

2½ cups shredded Mozzarella cheese
2 ounces (57 g) cream cheese, softened

1 cup blanched finely ground almond flour
48 slices pepperoni
2 teaspoons Italian seasoning

1. In a large microwave-safe bowl, combine Mozzarella, cream cheese, and flour. Microwave on high 90 seconds until cheese is melted.
2. Using a wooden spoon, mix melted mixture 2 minutes until a dough forms.
3. Once dough is cool enough to work with your hands, about 2 minutes, spread it out into a 12 × 4-inch rectangle on ungreased parchment paper. Line dough with pepperoni, divided into four even rows. Sprinkle Italian seasoning evenly over pepperoni.
4. Starting at the long end of the dough, roll up until a log is formed. Slice the log into twelve even pieces.
5. Place pizza rolls in an ungreased nonstick baking dish. Adjust the temperature to 375ºF (191ºC) and bake for 8 minutes. Rolls will be golden and firm when done. Allow cooked rolls to cool 10 minutes before serving.

Per Serving (2 rolls)
calories: 366 | fat: 27g | protein: 20g
carbs: 7g | net carbs: 5g | fiber: 2g

Mini Greek Meatballs

Prep time: 10 minutes | Cook time: 10 minutes | Makes 36 meatballs

1 cup fresh spinach leaves
¼ cup peeled and diced red onion
½ cup crumbled feta cheese
1 pound (454 g)

85/15 ground turkey
½ teaspoon salt
½ teaspoon ground cumin
¼ teaspoon ground black pepper

1. Place spinach, onion, and feta in a food processor, and pulse ten times until spinach is chopped. Scoop into a large bowl.
2. Add turkey to bowl and sprinkle with salt, cumin, and pepper. Mix until fully combined. Roll mixture into thirty-six meatballs (about 1 tablespoon each).
3. Place meatballs into ungreased air fryer basket, working in batches if needed. Adjust the temperature to 350ºF (177ºC) and air fry for 10 minutes, shaking basket twice during cooking. Meatballs will be browned and have an internal temperature of at least 165ºF (74ºC) when done. Serve warm.

Per Serving (4 meatballs)
calories: 115 | fat: 7g | protein: 10g
carbs: 1g | net carbs: 1g | fiber: 0g

Deviled Eggs

Prep time: 10 minutes | Cook time: 25 minutes | Makes 12 eggs

7 large eggs, divided
1 ounce (28 g) plain pork rinds, finely crushed
2 tablespoons

mayonnaise
¼ teaspoon salt
¼ teaspoon ground black pepper

1. Place 6 whole eggs into ungreased air fryer basket. Adjust the temperature to 220ºF (104ºC) and air fry for 20 minutes. When done, place eggs into a bowl of ice water to cool 5 minutes.
2. Peel cool eggs, then cut in half lengthwise. Remove yolks and place aside in a medium bowl.
3. In a separate small bowl, whisk remaining raw egg. Place pork rinds in a separate medium bowl. Dip each egg white into whisked egg, then gently coat with pork rinds. Spritz with cooking spray and place into ungreased air fryer basket. Adjust the temperature to 400ºF (204ºC) and air fry for 5 minutes, turning eggs halfway through cooking. Eggs will be golden when done.
4. Mash yolks in bowl with mayonnaise until smooth. Sprinkle with salt and pepper and mix.
5. Spoon 2 tablespoons yolk mixture into each fried egg white. Serve warm.

Per Serving (2 eggs)
calories: 141 | fat: 10g | protein: 10g
carbs: 1g | net carbs: 1g | fiber: 0g

Reuben Egg Rolls

Prep time: 15 minutes | Cook time: 10 minutes per batch | Makes 20 egg rolls

1 (8-ounce / 227-g) package cream cheese, softened
½ pound (227 g) cooked corned beef, chopped

½ cup drained and chopped sauerkraut
½ cup shredded Swiss cheese (about 2 ounces / 57 g)
20 slices prosciutto

Thousand Island Dipping Sauce:

¾ cup mayonnaise
¼ cup chopped dill pickles
¼ cup tomato sauce
2 tablespoons Swerve confectioners'-style sweetener or equivalent amount of liquid or powdered

sweetener
⅛ teaspoon fine sea salt
Fresh thyme leaves, for garnish
Ground black pepper, for garnish
Sauerkraut, for serving (optional)

1. Spray the air fryer basket with avocado oil. Preheat the air fryer to 400°F (204°C).
2. Make the filling: Place the cream cheese in a medium-sized bowl and stir to break it up. Add the corned beef, sauerkraut, and Swiss cheese and stir well to combine.
3. Assemble the egg rolls: Lay 1 slice of prosciutto on a sushi mat or a sheet of parchment paper with a short end toward you. Lay another slice of prosciutto on top of it at a right angle, forming a cross. Spoon 3 to 4 tablespoons of the filling into the center of the cross.
4. Fold the sides of the top slice up and over the filling to form the ends of the roll. Tightly roll up the long piece of prosciutto, starting at the edge closest to you, into a tight egg roll shape that overlaps by an inch or so. (Note: If the prosciutto rips, it's okay. It will seal when you fry it.) Repeat with the remaining prosciutto and filling.
5. Place the egg rolls in the air fryer seam side down, leaving space between them. (If you're using a smaller air fryer, cook in batches if necessary.) Air fry for 10 minutes, or until the outside is crispy.
6. While the egg rolls are cooking, make the dipping sauce: In a small bowl, combine the mayo, pickles, tomato sauce, sweetener, and salt. Stir well and garnish with thyme and ground black pepper. (The dipping sauce can be made up to 3 days ahead.)
7. Serve the egg rolls with the dipping sauce and sauerkraut if desired. Best served fresh. Store leftovers in an airtight container in the refrigerator for up to 5 days or in the freezer for up to a month. Reheat in a preheated 400°F (204°C) air fryer for 4 minutes, or until heated through and crispy.

Per Serving
calories: 321 | fat: 29g | protein: 13g
carbs: 1g | net carbs: 1g | fiber: 0g

Pepperoni Chips

Prep time: 5 minutes | Cook time: 8 minutes | Serves 2

14 slices pepperoni

1. Place pepperoni slices into ungreased air fryer basket. Adjust the temperature to 350°F (177°C) and air fry for 8 minutes. Pepperoni will be browned and crispy when done. Let cool 5 minutes before serving. Store in airtight container at room temperature up to 3 days.

Per Serving
calories: 69 | fat: 5g | protein: 3g
carbs: 0g | net carbs: 0g | fiber: 0g

Three Cheese Dip

Prep time: 5 minutes | Cook time: 12 minutes | Serves 8

8 ounces (227 g) cream cheese, softened
½ cup mayonnaise
¼ cup sour cream

½ cup shredded sharp Cheddar cheese
¼ cup shredded Monterey Jack cheese

1. In a large bowl, combine all ingredients. Scoop mixture into an ungreased 4-cup nonstick baking dish and place into air fryer basket.
2. Adjust the temperature to 375°F (191°C) and bake for 12 minutes. Dip will be browned on top and bubbling when done. Serve warm.

Per Serving (2 tablespoons)
calories: 245 | fat: 23g | protein: 5g
carbs: 2g | net carbs: 2g | fiber: 0g

Mozzarella Sticks

Prep time: 15 minutes | Cook time: 14 minutes per batch | Makes 24 Mozzarella sticks

Dough:

1¾ cups shredded Mozzarella cheese (about 7 ounces / 198 g)
2 tablespoons unsalted butter
1 large egg, beaten

¾ cup blanched almond flour
⅛ teaspoon fine sea salt
24 pieces of string cheese

Spice Mix:

¼ cup grated Parmesan cheese
3 tablespoons garlic powder
1 tablespoon dried oregano leaves

1 tablespoon onion powder

For Serving (Optional):
½ cup marinara sauce
½ cup pesto

1. Make the dough: Place the Mozzarella and butter in a large microwave-safe bowl and microwave for 1 to 2 minutes, until the cheese is entirely melted. Stir well.
2. Add the egg and, using a hand mixer on low, combine well. Add the almond flour and salt and combine well with the mixer.
3. Lay a piece of parchment paper on the countertop and place the dough on it. Knead it for about 3 minutes; the dough should be thick yet pliable. (Note: If the dough is too sticky, chill it in the refrigerator for an hour or overnight.)
4. Scoop up 3 tablespoons of the dough and flatten it into a very thin 3½ by 2-inch rectangle. Place one piece of string cheese in the center and use your hands to press the dough tightly around it. Repeat with the remaining string cheese and dough.
5. In a shallow dish, combine the spice mix ingredients. Place a wrapped piece of string cheese in the dish and roll while pressing down to form a nice crust. Repeat with the remaining pieces of string cheese. Place in the freezer for 2 hours.
6. Ten minutes before air frying, spray the air fryer basket with avocado oil and preheat the air fryer to 425°F (218°C).
7. Place the frozen Mozzarella sticks in the air fryer basket, leaving space between them, and air fry for 9 to 12 minutes, until golden brown. Remove from the air fryer and serve with marinara sauce and pesto, if desired.
8. Store leftovers in an airtight container in the refrigerator for up to 3 days or in the freezer for up to a month. Reheat in a preheated 425°F (218°C) air fryer for 4 minutes, or until warmed through.

Per Serving

calories: 337 | fat: 27g | protein: 23g
carbs: 4g | net carbs: 3g | fiber: 1g

Calamari Rings

Prep time: 10 minutes | Cook time: 15 minutes | Serves 4

2 large egg yolks
1 cup powdered Parmesan cheese
¼ cup coconut flour
3 teaspoons dried oregano leaves
½ teaspoon garlic powder
½ teaspoon onion powder

1 pound (454 g) calamari, sliced into rings
Fresh oregano leaves, for garnish (optional)
1 cup marinara sauce, for serving (optional)
Lemon slices, for serving (optional)

1. Spray the air fryer basket with avocado oil. Preheat the air fryer to 400°F (204°C).
2. In a shallow dish, whisk the egg yolks. In a separate bowl, mix together the Parmesan, coconut flour, and spices.
3. Dip the calamari rings in the egg yolks, tap off any excess egg, then dip them into the cheese mixture and coat well. Use your hands to press the coating onto the calamari if necessary. Spray the coated rings with avocado oil.
4. Place the calamari rings in the air fryer, leaving space between them, and air fry for 15 minutes, or until golden brown. Garnish with fresh oregano, if desired, and serve with marinara sauce for dipping and lemon slices, if desired.
5. Best served fresh. Store leftovers in an airtight container in the fridge for up to 5 days. Reheat in a preheated 400°F (204°C) air fryer for 3 minutes, or until heated through.

Per Serving

calories: 287 | fat: 13g | protein: 28g
carbs: 11g | net carbs: 8g | fiber: 1g

Prosciutto-Wrapped Guacamole Rings

Prep time: 10 minutes | Cook time: 6 minutes | Makes 8 rings

2 small onions (about 1½ inches in diameter), cut into **Guacamole:**

½-inch-thick slices
8 slices prosciutto

Guacamole:
2 avocados, halved, pitted, and peeled
3 tablespoons lime juice, plus more to taste
2 small plum tomatoes, diced
½ cup finely diced onions

2 small cloves garlic, smashed to a paste
3 tablespoons chopped fresh cilantro leaves
½ scant teaspoon fine sea salt
½ scant teaspoon ground cumin

1. Make the guacamole: Place the avocados and lime juice in a large bowl and mash with a fork until it reaches your desired consistency. Add the tomatoes, onions, garlic, cilantro, salt, and cumin and stir until well combined. Taste and add more lime juice if desired. Set aside half of the guacamole for serving. (Note: If you're making the guacamole ahead of time, place it in a large resealable plastic bag, squeeze out all the air, and seal it shut. It will keep in the refrigerator for up to 3 days when stored this way.)
2. Place a piece of parchment paper on a tray that fits in your freezer and place the onion slices on it, breaking the slices apart into 8 rings. Fill each ring with about 2 tablespoons of guacamole. Place the tray in the freezer for 2 hours.
3. Spray the air fryer basket with avocado oil. Preheat the air fryer to 400ºF (204ºC).
4. Remove the rings from the freezer and wrap each in a slice of prosciutto. Place them in the air fryer basket, leaving space between them (if you're using a smaller air fryer, work in batches if necessary), and air fry for 6 minutes, flipping halfway through. Use a spatula to remove the rings from the air fryer. Serve with the reserved half of the guacamole.
5. Store leftovers in an airtight container in the refrigerator for up to 4 days. Reheat in a preheated 400ºF (204ºC) air fryer for about 3 minutes, until heated through.

Per Serving
calories: 132 | fat: 9g | protein: 5g
carbs: 10g | net carbs: 6g | fiber: 4g

Pizza Rolls

Prep time: 15 minutes | Cook time: 10 minutes | Makes 24 rolls

2 cups shredded Mozzarella cheese
½ cup almond flour
2 large eggs
72 slices pepperoni
8 (1-ounce / 28-g) Mozzarella string cheese sticks, cut into 3 pieces each

2 tablespoons unsalted butter, melted
¼ teaspoon garlic powder
½ teaspoon dried parsley
2 tablespoons grated Parmesan cheese

1. In a large microwave-safe bowl, place Mozzarella and almond flour. Microwave for 1 minute. Remove bowl and mix until ball of dough forms. Microwave additional 30 seconds if necessary.
2. Crack eggs into the bowl and mix until smooth dough ball forms. Wet your hands with water and knead the dough briefly.
3. Tear off two large pieces of parchment paper and spray one side of each with nonstick cooking spray. Place the dough ball between the two sheets, with sprayed sides facing dough. Use a rolling pin to roll dough out to ¼-inch thickness.
4. Use a knife to slice into 24 rectangles. On each rectangle place 3 pepperoni slices and 1 piece string cheese.
5. Fold the rectangle in half, covering pepperoni and cheese filling. Pinch or roll sides closed. Cut a piece of parchment to fit your air fryer basket and place it into the basket. Put the rolls onto the parchment.
6. Adjust the temperature to 350ºF (177ºC) and air fry for 10 minutes.
7. After 5 minutes, open the fryer and flip the pizza rolls. Restart the fryer and continue cooking until pizza rolls are golden.
8. In a small bowl, place butter, garlic powder, and parsley. Brush the mixture over cooked pizza rolls and then sprinkle with Parmesan. Serve warm.

Per Serving
calories: 333 | fat: 24g | protein: 20g
carbs: 3g | net carbs: 2g | fiber: 1g

Prosciutto Pierogi

Prep time: 15 minutes | Cook time: 20 minutes | Serves 4

1 cup chopped cauliflower
2 tablespoons diced onions
1 tablespoon unsalted butter (or lard or bacon fat for dairy-free), melted
Pinch of fine sea salt
½ cup shredded

sharp Cheddar cheese (about 2 ounces / 57 g) (or Kite Hill brand cream cheese style spread, softened, for dairy-free)
8 slices prosciutto
Fresh oregano leaves, for garnish (optional)

1. Preheat the air fryer to 350ºF (177ºC). Lightly grease a pie pan or a casserole dish that will fit in your air fryer.
2. Make the filling: Place the cauliflower and onion in the pan. Drizzle with the melted butter and sprinkle with the salt. Using your hands, mix everything together, making sure the cauliflower is coated in the butter.
3. Place the cauliflower mixture in the air fryer and bake for 10 minutes, until fork-tender, stirring halfway through.
4. Transfer the cauliflower mixture to a food processor or high-powered blender. Spray the air fryer basket with avocado oil and increase the air fryer temperature to 400ºF (204ºC).
5. Pulse the cauliflower mixture in the food processor until smooth. Stir in the cheese.
6. Assemble the pierogi: Lay 1 slice of prosciutto on a sheet of parchment paper with a short end toward you. Lay another slice of prosciutto on top of it at a right angle, forming a cross. Spoon about 2 heaping tablespoons of the filling into the center of the cross.
7. Fold each arm of the prosciutto cross over the filling to form a square, making sure that the filling is well covered. Using your fingers, press down around the filling to even out the square shape. Repeat with the rest of the prosciutto and filling.
8. Spray the pierogi with avocado oil and place them in the air fryer basket. Air fry for 10 minutes, or until crispy.
9. Garnish with oregano before serving, if desired. Store leftovers in an airtight container in the fridge for up to 4 days. Reheat in a preheated 400ºF (204ºC) air fryer for 3 minutes, or until heated through.

Per Serving
calories: 150 | fat: 11g | protein: 11g
carbs: 2g | net carbs: 1g | fiber: 1g

Bacon and Egg Bites

Prep time: 10 minutes | Cook time: 10 minutes | Serves 4

6 ounces (170 g) reduced-sodium bacon
2 hard-boiled eggs, chopped
Flesh of ½ avocado, chopped
2 tablespoons unsalted butter, softened
2 tablespoons

mayonnaise
1 jalapeño pepper, seeded and finely chopped
2 tablespoons chopped fresh cilantro
Juice of ½ lime
Salt and freshly ground black pepper, to taste

1. Arrange the bacon in a single layer in the air fryer basket (it's OK if the bacon sits a bit on the sides). Set the air fryer to 350ºF (177ºC) and air fry for 10 minutes. Check for crispiness and cook for 2 to 3 minutes longer if needed. Transfer the bacon to a paper towel-lined plate and let cool completely. Reserve 2 tablespoons of bacon grease from the bottom of the air fryer basket. Finely chop the bacon and set aside in a small, shallow bowl.
2. In a large bowl, combine the eggs, avocado, butter, mayonnaise, jalapeño, cilantro, and lime juice. Mash into a smooth paste with a fork or potato smasher. Season to taste with salt and pepper.
3. Add the reserved bacon grease to the egg mixture and stir gently until thoroughly combined. Cover and refrigerate for 30 minutes, or until the mixture is firm.
4. Divide the mixture into 12 equal portions and shape into balls. Roll the balls in the chopped bacon bits until completely coated.

Per Serving (3 balls)
calories: 330 | fat: 31g | protein: 10g
carbs: 2g | net carbs: 2g | fiber: 0g

Bacon-Pickle Bites

Prep time: 5 minutes | Cook time: 10 minutes | Serves 4

4 dill pickles
8 slices reduced-sodium bacon, cut in

half
¼ cup ranch dressing

1. Slice each pickle into 4 spears by cutting lengthwise. Wrap a piece of bacon around each pickle spear.
2. Arrange the pickles seam-side down in a single layer in the air fryer basket. Set the air fryer to 350ºF (177ºC) and air fry for 10 minutes. Check for crispiness and cook for 2 to 3 minutes longer if needed. Serve with the ranch dressing for dipping.

Per Serving
calories: 230 | fat: 21g | protein: 7g
carbs: 5g | net carbs: 1g | fiber: 1g

Bacon-Wrapped Cabbage Bites

Prep time: 10 minutes | Cook time: 12 minutes | Serves 6

3 tablespoons Sriracha hot chili sauce, divided
1 medium head cabbage, cored and cut into 12 bite-sized pieces
2 tablespoons coconut

oil, melted
½ teaspoon salt
12 slices sugar-free bacon
½ cup mayonnaise
¼ teaspoon garlic powder

1. Evenly brush 2 tablespoons Sriracha onto cabbage pieces. Drizzle evenly with coconut oil, then sprinkle with salt.
2. Wrap each cabbage piece with bacon and secure with a toothpick. Place into ungreased air fryer basket. Adjust the temperature to 375ºF (191ºC) and air fry for 12 minutes, turning cabbage halfway through cooking. Bacon will be cooked and crispy when done.
3. In a small bowl, whisk together mayonnaise, garlic powder, and remaining Sriracha. Use as a dipping sauce for cabbage bites.

Per Serving
calories: 316 | fat: 26g | protein: 10g
carbs: 11g | net carbs: 7g | fiber: 4g

Sausage-Cheddar Bites

Prep time: 5 minutes | Cook time: 25 minutes | Serves 12

1 pound (454 g) bulk Italian sausage
½ cup almond flour
¼ cup coconut flour
1 teaspoon garlic powder
½ teaspoon baking powder
½ teaspoon smoked

paprika
½ teaspoon dried oregano
3 eggs
¼ cup coconut oil, melted
½ cup sour cream
2 cups shredded Cheddar cheese

1. Crumble the sausage into small pieces in the air fryer basket. Set the air fryer to 400ºF (204ºC) and air fry for 10 to 15 minutes until browned. Transfer the sausage to a bowl and set aside. When the air fryer basket is cool enough to handle, drain the grease and wash the basket.
2. Meanwhile, in a small bowl, combine the almond flour, coconut flour, garlic powder, baking powder, paprika, and oregano.
3. In a large bowl, whisk together the eggs, coconut oil, and sour cream.
4. Add the flour mixture to the egg mixture. Use a silicone spatula to gently fold the ingredients until thoroughly combined (do not overmix). Stir in the reserved sausage and the Cheddar. Let the batter rest for 5 minutes.
5. Using a small cookie scoop, shape the dough into 24 balls and arrange them on a rimmed baking sheet. Refrigerate for 10 minutes.
6. Preheat the air fryer to 370ºF (188ºC).
7. Working in batches, arrange the balls in a single layer in the air fryer basket (about 1 inch apart). Spray generously with olive oil. Pausing halfway through the cooking time to shake the basket, air fry for 10 to 12 minutes until golden brown.

Per Serving
calories: 280 | fat: 23g | protein: 13g
carbs: 4g | net carbs: 4g | fiber: 0g

Spicy Turkey Meatballs

Prep time: 10 minutes | Cook time: 15 minutes | Makes 18 meatballs

1 pound (454 g) 85/15 ground turkey
1 large egg, whisked
¼ cup Sriracha hot chili sauce
½ teaspoon salt
½ teaspoon paprika
¼ teaspoon ground black pepper

1. Combine all ingredients in a large bowl. Roll mixture into eighteen meatballs, about 3 tablespoons each.
2. Place meatballs into ungreased air fryer basket. Adjust the temperature to 375°F (191°C) and air fry for 15 minutes, shaking the basket three times during cooking. Meatballs will be done when browned and internal temperature is at least 165°F (74°C). Serve warm.

Per Serving (3 meatballs)
calories: 146 | fat: 9g | protein: 13g
carbs: 2g | net carbs: 2g | fiber: 0g

Sausage-Stuffed Mushrooms

Prep time: 10 minutes | Cook time: 20 minutes | Serves 6

½ pound (227 g) ground pork sausage
¼ teaspoon salt
¼ teaspoon garlic powder
2 medium scallions, trimmed and chopped
½ ounce (14 g) plain pork rinds, finely crushed
1 pound (454 g) cremini mushrooms, stems removed

1. In a large bowl, mix sausage, salt, garlic powder, scallions, and pork rinds. Scoop 1 tablespoon mixture into center of each mushroom cap.
2. Place mushrooms into ungreased air fryer basket. Adjust the temperature to 375°F (191°C) and roast for 20 minutes. Pork will be fully cooked to at least 145°F (63°C) in the center and browned when done. Serve warm.

Per Serving
calories: 161 | fat: 12g | protein: 9g
carbs: 4g | net carbs: 3g | fiber: 1g

Salami Roll-Ups

Prep time: 5 minutes | Cook time: 4 minutes | Makes 16 roll-ups

4 ounces (113 g) cream cheese, broken into 16 equal pieces
16 (½-ounce / 14-g) deli slices Genoa salami

1. Place a piece of cream cheese at the edge of a slice of salami and roll to close. Secure with a toothpick. Repeat with remaining cream cheese pieces and salami.
2. Place roll-ups in an ungreased round nonstick baking dish and place into air fryer basket. Adjust the temperature to 350°F (177°C) and bake for 4 minutes. Salami will be crispy and cream cheese will be warm when done. Let cool 5 minutes before serving.

Per Serving (4 roll-ups)
calories: 269 | fat: 22g | protein: 11g
carbs: 2g | net carbs: 2g | fiber: 0g

Cheese Crisps

Prep time: 5 minutes | Cook time: 10 to 12 minutes | Serves 2

½ cup shredded Cheddar cheese
1 egg white

1. Preheat the air fryer to 400°F (204°C). Place a piece of parchment paper in the bottom of the air fryer basket.
2. In a medium bowl, combine the cheese and egg white, stirring with a fork until thoroughly combined.
3. Place small scoops of the cheese mixture in a single layer in the basket of the air fryer (about 1 inch apart). Use the fork to spread the mixture as thin as possible. Air fry for 10 to 12 minutes until the crisps are golden brown. Let cool for a few minutes before transferring them to a plate. Store at room temperature in an airtight container for up to 3 days.

Per Serving
calories: 120 | fat: 10g | protein: 9g
carbs: 1g | net carbs: 1g | fiber: 0g

Savory Ranch Chicken Bites

Prep time: 10 minutes | Cook time: 15 minutes | Serves 6

2 (6-ounce / 170-g) boneless, skinless chicken breasts, cut into 1-inch cubes
1 tablespoon coconut oil
½ teaspoon salt
¼ teaspoon ground black pepper
1/3 cup ranch dressing
½ cup shredded Colby cheese
4 slices cooked sugar-free bacon, crumbled

1. Drizzle chicken with coconut oil. Sprinkle with salt and pepper, and place into an ungreased round nonstick baking dish.
2. Place dish into air fryer basket. Adjust the temperature to 370ºF (188ºC) and bake for 10 minutes, stirring chicken halfway through cooking.
3. Drizzle ranch dressing over chicken and top with Colby and bacon. Adjust the temperature to 400ºF (204ºC) and bake for 5 minutes. When done, chicken will be browned and have an internal temperature of at least 165ºF (74ºC). Serve warm.

Per Serving
calories: 164 | fat: 9g | protein: 18g
carbs: 0g | net carbs: 0g | fiber: 0g

Avocado Fries

Prep time: 10 minutes | Cook time: 7 to 8 minutes | Serves 4

¼ cup almond flour
¼ cup grated Parmesan cheese
½ teaspoon smoked paprika
¼ teaspoon garlic powder
2 eggs
Flesh of 3 avocados,
each sliced into 8 pieces (24 wedges total)
Salt and freshly ground black pepper, to taste
4 lime wedges, for garnish (optional)

1. Preheat the air fryer to 400ºF (204ºC).
2. In a shallow bowl, combine the almond flour, Parmesan cheese, paprika, and garlic powder.
3. In a separate shallow bowl, whisk the eggs.

4. Working one at a time, dip the avocado wedges first in the egg and then dredge in the almond flour mixture, pressing lightly to coat evenly. Arrange the avocado fries on a plate lined with parchment paper.
5. Working in batches if necessary, arrange the avocado fries in a single layer in the air fryer basket, making sure they do not touch. Spray generously with olive oil. Pausing halfway through the cooking time to turn the fries, air fry for 7 to 8 minutes until the coating is brown and crispy. Serve with the lime wedges (if desired).

Per Serving
calories: 270 | fat: 22g | protein: 9g
carbs: 12g | net carbs: 5g | fiber: 7g

Cajun-Spiced Kale Chips

Prep time: 10 minutes | Cook time: 8 to 10 minutes | Serves 2

1 large bunch kale, stems removed and torn into chip-size pieces (about 6 cups)
2 tablespoons olive oil
1 teaspoon garlic powder
1 teaspoon Creole seasoning

1. Preheat the air fryer to 360ºF (182ºC).
2. In a large bowl, combine the kale, olive oil, garlic powder, and Creole seasoning. Toss until the kale is thoroughly coated.
3. Working in batches, arrange about 2 cups of the kale in an even layer in the basket of the air fryer. (Allow the mixture to stay as fluffy as possible to help air circulate in the basket.) Pausing halfway through to shake the basket, air fry for 8 to 10 minutes. Spread the kale chips on a baking sheet to cool completely. Repeat with the remaining kale. Store in an airtight container at room temperature for up to 2 days.

Per Serving
calories: 150 | fat: 14g | protein: 2g
carbs: 5g | net carbs: 3g | fiber: 2g

Chapter 5 Side Dishes

Cheesy Loaded Broccoli

Prep time: 10 minutes | Cook time: 10 minutes | Serves 2

3 cups fresh broccoli florets
1 tablespoon coconut oil
¼ teaspoon salt
½ cup shredded sharp Cheddar cheese
¼ cup sour cream
4 slices cooked sugar-free bacon, crumbled
1 medium scallion, trimmed and sliced on the bias

1. Place broccoli into ungreased air fryer basket, drizzle with coconut oil, and sprinkle with salt. Adjust the temperature to 350°F (177°C) and roast for 8 minutes. Shake basket three times during cooking to avoid burned spots.
2. Sprinkle broccoli with Cheddar and cook for 2 additional minutes. When done, cheese will be melted and broccoli will be tender.
3. Serve warm in a large serving dish, topped with sour cream, crumbled bacon, and scallion slices.

Per Serving
calories: 381 | fat: 27g | protein: 19g
carbs: 11g | net carbs: 7g | fiber: 4g

Buttery Mushrooms

Prep time: 10 minutes | Cook time: 10 minutes | Serves 4

8 ounces (227 g) cremini mushrooms, halved
2 tablespoons salted butter, melted
¼ teaspoon salt
¼ teaspoon ground black pepper

1. In a medium bowl, toss mushrooms with butter, then sprinkle with salt and pepper. Place into ungreased air fryer basket. Adjust the temperature to 400°F (204°C) and air fry for 10 minutes, shaking the basket halfway through cooking. Mushrooms will be tender when done. Serve warm.

Per Serving
calories: 63 | fat: 5g | protein: 1g
carbs: 8g | net carbs: 3g | fiber: 5g

Lemon-Thyme Asparagus

Prep time: 5 minutes | Cook time: 4 to 8 minutes | Serves 4

1 pound (454 g) asparagus, woody ends trimmed off
1 tablespoon avocado oil
½ teaspoon dried thyme or ½ tablespoon chopped fresh thyme
Sea salt and freshly ground black pepper, to taste
2 ounces (57 g) goat cheese, crumbled
Zest and juice of 1 lemon
Flaky sea salt, for serving (optional)

1. In a medium bowl, toss together the asparagus, avocado oil, and thyme, and season with sea salt and pepper.
2. Place the asparagus in the air fryer basket in a single layer. Set the air fryer to 400°F (204°C) and air fry for 4 to 8 minutes, to your desired doneness.
3. Transfer to a serving platter. Top with the goat cheese, lemon zest, and lemon juice. If desired, season with a pinch of flaky salt.

Per Serving
calories: 103 | fat: 7g | protein: 5g
carbs: 7g | net carbs: 4g | fiber: 3g

Parmesan-Rosemary Radishes

Prep time: 5 minutes | Cook time: 15 to 20 minutes | Serves 4

1 bunch radishes, stemmed, trimmed, and quartered
1 tablespoon avocado oil
2 tablespoons finely grated fresh
Parmesan cheese
1 tablespoon chopped fresh rosemary
Sea salt and freshly ground black pepper, to taste

1. Place the radishes in a medium bowl and toss them with the avocado oil, Parmesan cheese, rosemary, salt, and pepper.
2. Set the air fryer to 375°F (191°C). Arrange the radishes in a single layer in the air fryer basket. Roast for 15 to 20 minutes, until golden brown and tender. Let cool for 5 minutes before serving.

Per Serving
calories: 47 | fat: 4g | protein: 1g
carbs: 1g | net carbs: 1g | fiber: 0g

Roasted Garlic

Prep time: 5 minutes | Cook time: 20 minutes | Makes 12 cloves

1 medium head garlic
2 teaspoons avocado oil

1. Remove any hanging excess peel from the garlic but leave the cloves covered. Cut off ¼ of the head of garlic, exposing the tips of the cloves.
2. Drizzle with avocado oil. Place the garlic head into a small sheet of aluminum foil, completely enclosing it. Place it into the air fryer basket.
3. Adjust the temperature to 400ºF (204ºC) and air fry for 20 minutes. If your garlic head is a bit smaller, check it after 15 minutes.
4. When done, garlic should be golden brown and very soft.
5. To serve, cloves should pop out and easily be spread or sliced. Store in an airtight container in the refrigerator up to 5 days. You may also freeze individual cloves on a baking sheet, then store together in a freezer-safe storage bag once frozen.

Per Serving
calories: 11 | fat: 0g | protein: 0g
carbs: 1g | net carbs: 1g | fiber: 0g

Buffalo Cauliflower

Prep time: 5 minutes | Cook time: 5 minutes | Serves 4

4 cups cauliflower florets
2 tablespoons salted butter, melted
½ (1-ounce / 28-g) dry ranch seasoning packet
¼ cup buffalo sauce

1. In a large bowl, toss cauliflower with butter and dry ranch. Place into the air fryer basket.
2. Adjust the temperature to 400ºF (204ºC) and air fry for 5 minutes.
3. Shake the basket two or three times during cooking. When tender, remove cauliflower from fryer basket and toss in buffalo sauce. Serve warm.

Per Serving
calories: 87 | fat: 5g | protein: 2g
carbs: 7g | net carbs: 5g | fiber: 2g

Buttery Green Beans

Prep time: 5 minutes | Cook time: 8 to 10 minutes | Serves 6

1 pound (454 g) green beans, trimmed
1 tablespoon avocado oil
1 teaspoon garlic powder
Sea salt and freshly
ground black pepper, to taste
¼ cup (4 tablespoons) unsalted butter, melted
¼ cup freshly grated Parmesan cheese

1. In a large bowl, toss together the green beans, avocado oil, and garlic powder and season with salt and pepper.
2. Set the air fryer to 400ºF (204ºC). Arrange the green beans in a single layer in the air fryer basket. Air fry for 8 to 10 minutes, tossing halfway through.
3. Transfer the beans to a large bowl and toss with the melted butter. Top with the Parmesan cheese and serve warm.

Per Serving
calories: 134 | fat: 11g | protein: 3g
carbs: 6g | net carbs: 3g | fiber: 3g

Garlic Parmesan-Roasted Cauliflower

Prep time: 5 minutes | Cook time: 15 minutes | Serves 6

1 medium head cauliflower, leaves and core removed, cut into florets
2 tablespoons salted butter, melted
½ tablespoon salt
2 cloves garlic, peeled and finely minced
½ cup grated Parmesan cheese, divided

1. Toss cauliflower in a large bowl with butter. Sprinkle with salt, garlic, and ¼ cup Parmesan.
2. Place florets into ungreased air fryer basket. Adjust the temperature to 350ºF (177ºC) and roast for 15 minutes, shaking basket halfway through cooking. Cauliflower will be browned at the edges and tender when done.
3. Transfer florets to a large serving dish and sprinkle with remaining Parmesan. Serve warm.

Per Serving
calories: 94 | fat: 6g | protein: 4g
carbs: 6g | net carbs: 4g | fiber: 2g

Garlic Roasted Broccoli

Prep time: 8 minutes | Cook time: 10 to 14 minutes | Serves 6

1 head broccoli, cut into bite-size florets	Sea salt and freshly ground black pepper, to taste
1 tablespoon avocado oil	1 tablespoon freshly squeezed lemon juice
2 teaspoons minced garlic	½ teaspoon lemon zest
⅛ teaspoon red pepper flakes	

1. In a large bowl, toss together the broccoli, avocado oil, garlic, red pepper flakes, salt, and pepper.
2. Set the air fryer to 375ºF (191ºC). Arrange the broccoli in a single layer in the air fryer basket, working in batches if necessary. Roast for 10 to 14 minutes, until the broccoli is lightly charred.
3. Place the florets in a medium bowl and toss with the lemon juice and lemon zest. Serve.

Per Serving
calories: 52 | fat: 3g | protein: 3g
carbs: 6g | net carbs: 3g | fiber: 3g

Fried Green Tomatoes

Prep time: 10 minutes | Cook time: 7 minutes | Serves 4

2 medium green tomatoes	ground almond flour
1 large egg	⅓ cup grated Parmesan cheese
¼ cup blanched finely	

1. Slice tomatoes into ½-inch-thick slices. In a medium bowl, whisk the egg. In a large bowl, mix the almond flour and Parmesan.
2. Dip each tomato slice into the egg, then dredge in the almond flour mixture. Place the slices into the air fryer basket.
3. Adjust the temperature to 400ºF (204ºC) and air fry for 7 minutes.
4. Flip the slices halfway through the cooking time. Serve immediately.

Per Serving
calories: 106 | fat: 7g | protein: 6g
carbs: 6g | net carbs: 4g | fiber: 2g

Bacon-Wrapped Asparagus

Prep time: 10 minutes | Cook time: 10 minutes | Serves 4

8 slices reduced-sodium bacon, cut in half	1 pound / 454 g) asparagus spears, trimmed of woody ends
16 thick (about	

1. Preheat the air fryer to 350ºF (177ºC).
2. Wrap a half piece of bacon around the center of each stalk of asparagus.
3. Working in batches, if necessary, arrange seam-side down in a single layer in the air fryer basket. Air fry for 10 minutes until the bacon is crisp and the stalks are tender.

Per Serving
calories: 110 | fat: 7g | protein: 8g
carbs: 5g | net carbs: 3g | fiber: 2g

Flatbread

Prep time: 5 minutes | Cook time: 7 minutes | Serves 2

1 cup shredded Mozzarella cheese	1 ounce (28 g) full-fat cream cheese, softened
¼ cup blanched finely ground almond flour	

1. In a large microwave-safe bowl, melt Mozzarella in the microwave for 30 seconds. Stir in almond flour until smooth and then add cream cheese. Continue mixing until dough forms, gently kneading it with wet hands if necessary.
2. Divide the dough into two pieces and roll out to ¼-inch thickness between two pieces of parchment. Cut another piece of parchment to fit your air fryer basket.
3. Place a piece of flatbread onto your parchment and into the air fryer, working in two batches if needed.
4. Adjust the temperature to 320ºF (160ºC) and air fry for 7 minutes.
5. Halfway through the cooking time flip the flatbread. Serve warm.

Per Serving
calories: 296 | fat: 23g | protein: 16g
carbs: 5g | net carbs: 3g | fiber: 2g

Burger Bun for One

Prep time: 2 minutes | Cook time: 5 minutes | Serves 1

2 tablespoons salted butter, melted
¼ cup blanched finely ground almond flour
¼ teaspoon baking powder
⅛ teaspoon apple cider vinegar
1 large egg, whisked

1. Pour butter into an ungreased ramekin. Add flour, baking powder, and vinegar to ramekin and stir until combined. Add egg and stir until batter is mostly smooth.
2. Place ramekin into air fryer basket. Adjust the temperature to 350°F (177°C) and bake for 5 minutes. When done, the center will be firm and the top slightly browned. Let cool, about 5 minutes, then remove from ramekin and slice in half. Serve.

Per Serving
calories: 444 | fat: 41g | protein: 13g
carbs: 6g | net carbs: 3g | fiber: 3g

Dijon Roast Cabbage

Prep time: 10 minutes | Cook time: 10 minutes | Serves 4

1 small head cabbage, cored and sliced into 1-inch-thick slices
2 tablespoons olive oil, divided
½ teaspoon salt
1 tablespoon Dijon mustard
1 teaspoon apple cider vinegar
1 teaspoon granular erythritol

1. Drizzle each cabbage slice with 1 tablespoon olive oil, then sprinkle with salt. Place slices into ungreased air fryer basket, working in batches if needed. Adjust the temperature to 350°F (177°C) and air fry for 10 minutes. Cabbage will be tender and edges will begin to brown when done.
2. In a small bowl, whisk remaining olive oil with mustard, vinegar, and erythritol. Drizzle over cabbage in a large serving dish. Serve warm.

Per Serving
calories: 111 | fat: 7g | protein: 3g
carbs: 11g | net carbs: 7g | fiber: 4g

"Faux-Tato" Hash

Prep time: 10 minutes | Cook time: 12 minutes | Serves 4

1 pound (454 g) radishes, ends removed, quartered
¼ medium yellow onion, peeled and diced
½ medium green bell pepper, seeded and chopped
2 tablespoons salted butter, melted
½ teaspoon garlic powder
¼ teaspoon ground black pepper

1. In a large bowl, combine radishes, onion, and bell pepper. Toss with butter.
2. Sprinkle garlic powder and black pepper over mixture in bowl, then spoon into ungreased air fryer basket.
3. Adjust the temperature to 320°F (160°C) and air fry for 12 minutes. Shake basket halfway through cooking. Radishes will be tender when done. Serve warm.

Per Serving
calories: 69 | fat: 5g | protein: 1g
carbs: 4g | net carbs: 2g | fiber: 2g

Mediterranean Zucchini Boats

Prep time: 5 minutes | Cook time: 10 minutes | Serves 4

1 large zucchini, ends removed, halved lengthwise
6 grape tomatoes, quartered
¼ teaspoon salt
¼ cup feta cheese
1 tablespoon balsamic vinegar
1 tablespoon olive oil

1. Use a spoon to scoop out 2 tablespoons from center of each zucchini half, making just enough space to fill with tomatoes and feta.
2. Place tomatoes evenly in centers of zucchini halves and sprinkle with salt. Place into ungreased air fryer basket. Adjust the temperature to 350°F (177°C) and roast for 10 minutes. When done, zucchini will be tender.
3. Transfer boats to a serving tray and sprinkle with feta, then drizzle with vinegar and olive oil. Serve warm.

Per Serving
calories: 74 | fat: 5g | protein: 2g
carbs: 4g | net carbs: 3g | fiber: 1g

Cabbage Wedges with Caraway Butter

Prep time: 15 minutes | Cook time: 35 to 40 minutes | Serves 6

1 tablespoon caraway seeds	red cabbage, cut into 6 wedges
½ cup (1 stick) unsalted butter, at room temperature	1 tablespoon avocado oil
½ teaspoon grated lemon zest	½ teaspoon sea salt
1 small head green or	¼ teaspoon freshly ground black pepper

1. Place the caraway seeds in a small dry skillet over medium-high heat. Toast the seeds for 2 to 3 minutes, then remove them from the heat and let cool. Lightly crush the seeds using a mortar and pestle or with the back of a knife.
2. Place the butter in a small bowl and stir in the crushed caraway seeds and lemon zest. Form the butter into a log and wrap it in parchment paper or plastic wrap. Refrigerate for at least 1 hour or freeze for 20 minutes.
3. Brush or spray the cabbage wedges with the avocado oil, and sprinkle with the salt and pepper.
4. Set the air fryer to 375°F (191°C). Place the cabbage in a single layer in the air fryer basket and roast for 20 minutes. Flip and cook for 15 to 20 minutes more, until the cabbage is tender and lightly charred.
5. Plate the cabbage and dot with caraway butter. Tent with foil for 5 minutes to melt the butter, and serve.

Per Serving
calories: 191 | fat: 18g | protein: 2g
carbs: 7g | net carbs: 4g | fiber: 3g

Brussels Sprouts with Bacon

Prep time: 10 minutes | Cook time: 15 to 18 minutes | Serves 6

1 pound (454 g) Brussels sprouts, trimmed and halved	powder
	1 teaspoon smoked paprika
1 tablespoon avocado oil	Sea salt and freshly ground black pepper, to taste
1 tablespoon coconut aminos	
1 teaspoon garlic	4 strips cooked bacon, crumbled

1. Place the Brussels sprouts in a large bowl and toss them with the avocado oil, coconut aminos, garlic powder, smoked paprika, salt, and pepper.
2. Set the air fryer to 375°F (191°C) and arrange the Brussels sprouts in a single layer in the air fryer basket, working in batches if necessary.
3. Roast for 15 to 18 minutes, stirring halfway through, until the sprouts are brown and crispy.
4. Transfer the sprouts to a bowl and toss with the bacon. Serve warm.

Per Serving
calories: 89 | fat: 5g | protein: 11g
carbs: 8g | net carbs: 5g | fiber: 3g

Lemon-Garlic Mushrooms

Prep time: 10 minutes | Cook time: 10 to 15 minutes | Serves 6

12 ounces (340 g) sliced mushrooms	1 teaspoon minced garlic
1 tablespoon avocado oil	1 teaspoon freshly squeezed lemon juice
Sea salt and freshly ground black pepper, to taste	½ teaspoon red pepper flakes
3 tablespoons unsalted butter	2 tablespoons chopped fresh parsley

1. Place the mushrooms in a medium bowl and toss with the oil. Season to taste with salt and pepper.
2. Place the mushrooms in a single layer in the air fryer basket. Set your air fryer to 375°F (191°C) and roast for 10 to 15 minutes, until the mushrooms are tender.
3. While the mushrooms cook, melt the butter in a small pot or skillet over medium-low heat. Stir in the garlic and cook for 30 seconds. Remove the pot from the heat and stir in the lemon juice and red pepper flakes.
4. Toss the mushrooms with the lemon-garlic butter and garnish with the parsley before serving.

Per Serving
calories: 80 | fat: 8g | protein: 1g
carbs: 1g | net carbs: 1g | fiber: 0g

Dinner Rolls

Prep time: 10 minutes | Cook time: 12 minutes | Serves 6

1 cup shredded Mozzarella cheese
1 ounce (28 g) full-fat cream cheese
1 cup blanched finely ground almond flour
¼ cup ground flaxseed
½ teaspoon baking powder
1 large egg

1. Place Mozzarella, cream cheese, and almond flour in a large microwave-safe bowl. Microwave for 1 minute. Mix until smooth.
2. Add flaxseed, baking powder, and egg until fully combined and smooth. Microwave an additional 15 seconds if it becomes too firm.
3. Separate the dough into six pieces and roll into balls. Place the balls into the air fryer basket.
4. Adjust the temperature to 320ºF (160ºC) and air fry for 12 minutes.
5. Allow rolls to cool completely before serving.

Per Serving
calories: 228 | fat: 18g | protein: 11g
carbs: 7g | net carbs: 3g | fiber: 4g

Radish Chips

Prep time: 10 minutes | Cook time: 5 minutes | Serves 4

2 cups water
1 pound (454 g) radishes
¼ teaspoon onion powder
¼ teaspoon paprika
½ teaspoon garlic powder
2 tablespoons coconut oil, melted

1. Place water in a medium saucepan and bring to a boil on stovetop.
2. Remove the top and bottom from each radish, then use a mandoline to slice each radish thin and uniformly. You may also use the slicing blade in the food processor for this step.
3. Place the radish slices into the boiling water for 5 minutes or until translucent. Remove them from the water and place them into a clean kitchen towel to absorb excess moisture.
4. Toss the radish chips in a large bowl with remaining ingredients until fully coated in oil and seasoning. Place radish chips into the air fryer basket.
5. Adjust the temperature to 320ºF (160ºC) and air fry for 5 minutes.
6. Shake the basket two or three times during the cooking time. Serve warm.

Per Serving
calories: 77 | fat: 6g | protein: 1g
carbs: 4g | net carbs: 2g | fiber: 2g

Garlic-Parmesan Jícama Fries

Prep time: 10 minutes | Cook time: 25 to 35 minutes | Serves 4

1 medium jícama, peeled
1 tablespoon avocado oil
¼ cup (4 tablespoons) unsalted butter
1 tablespoon minced garlic
¾ teaspoon chopped dried rosemary
¾ teaspoon sea salt
½ teaspoon freshly ground black pepper
⅓ cup grated Parmesan cheese
Chopped fresh parsley, for garnish
Maldon sea salt, for garnish

1. Using a spiralizer or julienne peeler, cut the jícama into shoestrings, then cut them into 3-inch-long sticks.
2. Bring a large pot of water to boil. Add the jícama and cook for about 10 minutes. Drain and dry on paper towels. Transfer to a medium bowl and toss with the oil.
3. Set the air fryer to 400ºF (204ºC). Arrange the jícama in a single layer in the basket, working in batches if necessary. Air fry for 15 to 25 minutes, checking at intervals, until tender and golden brown.
4. While the fries cook, melt the butter over medium-high heat. Add the garlic, rosemary, salt, and pepper. Cook for about 1 minute.
5. Toss the fries with the garlic butter. Top with the Parmesan cheese, and sprinkle with parsley and Maldon sea salt.

Per Serving
calories: 239 | fat: 18g | protein: 5g
carbs: 16g | net carbs: 8g | fiber: 8g

Brussels Sprouts with Pecans and Gorgonzola

Prep time: 10 minutes | Cook time: 25 minutes | Serves 4

½ cup pecans
1½ pounds (680 g) fresh Brussels sprouts, trimmed and quartered
2 tablespoons olive oil
Salt and freshly ground black pepper, to taste
¼ cup crumbled Gorgonzola cheese

1. Spread the pecans in a single layer of the air fryer and set the heat to 350ºF (177ºC). Air fry for 3 to 5 minutes until the pecans are lightly browned and fragrant. Transfer the pecans to a plate and continue preheating the air fryer, increasing the heat to 400ºF (204ºC).
2. In a large bowl, toss the Brussels sprouts with the olive oil and season with salt and black pepper to taste.
3. Working in batches if necessary, arrange the Brussels sprouts in a single layer in the air fryer basket. Pausing halfway through the baking time to shake the basket, air fry for 20 to 25 minutes until the sprouts are tender and starting to brown on the edges.
4. Transfer the sprouts to a serving bowl and top with the toasted pecans and Gorgonzola. Serve warm or at room temperature.

Per Serving
calories: 250 | fat: 19g | protein: 9g
carbs: 17g | net carbs: 9g | fiber: 8g

Zucchini Fritters

Prep time: 10 minutes | Cook time: 10 minutes | Serves 4

2 zucchini, grated (about 1 pound / 454 g)
1 teaspoon salt
¼ cup almond flour
¼ cup grated Parmesan cheese
1 large egg
¼ teaspoon dried
thyme
¼ teaspoon ground turmeric
¼ teaspoon freshly ground black pepper
1 tablespoon olive oil
½ lemon, sliced into wedges

1. Preheat the air fryer to 400ºF (204ºC). Cut a piece of parchment paper to fit slightly smaller than the bottom of the air fryer.
2. Place the zucchini in a large colander and sprinkle with the salt. Let sit for 5 to 10 minutes. Squeeze as much liquid as you can from the zucchini and place in a large mixing bowl. Add the almond flour, Parmesan, egg, thyme, turmeric, and black pepper. Stir gently until thoroughly combined.
3. Shape the mixture into 8 patties and arrange on the parchment paper. Brush lightly with the olive oil. Pausing halfway through the cooking time to turn the patties, air fry for 10 minutes until golden brown. Serve warm with the lemon wedges.

Per Serving
calories: 190 | fat: 16g | protein: 6g
carbs: 8g | net carbs: 6g | fiber: 2g

Roasted Salsa

Prep time: 5 minutes | Cook time: 30 minutes | Makes 2 cups

2 large San Marzano tomatoes, cored and cut into large chunks
½ medium white onion, peeled and large-diced
½ medium jalapeño, seeded and large-
diced
2 cloves garlic, peeled and diced
½ teaspoon salt
1 tablespoon coconut oil
¼ cup fresh lime juice

1. Place tomatoes, onion, and jalapeño into an ungreased round nonstick baking dish. Add garlic, then sprinkle with salt and drizzle with coconut oil.
2. Place dish into air fryer basket. Adjust the temperature to 300ºF (149ºC) and bake for 30 minutes. Vegetables will be dark brown around the edges and tender when done.
3. Pour mixture into a food processor or blender. Add lime juice. Process on low speed 30 seconds until only a few chunks remain.
4. Transfer salsa to a sealable container and refrigerate at least 1 hour. Serve chilled.

Per Serving (¼ cup)
calories: 28 | fat: 2g | protein: 1g
carbs: 3g | net carbs: 2g | fiber: 1g

Fried Zucchini Salad

Prep time: 10 minutes | Cook time: 5 to 7 minutes | Serves 4

2 medium zucchini, thinly sliced
5 tablespoons olive oil, divided
¼ cup chopped fresh parsley
2 tablespoons chopped fresh mint
Zest and juice of ½ lemon
1 clove garlic, minced
¼ cup crumbled feta cheese
Freshly ground black pepper, to taste

1. Preheat the air fryer to 400ºF (204ºC).
2. In a large bowl, toss the zucchini slices with 1 tablespoon of the olive oil.
3. Working in batches if necessary, arrange the zucchini slices in an even layer in the air fryer basket. Pausing halfway through the cooking time to shake the basket, air fry for 5 to 7 minutes until soft and lightly browned on each side.
4. Meanwhile, in a small bowl, combine the remaining 4 tablespoons olive oil, parsley, mint, lemon zest, lemon juice, and garlic.
5. Arrange the zucchini on a plate and drizzle with the dressing. Sprinkle the feta and black pepper on top. Serve warm or at room temperature.

Per Serving
calories: 195 | fat: 19g | protein: 3g
carbs: 5g | net carbs: 4g | fiber: 1g

Curry Roasted Cauliflower

Prep time: 10 minutes | Cook time: 20 minutes | Serves 4

¼ cup olive oil
2 teaspoons curry powder
½ teaspoon salt
¼ teaspoon freshly ground black pepper
1 head cauliflower,
cut into bite-size florets
½ red onion, sliced
2 tablespoons freshly chopped parsley, for garnish (optional)

1. Preheat the air fryer to 400ºF (204ºC).
2. In a large bowl, combine the olive oil, curry powder, salt, and pepper. Add the cauliflower and onion. Toss gently until the vegetables are completely coated with the oil mixture. Transfer the vegetables to the basket of the air fryer.
3. Pausing about halfway through the cooking time to shake the basket, air fry for 20 minutes until the cauliflower is tender and beginning to brown. Top with the parsley, if desired, before serving.

Per Serving
calories: 165 | fat: 14g | protein: 3g
carbs: 10g | net carbs: 6g | fiber: 4g

Green Tomato Salad

Prep time: 5 minutes | Cook time: 8 to 10 minutes | Serves 4

4 green tomatoes
½ teaspoon salt
1 large egg, lightly beaten
½ cup peanut flour
1 tablespoon Creole seasoning
1 (5-ounce / 142-g) bag arugula
Buttermilk Dressing:
1 cup mayonnaise
½ cup sour cream
2 teaspoons fresh lemon juice
2 tablespoons finely chopped fresh parsley
1 teaspoon dried dill
1 teaspoon dried chives
½ teaspoon salt
½ teaspoon garlic powder
½ teaspoon onion powder

1. Preheat the air fryer to 400ºF (204ºC).
2. Slice the tomatoes into ½-inch slices and sprinkle with the salt. Let sit for 5 to 10 minutes.
3. Place the egg in a small shallow bowl. In another small shallow bowl, combine the peanut flour and Creole seasoning. Dip each tomato slice into the egg wash, then dip into the peanut flour mixture, turning to coat evenly.
4. Working in batches if necessary, arrange the tomato slices in a single layer in the air fryer basket and spray both sides lightly with olive oil. Air fry until browned and crisp, 8 to 10 minutes.
5. To make the buttermilk dressing: In a small bowl, whisk together the mayonnaise, sour cream, lemon juice, parsley, dill, chives, salt, garlic powder, and onion powder.
6. Serve the tomato slices on top of a bed of the arugula with the dressing on the side.

Per Serving
calories: 560 | fat: 54g | protein: 9g
carbs: 16g | net carbs: 13g | fiber: 3g

Air-Fried Okra

Prep time: 10 minutes | Cook time: 10 minutes | Serves 4

1 egg
½ cup almond milk
½ cup crushed pork rinds
¼ cup grated Parmesan cheese
¼ cup almond flour
1 teaspoon garlic powder
¼ teaspoon freshly ground black pepper
½ pound (227 g) fresh okra, stems removed and chopped into 1-inch slices

1. Preheat the air fryer to 400ºF (204ºC).
2. In a shallow bowl, whisk together the egg and milk.
3. In a second shallow bowl, combine the pork rinds, Parmesan, almond flour, garlic powder, and black pepper.
4. Working with a few slices at a time, dip the okra into the egg mixture followed by the crumb mixture. Press lightly to ensure an even coating.
5. Working in batches if necessary, arrange the okra in a single layer in the air fryer basket and spray lightly with olive oil. Pausing halfway through the cooking time to turn the okra, air fry for 10 minutes until tender and golden brown. Serve warm.

Per Serving
calories: 180 | fat: 10g | protein: 14g
carbs: 9g | net carbs: 7g | fiber: 2g

Parmesan Herb Focaccia Bread

Prep time: 10 minutes | Cook time: 10 minutes | Serves 6

1 cup shredded Mozzarella cheese
1 ounce (28 g) full-fat cream cheese
1 cup blanched finely ground almond flour
¼ cup ground golden flaxseed
¼ cup grated Parmesan cheese
½ teaspoon baking soda
2 large eggs
½ teaspoon garlic powder
¼ teaspoon dried basil
¼ teaspoon dried rosemary
2 tablespoons salted butter, melted and divided

1. Place Mozzarella, cream cheese, and almond flour into a large microwave-safe bowl and microwave for 1 minute. Add the flaxseed, Parmesan, and baking soda and stir until smooth ball forms. If the mixture cools too much, it will be hard to mix. Return to microwave for 10 to 15 seconds to rewarm if necessary.
2. Stir in eggs. You may need to use your hands to get them fully incorporated. Just keep stirring and they will absorb into the dough.
3. Sprinkle dough with garlic powder, basil, and rosemary and knead into dough. Grease a baking pan with 1 tablespoon melted butter. Press the dough evenly into the pan. Place pan into the air fryer basket.
4. Adjust the temperature to 400ºF (204ºC) and bake for 10 minutes.
5. At 7 minutes, cover with foil if bread begins to get too dark.
6. Remove and let cool at least 30 minutes. Drizzle with remaining butter and serve.

Per Serving
calories: 292 | fat: 23g | protein: 13g
carbs: 7g | net carbs: 3g | fiber: 4g

Spinach and Sweet Pepper Poppers

Prep time: 10 minutes | Cook time: 8 minutes | Makes 16 poppers

4 ounces (113 g) cream cheese, softened
1 cup chopped fresh spinach leaves
½ teaspoon garlic powder
8 mini sweet bell peppers, tops removed, seeded, and halved lengthwise

1. In a medium bowl, mix cream cheese, spinach, and garlic powder. Place 1 tablespoon mixture into each sweet pepper half and press down to smooth.
2. Place poppers into ungreased air fryer basket. Adjust the temperature to 400ºF (204ºC) and air fry for 8 minutes. Poppers will be done when cheese is browned on top and peppers are tender-crisp. Serve warm.

Per Serving (4 poppers)
calories: 116 | fat: 8g | protein: g
carbs: 5g | net carbs: 4g | fiber: 1g

Spicy Roasted Bok Choy

Prep time: 10 minutes | Cook time: 7 to 10 minutes | Serves 4

2 tablespoons olive oil
2 tablespoons reduced-sodium coconut aminos
2 teaspoons sesame oil
2 teaspoons chili-garlic sauce
2 cloves garlic, minced
1 head (about 1 pound / 454 g) bok choy, sliced lengthwise into quarters
2 teaspoons black sesame seeds

1. Preheat the air fryer to 400°F (204°C).
2. In a large bowl, combine the olive oil, coconut aminos, sesame oil, chili-garlic sauce, and garlic. Add the bok choy and toss, massaging the leaves with your hands if necessary, until thoroughly coated.
3. Arrange the bok choy in the basket of the air fryer. Pausing about halfway through the cooking time to shake the basket, air fry for 7 to 10 minutes until the bok choy is tender and the tips of the leaves begin to crisp. Remove from the basket and let cool for a few minutes before coarsely chopping. Serve sprinkled with the sesame seeds.

Per Serving
calories: 100 | fat: 8g | protein: 2g
carbs: 4g | net carbs: 3g | fiber: 1g

Green Bean Casserole

Prep time: 10 minutes | Cook time: 20 minutes | Serves 4

1 pound (454 g) fresh green beans, ends trimmed, strings removed, and chopped into 2-inch pieces
1 (8-ounce / 227-g) package sliced brown mushrooms
½ onion, sliced
1 clove garlic, minced
1 tablespoon olive oil
½ teaspoon salt
¼ teaspoon freshly ground black pepper
4 ounces (113 g) cream cheese
½ cup chicken stock
¼ teaspoon ground nutmeg
½ cup grated Cheddar cheese

1. Preheat the air fryer to 400°F (204°C). Coat a 6-cup casserole dish with olive oil and set aside.
2. In a large bowl, combine the green beans, mushrooms, onion, garlic, olive oil, salt, and pepper. Toss until the vegetables are thoroughly coated with the oil and seasonings.
3. Transfer the mixture to the air fryer basket. Pausing halfway through the cooking time to shake the basket, air fry for 10 minutes until tender.
4. While the vegetables are cooking, in a 2-cup glass measuring cup, warm the cream cheese and chicken stock in the microwave on high for 1 to 2 minutes until the cream cheese is melted. Add the nutmeg and whisk until smooth.
5. Transfer the vegetables to the prepared casserole dish and pour the cream cheese mixture over the top. Top with the Cheddar cheese. Air fry for another 10 minutes until the cheese is melted and beginning to brown.

Per Serving
calories: 250 | fat: 19g | protein: 10g
carbs: 14g | net carbs: 10g | fiber: 4g

Baked Jalapeño and Cheese Cauliflower Mash

Prep time: 10 minutes | Cook time: 15 minutes | Serves 6

1 (12-ounce / 340-g) steamer bag cauliflower florets, cooked according to package instructions
2 tablespoons salted butter, softened
2 ounces (57 g) cream cheese, softened
½ cup shredded sharp Cheddar cheese
¼ cup pickled jalapeños
½ teaspoon salt
¼ teaspoon ground black pepper

1. Place cooked cauliflower into a food processor with remaining ingredients. Pulse twenty times until cauliflower is smooth and all ingredients are combined.
2. Spoon mash into an ungreased round nonstick baking dish. Place dish into air fryer basket. Adjust the temperature to 380°F (193°C) and bake for 15 minutes. The top will be golden brown when done. Serve warm.

Per Serving
calories: 117 | fat: 9g | protein: 4g
carbs: 3g | net carbs: 2g | fiber: 1g

Cauliflower Rice Balls

Prep time: 10 minutes | Cook time: 8 minutes | Serves 4

1 (10-ounce / 283-g) steamer bag cauliflower rice, cooked according to package instructions
½ cup shredded Mozzarella cheese

1 large egg
2 ounces (57 g) plain pork rinds, finely crushed
¼ teaspoon salt
½ teaspoon Italian seasoning

1. Place cauliflower into a large bowl and mix with Mozzarella.
2. Whisk egg in a separate medium bowl. Place pork rinds into another large bowl with salt and Italian seasoning.
3. Separate cauliflower mixture into four equal sections and form each into a ball. Carefully dip a ball into whisked egg, then roll in pork rinds. Repeat with remaining balls.
4. Place cauliflower balls into ungreased air fryer basket. Adjust the temperature to 400°F (204°C) and air fry for 8 minutes. Rice balls will be golden when done.
5. Use a spatula to carefully move cauliflower balls to a large dish for serving. Serve warm.

Per Serving
calories: 158 | fat: 9g | protein: 15g
carbs: 4g | net carbs: 2g | fiber: 2g

Kohlrabi Fries

Prep time: 10 minutes | Cook time: 20 to 30 minutes | Serves 4

2 pounds (907 g) kohlrabi, peeled and cut into ¼ to ½-inch fries

2 tablespoons olive oil
Salt and freshly ground black pepper, to taste

1. Preheat the air fryer to 400°F (204°C).
2. In a large bowl, combine the kohlrabi and olive oil. Season to taste with salt and black pepper. Toss gently until thoroughly coated.
3. Working in batches if necessary, spread the kohlrabi in a single layer in the air fryer basket. Pausing halfway through the cooking time to shake the basket, air fry for 20 to 30 minutes until the fries are lightly browned and crunchy.

Per Serving
calories: 120 | fat: 7g | protein: 4g
carbs: 14g | net carbs: 12g | fiber: 2g

Buffalo Cauliflower Wings

Prep time: 20 minutes | Cook time: 10 to 12 minutes | Serves 6

1 head cauliflower
3 large eggs
¾ cup finely ground blanched almond flour
¾ cup finely grated Parmesan cheese
1 teaspoon garlic powder
½ teaspoon smoked paprika
½ teaspoon sea salt

½ teaspoon freshly ground black pepper
Avocado oil spray
1 cup Buffalo hot sauce, such as Frank's RedHot
4 tablespoons unsalted butter
Garlic Ranch Dressing or Blue Cheese Dressing, for serving

1. Line a baking sheet or platter with parchment paper.
2. Core the cauliflower and cut it into large florets.
3. Beat the eggs together in a small bowl. In a separate bowl, combine the almond flour, Parmesan, garlic powder, smoked paprika, salt, and pepper.
4. Dip a cauliflower floret into the egg, then coat it in the almond flour mixture, making sure to firmly press the mixture into the cauliflower. Transfer the coated floret to the prepared baking sheet. Continue with the remaining cauliflower, egg, and almond flour mixture.
5. Set the air fryer to 400°F (204°C). Spray the cauliflower with oil. Place the florets in the air fryer basket in a single layer, working in batches if necessary, and air fry for 5 minutes. Flip the florets and spray them with more oil. Continue cooking for 5 to 7 minutes more.
6. While the cauliflower is cooking, make the sauce. Place the hot sauce and butter in a small saucepan over medium-low heat. Heat, stirring occasionally, until the butter melts.
7. Toss the crispy cauliflower in the sauce, then use a slotted spoon to transfer the coated cauliflower to a plate or platter. Serve warm with the dressing.

Per Serving
calories: 306 | fat: 21g | protein: 13g
carbs: 9g | net carbs: 5g | fiber: 4g

Chapter 6 Vegetarian Mains

Loaded Cauliflower Steak

Prep time: 5 minutes | Cook time: 7 minutes | Serves 4

1 medium head cauliflower	¼ cup blue cheese crumbles
¼ cup hot sauce	¼ cup full-fat ranch dressing
2 tablespoons salted butter, melted	

1. Remove cauliflower leaves. Slice the head in ½-inch-thick slices.
2. In a small bowl, mix hot sauce and butter. Brush the mixture over the cauliflower.
3. Place each cauliflower steak into the air fryer, working in batches if necessary.
4. Adjust the temperature to 400ºF (204ºC) and air fry for 7 minutes.
5. When cooked, edges will begin turning dark and caramelized.
6. To serve, sprinkle steaks with crumbled blue cheese. Drizzle with ranch dressing.

Per Serving
calories: 122 | fat: 8g | protein: 5g
carbs: 7g | net carbs: 5g | fiber: 2g

Mediterranean Pan Pizza

Prep time: 5 minutes | Cook time: 8 minutes | Serves 2

1 cup shredded Mozzarella cheese	spinach leaves
¼ medium red bell pepper, seeded and chopped	2 tablespoons chopped black olives
½ cup chopped fresh	2 tablespoons crumbled feta cheese

1. Sprinkle Mozzarella into an ungreased round nonstick baking dish in an even layer. Add remaining ingredients on top.
2. Place dish into air fryer basket. Adjust the temperature to 350ºF (177ºC) and bake for 8 minutes, checking halfway through to avoid burning. Top of pizza will be golden brown and the cheese melted when done.
3. Remove dish from fryer and let cool 5 minutes before slicing and serving.

Per Serving
calories: 215 | fat: 13g | protein: 16g
carbs: 5g | net carbs: 5g | fiber: 0g

Roasted Broccoli Salad

Prep time: 10 minutes | Cook time: 7 minutes | Serves 2

3 cups fresh broccoli florets	butter, melted
2 tablespoons salted	¼ cup sliced almonds
	½ medium lemon

1. Place broccoli into a round baking dish. Pour butter over broccoli. Add almonds and toss. Place dish into the air fryer basket.
2. Adjust the temperature to 380ºF (193ºC) and bake for 7 minutes.
3. Stir halfway through the cooking time.
4. When done, zest lemon onto broccoli and squeeze juice into pan. Toss. Serve warm.

Per Serving
calories: 215 | fat: 16g | protein: 6g
carbs: 12g | net carbs: 8g | fiber: 4g

Zucchini Cauliflower Fritters

Prep time: 15 minutes | Cook time: 12 minutes | Serves 2

1 (12-ounce / 340-g) cauliflower steamer bag	1 large egg
1 medium zucchini, shredded	½ teaspoon garlic powder
¼ cup almond flour	¼ cup grated vegetarian Parmesan cheese

1. Cook cauliflower according to package instructions and drain excess moisture in cheesecloth or paper towel. Place into a large bowl.
2. Place zucchini into paper towel and pat down to remove excess moisture. Add to bowl with cauliflower. Add remaining ingredients.
3. Divide the mixture evenly and form four patties. Press into ¼-inch-thick patties. Place each into the air fryer basket.
4. Adjust the temperature to 320ºF (160ºC) and air fry for 12 minutes.
5. Fritters will be firm when fully cooked. Allow to cool 5 minutes before moving. Serve warm.

Per Serving
calories: 217 | fat: 12g | protein: 14g
carbs: 16g | net carbs: 8g | fiber: 8g

Parmesan Artichokes

Prep time: 10 minutes | Cook time: 10 minutes | Serves 4

2 medium artichokes, trimmed and quartered, center removed
2 tablespoons coconut oil
1 large egg, beaten
½ cup grated vegetarian Parmesan cheese
¼ cup blanched finely ground almond flour
½ teaspoon crushed red pepper flakes

1. In a large bowl, toss artichokes in coconut oil and then dip each piece into the egg.
2. Mix the Parmesan and almond flour in a large bowl. Add artichoke pieces and toss to cover as completely as possible, sprinkle with pepper flakes. Place into the air fryer basket.
3. Adjust the temperature to 400ºF (204ºC) and air fry for 10 minutes.
4. Toss the basket two times during cooking. Serve warm.

Per Serving

calories: 189 | fat: 13g | protein: 8g
carbs: 10g | net carbs: 6g | fiber: 4g

Basic Spaghetti Squash

Prep time: 10 minutes | Cook time: 45 minutes | Serves 2

½ large spaghetti squash
1 tablespoon coconut oil
2 tablespoons salted
butter, melted
½ teaspoon garlic powder
1 teaspoon dried parsley

1. Brush shell of spaghetti squash with coconut oil. Place the skin side down and brush the inside with butter. Sprinkle with garlic powder and parsley.
2. Place squash with the skin side down into the air fryer basket.
3. Adjust the temperature to 350ºF (177ºC) and air fry for 30 minutes.
4. Flip the squash so skin side is up and cook an additional 15 minutes or until fork tender. Serve warm.

Per Serving

calories: 182 | fat: 12g | protein: 2g
carbs: 18g | net carbs: 14g | fiber: 4g

Caprese Eggplant Stacks

Prep time: 5 minutes | Cook time: 12 minutes | Serves 4

1 medium eggplant, cut into ¼-inch slices
2 large tomatoes, cut into ¼-inch slices
4 ounces (113 g) fresh Mozzarella, cut
into ½-ounce / 14-g slices
2 tablespoons olive oil
¼ cup fresh basil, sliced

1. In a baking dish, place four slices of eggplant on the bottom. Place a slice of tomato on top of each eggplant round, then Mozzarella, then eggplant. Repeat as necessary.
2. Drizzle with olive oil. Cover dish with foil and place dish into the air fryer basket.
3. Adjust the temperature to 350ºF (177ºC) and bake for 12 minutes.
4. When done, eggplant will be tender. Garnish with fresh basil to serve.

Per Serving

calories: 195 | fat: 13g | protein: 8g
carbs: 13g | net carbs: 8g | fiber: 5g

Sweet Pepper Nachos

Prep time: 10 minutes | Cook time: 5 minutes | Serves 2

6 mini sweet peppers, seeded and sliced in half
¾ cup shredded Colby jack cheese
¼ cup sliced pickled
jalapeños
½ medium avocado, peeled, pitted, and diced
2 tablespoons sour cream

1. Place peppers into an ungreased round nonstick baking dish. Sprinkle with Colby and top with jalapeños.
2. Place dish into air fryer basket. Adjust the temperature to 350ºF (177ºC) and bake for 5 minutes. Cheese will be melted and bubbly when done.
3. Remove dish from air fryer and top with avocado. Drizzle with sour cream. Serve warm.

Per Serving

calories: 310 | fat: 23g | protein: 12g
carbs: 11g | net carbs: 6g | fiber: 5g

Cauliflower Rice-Stuffed Peppers

Prep time: 10 minutes | Cook time: 15 minutes | Serves 4

2 cups uncooked cauliflower rice
¾ cup drained canned petite diced tomatoes
2 tablespoons olive oil
1 cup shredded Mozzarella cheese
¼ teaspoon salt
¼ teaspoon ground black pepper
4 medium green bell peppers, tops removed, seeded

1. In a large bowl, mix all ingredients except bell peppers. Scoop mixture evenly into peppers.
2. Place peppers into ungreased air fryer basket. Adjust the temperature to 350°F (177°C) and air fry for 15 minutes. Peppers will be tender and cheese will be melted when done. Serve warm.

Per Serving
calories: 185 | fat: 12g | protein: 9g
carbs: 11g | net carbs: 7g | fiber: 4g

Vegetable Burgers

Prep time: 10 minutes | Cook time: 12 minutes | Serves 4

8 ounces (227 g) cremini mushrooms
2 large egg yolks
½ medium zucchini, trimmed and chopped
¼ cup peeled and
chopped yellow onion
1 clove garlic, peeled and finely minced
½ teaspoon salt
¼ teaspoon ground black pepper

1. Place all ingredients into a food processor and pulse twenty times until finely chopped and combined.
2. Separate mixture into four equal sections and press each into a burger shape. Place burgers into ungreased air fryer basket. Adjust the temperature to 375°F (191°C) and air fry for 12 minutes, turning burgers halfway through cooking. Burgers will be browned and firm when done.
3. Place burgers on a large plate and let cool 5 minutes before serving.

Per Serving
calories: 48 | fat: 2g | protein: 3g
carbs: 5g | net carbs: 4g | fiber: 1g

Crustless Spinach Cheese Pie

Prep time: 10 minutes | Cook time: 20 minutes | Serves 4

6 large eggs
¼ cup heavy whipping cream
1 cup frozen chopped spinach, drained
1 cup shredded sharp Cheddar cheese
¼ cup diced yellow onion

1. In a medium bowl, whisk eggs and add cream. Add remaining ingredients to bowl.
2. Pour into a round baking dish. Place into the air fryer basket.
3. Adjust the temperature to 320°F (160°C) and bake for 20 minutes.
4. Eggs will be firm and slightly browned when cooked. Serve immediately.

Per Serving
calories: 288 | fat: 20g | protein: 18g
carbs: 4g | net carbs: 2g | fiber: 2g

Quiche-Stuffed Peppers

Prep time: 5 minutes | Cook time: 15 minutes | Serves 2

2 medium green bell peppers
3 large eggs
¼ cup full-fat ricotta cheese
¼ cup diced yellow
onion
½ cup chopped broccoli
½ cup shredded medium Cheddar cheese

1. Cut the tops off of the peppers and remove the seeds and white membranes with a small knife.
2. In a medium bowl, whisk eggs and ricotta.
3. Add onion and broccoli. Pour the egg and vegetable mixture evenly into each pepper. Top with Cheddar. Place peppers into a 4-cup round baking dish and place into the air fryer basket.
4. Adjust the temperature to 350°F (177°C) and bake for 15 minutes.
5. Eggs will be mostly firm and peppers tender when fully cooked. Serve immediately.

Per Serving
calories: 314 | fat: 19g | protein: 22g
carbs: 11g | net carbs: 8g | fiber: 3g

Spinach-Artichoke Stuffed Mushrooms

Prep time: 10 minutes | Cook time: 10 to 14 minutes | Serves 4

2 tablespoons olive oil
4 large portobello mushrooms, stems removed and gills scraped out
½ teaspoon salt
¼ teaspoon freshly ground pepper
4 ounces (113 g) goat cheese, crumbled
½ cup chopped marinated artichoke hearts
1 cup frozen spinach, thawed and squeezed dry
½ cup grated Parmesan cheese
2 tablespoons chopped fresh parsley

1. Preheat the air fryer to 400ºF (204ºC).
2. Rub the olive oil over the portobello mushrooms until thoroughly coated. Sprinkle both sides with the salt and black pepper. Place top-side down on a clean work surface.
3. In a small bowl, combine the goat cheese, artichoke hearts, and spinach. Mash with the back of a fork until thoroughly combined. Divide the cheese mixture among the mushrooms and sprinkle with the Parmesan cheese.
4. Air fry for 10 to 14 minutes until the mushrooms are tender and the cheese has begun to brown. Top with the fresh parsley just before serving.

Per Serving
calories: 270 | fat: 23g | protein: 8g
carbs: 11g | net carbs: 7g | fiber: 4g

Three-Cheese Zucchini Boats

Prep time: 15 minutes | Cook time: 20 minutes | Serves 2

2 medium zucchini
1 tablespoon avocado oil
¼ cup low-carb, no-sugar-added pasta sauce
¼ cup full-fat ricotta cheese
¼ cup shredded Mozzarella cheese
¼ teaspoon dried oregano
¼ teaspoon garlic powder
½ teaspoon dried parsley
2 tablespoons grated vegetarian Parmesan cheese

1. Cut off 1 inch from the top and bottom of each zucchini. Slice zucchini in half lengthwise and use a spoon to scoop out a bit of the inside, making room for filling. Brush with oil and spoon 2 tablespoons pasta sauce into each shell.
2. In a medium bowl, mix ricotta, Mozzarella, oregano, garlic powder, and parsley. Spoon the mixture into each zucchini shell. Place stuffed zucchini shells into the air fryer basket.
3. Adjust the temperature to 350ºF (177ºC) and air fry for 20 minutes.
4. To remove from the fryer basket, use tongs or a spatula and carefully lift out. Top with Parmesan. Serve immediately.

Per Serving
calories: 215 | fat: 15g | protein: 10g
carbs: 9g | net carbs: 6g | fiber: 3g

Pesto Vegetable Skewers

Prep time: 30 minutes | Cook time: 8 minutes | Makes 8 skewers

1 medium zucchini, trimmed and cut into ½-inch slices
½ medium yellow onion, peeled and cut into 1-inch squares
1 medium red bell pepper, seeded
and cut into 1-inch squares
16 whole cremini mushrooms
⅓ cup basil pesto
½ teaspoon salt
¼ teaspoon ground black pepper

1. Divide zucchini slices, onion, and bell pepper into eight even portions. Place on 6-inch skewers for a total of eight kebabs. Add 2 mushrooms to each skewer and brush kebabs generously with pesto.
2. Sprinkle each kebab with salt and black pepper on all sides, then place into ungreased air fryer basket. Adjust the temperature to 375ºF (191ºC) and air fry for 8 minutes, turning kebabs halfway through cooking. Vegetables will be browned at the edges and tender-crisp when done. Serve warm.

Per Serving (2 skewers)
calories: 107 | fat: 8g | protein: 5g
carbs: 10g | net carbs: 8g | fiber: 2g

Crispy Eggplant Rounds

Prep time: 15 minutes | Cook time: 10 minutes | Serves 4

1 large eggplant, ends trimmed, cut into ½-inch slices	cheese crisps, finely ground
½ teaspoon salt	½ teaspoon paprika
2 ounces (57 g) Parmesan 100%	¼ teaspoon garlic powder
	1 large egg

1. Sprinkle eggplant rounds with salt. Place rounds on a kitchen towel for 30 minutes to draw out excess water. Pat rounds dry.
2. In a medium bowl, mix cheese crisps, paprika, and garlic powder. In a separate medium bowl, whisk egg. Dip each eggplant round in egg, then gently press into cheese crisps to coat both sides.
3. Place eggplant rounds into ungreased air fryer basket. Adjust the temperature to 400ºF (204ºC) and air fry for 10 minutes, turning rounds halfway through cooking. Eggplant will be golden and crispy when done. Serve warm.

Per Serving
calories: 93 | fat: 4g | protein: 7g
carbs: 9g | net carbs: 5g | fiber: 4g

Broccoli Crust Pizza

Prep time: 15 minutes | Cook time: 12 minutes | Serves 4

3 cups riced broccoli, steamed and drained well	cheese
1 large egg	3 tablespoons low-carb Alfredo sauce
½ cup grated vegetarian Parmesan	½ cup shredded Mozzarella cheese

1. In a large bowl, mix broccoli, egg, and Parmesan.
2. Cut a piece of parchment to fit your air fryer basket. Press out the pizza mixture to fit on the parchment, working in two batches if necessary. Place into the air fryer basket.
3. Adjust the temperature to 370ºF (188ºC) and air fry for 5 minutes.
4. The crust should be firm enough to flip. If not, add 2 additional minutes. Flip crust.

5. Top with Alfredo sauce and Mozzarella. Return to the air fryer basket and cook an additional 7 minutes or until cheese is golden and bubbling. Serve warm.

Per Serving
calories: 136 | fat: 7g | protein: 10g
carbs: 6g | net carbs: 4g | fiber: 2g

Cauliflower Steak with Gremolata

Prep time: 15 minutes | Cook time: 25 minutes | Serves 4

2 tablespoons olive oil	through the core into thick "steaks"
1 tablespoon Italian seasoning	Salt and freshly ground black pepper, to taste
1 large head cauliflower, outer leaves removed and sliced lengthwise	¼ cup Parmesan cheese
Gremolata:	
1 bunch Italian parsley (about 1 cup packed)	plus 1 to 2 teaspoons lemon juice
2 cloves garlic	½ cup olive oil
Zest of 1 small lemon,	Salt and pepper, to taste

1. Preheat the air fryer to 400ºF (204ºC).
2. In a small bowl, combine the olive oil and Italian seasoning. Brush both sides of each cauliflower "steak" generously with the oil. Season to taste with salt and black pepper.
3. Working in batches if necessary, arrange the cauliflower in a single layer in the air fryer basket. Pausing halfway through the cooking time to turn the "steaks," air fry for 15 to 20 minutes until the cauliflower is tender and the edges begin to brown. Sprinkle with the Parmesan and air fry for 5 minutes longer.
4. To make the gremolata: In a food processor fitted with a metal blade, combine the parsley, garlic, and lemon zest and juice. With the motor running, add the olive oil in a steady stream until the mixture forms a bright green sauce. Season to taste with salt and black pepper. Serve the cauliflower steaks with the gremolata spooned over the top.

Per Serving
calories: 390 | fat: 36g | protein: 7g
carbs: 14g | net carbs: 8g | fiber: 6g

Pesto Spinach Flatbread

Prep time: 10 minutes | Cook time: 8 minutes | Serves 4

1 cup blanched finely ground almond flour
2 ounces (57 g) cream cheese
2 cups shredded Mozzarella cheese
1 cup chopped fresh spinach leaves
2 tablespoons basil pesto

1. Place flour, cream cheese, and Mozzarella in a large microwave-safe bowl and microwave on high 45 seconds, then stir.
2. Fold in spinach and microwave an additional 15 seconds. Stir until a soft dough ball forms.
3. Cut two pieces of parchment paper to fit air fryer basket. Separate dough into two sections and press each out on ungreased parchment to create 6-inch rounds.
4. Spread 1 tablespoon pesto over each flatbread and place rounds on parchment into ungreased air fryer basket. Adjust the temperature to 350°F (177°C) and air fry for 8 minutes, turning crusts halfway through cooking. Flatbread will be golden when done.
5. Let cool 5 minutes before slicing and serving.

Per Serving
calories: 414 | fat: 31g | protein: 21g
carbs: 10g | net carbs: 7g | fiber: 3g

Stuffed Portobellos

Prep time: 10 minutes | Cook time: 8 minutes | Serves 4

3 ounces (85 g) cream cheese, softened
½ medium zucchini, trimmed and chopped
¼ cup seeded and chopped red bell pepper
1½ cups chopped fresh spinach leaves
4 large portobello mushrooms, stems removed
2 tablespoons coconut oil, melted
½ teaspoon salt

1. In a medium bowl, mix cream cheese, zucchini, pepper, and spinach.
2. Drizzle mushrooms with coconut oil and sprinkle with salt. Scoop ¼ zucchini mixture into each mushroom.

3. Place mushrooms into ungreased air fryer basket. Adjust the temperature to 400°F (204°C) and air fry for 8 minutes. Portobellos will be tender and tops will be browned when done. Serve warm.

Per Serving
calories: 158 | fat: 13g | protein: 4g
carbs: 6g | net carbs: 4g | fiber: 2g

Almond-Cauliflower Gnocchi

Prep time: 5 minutes | Cook time: 25 to 30 minutes | Serves 4

5 cups cauliflower florets
⅔ cup almond flour
½ teaspoon salt
¼ cup unsalted butter, melted
¼ cup grated Parmesan cheese

1. In a food processor fitted with a metal blade, pulse the cauliflower until finely chopped. Transfer the cauliflower to a large microwave-safe bowl and cover it with a paper towel. Microwave for 5 minutes. Spread the cauliflower on a towel to cool.
2. When cool enough to handle, draw up the sides of the towel and squeeze tightly over a sink to remove the excess moisture. Return the cauliflower to the food processor and whirl until creamy. Sprinkle in the flour and salt and pulse until a sticky dough comes together.
3. Transfer the dough to a workspace lightly floured with almond flour. Shape the dough into a ball and divide into 4 equal sections. Roll each section into a rope 1 inch thick. Slice the dough into squares with a sharp knife.
4. Preheat the air fryer to 400°F (204°C).
5. Working in batches if necessary, place the gnocchi in a single layer in the basket of the air fryer and spray generously with olive oil. Pausing halfway through the cooking time to turn the gnocchi, air fry for 25 to 30 minutes until golden brown and crispy on the edges. Transfer to a large bowl and toss with the melted butter and Parmesan cheese.

Per Serving
calories: 360 | fat: 20g | protein: 9g
carbs: 14g | net carbs: 10g | fiber: 4g

White Cheddar and Mushroom Soufflés

Prep time: 15 minutes | Cook time: 12 minutes | Serves 4

3 large eggs, whites and yolks separated
½ cup sharp white Cheddar cheese
3 ounces (85 g) cream cheese, softened

¼ teaspoon cream of tartar
¼ teaspoon salt
¼ teaspoon ground black pepper
½ cup cremini mushrooms, sliced

1. In a large bowl, whip egg whites until stiff peaks form, about 2 minutes. In a separate large bowl, beat Cheddar, egg yolks, cream cheese, cream of tartar, salt, and pepper together until combined.
2. Fold egg whites into cheese mixture, being careful not to stir. Fold in mushrooms, then pour mixture evenly into four ungreased ramekins.
3. Place ramekins into air fryer basket. Adjust the temperature to 350ºF (177ºC) and bake for 12 minutes. Eggs will be browned on the top and firm in the center when done. Serve warm.

Per Serving
calories: 185 | fat: 14g | protein: 10g
carbs: 2g | net carbs: 2g | fiber: 0g

Crispy Tofu

Prep time: 5 minutes | Cook time: 15 to 20 minutes | Serves 4

1 (16-ounce / 454-g) block extra-firm tofu
2 tablespoons coconut aminos
1 tablespoon toasted sesame oil
1 tablespoon olive oil

1 tablespoon chili-garlic sauce
1½ teaspoons black sesame seeds
1 scallion, thinly sliced

1. Press the tofu for at least 15 minutes by wrapping it in paper towels and setting a heavy pan on top so that the moisture drains.
2. Slice the tofu into bite-size cubes and transfer to a bowl. Drizzle with the coconut aminos, sesame oil, olive oil, and chili-garlic sauce. Cover and refrigerate for 1 hour or up to overnight.

3. Preheat the air fryer to 400ºF (204ºC).
4. Arrange the tofu in a single layer in the air fryer basket. Pausing to shake the pan halfway through the cooking time, air fry for 15 to 20 minutes until crisp. Serve with any juices that accumulate in the bottom of the air fryer, sprinkled with the sesame seeds and sliced scallion.

Per Serving
calories: 180 | fat: 13g | protein: 11g
carbs: 5g | net carbs: 4g | fiber: 1g

Eggplant Parmesan

Prep time: 15 minutes | Cook time: 17 minutes | Serves 4

1 medium eggplant, ends trimmed, sliced into ½-inch rounds
¼ teaspoon salt
2 tablespoons coconut oil
½ cup grated Parmesan cheese

1 ounce (28 g) 100% cheese crisps, finely crushed
½ cup low-carb marinara sauce
½ cup shredded Mozzarella cheese

1. Sprinkle eggplant rounds with salt on both sides and wrap in a kitchen towel for 30 minutes. Press to remove excess water, then drizzle rounds with coconut oil on both sides.
2. In a medium bowl, mix Parmesan and cheese crisps. Press each eggplant slice into mixture to coat both sides.
3. Place rounds into ungreased air fryer basket. Adjust the temperature to 350ºF (177ºC) and air fry for 15 minutes, turning rounds halfway through cooking. They will be crispy around the edges when done.
4. Spoon marinara over rounds and sprinkle with Mozzarella. Continue cooking an additional 2 minutes at 350ºF (177ºC) until cheese is melted. Serve warm.

Per Serving
calories: 255 | fat: 17g | protein: 11g
carbs: 12g | net carbs: 8g | fiber: 4g

Roasted Veggie Bowl

Prep time: 10 minutes | Cook time: 15 minutes | Serves 2

1 cup broccoli florets
1 cup quartered Brussels sprouts
½ cup cauliflower florets
¼ medium white onion, peeled and sliced ¼ inch thick
½ medium green bell pepper, seeded and sliced ¼ inch thick
1 tablespoon coconut oil
2 teaspoons chili powder
½ teaspoon garlic powder
½ teaspoon cumin

1. Toss all ingredients together in a large bowl until vegetables are fully coated with oil and seasoning.
2. Pour vegetables into the air fryer basket.
3. Adjust the temperature to 360ºF (182ºC) and roast for 15 minutes.
4. Shake two or three times during cooking. Serve warm.

Per Serving
calories: 121 | fat: 7g | protein: 4g
carbs: 13g | net carbs: 8g | fiber: 5g

Greek Stuffed Eggplant

Prep time: 15 minutes | Cook time: 20 minutes | Serves 2

1 large eggplant
2 tablespoons unsalted butter
¼ medium yellow onion, diced
¼ cup chopped artichoke hearts
1 cup fresh spinach
2 tablespoons diced red bell pepper
½ cup crumbled feta

1. Slice eggplant in half lengthwise and scoop out flesh, leaving enough inside for shell to remain intact. Take eggplant that was scooped out, chop it, and set aside.
2. In a medium skillet over medium heat, add butter and onion. Sauté until onions begin to soften, about 3 to 5 minutes. Add chopped eggplant, artichokes, spinach, and bell pepper. Continue cooking 5 minutes until peppers soften and spinach wilts. Remove from the heat and gently fold in the feta.
3. Place filling into each eggplant shell and place into the air fryer basket.

4. Adjust the temperature to 320ºF (160ºC) and air fry for 20 minutes.
5. Eggplant will be tender when done. Serve warm.

Per Serving
calories: 291 | fat: 19g | protein: 9g
carbs: 23g | net carbs: 12g | fiber: 11g

Italian Baked Egg and Veggies

Prep time: 10 minutes | Cook time: 10 minutes | Serves 2

2 tablespoons salted butter
1 small zucchini, sliced lengthwise and quartered
½ medium green bell pepper, seeded and diced
1 cup fresh spinach, chopped
1 medium Roma tomato, diced
2 large eggs
¼ teaspoon onion powder
¼ teaspoon garlic powder
½ teaspoon dried basil
¼ teaspoon dried oregano

1. Grease two ramekins with 1 tablespoon butter each.
2. In a large bowl, toss zucchini, bell pepper, spinach, and tomatoes. Divide the mixture in two and place half in each ramekin.
3. Crack an egg on top of each ramekin and sprinkle with onion powder, garlic powder, basil, and oregano. Place into the air fryer basket.
4. Adjust the temperature to 330ºF (166ºC) and bake for 10 minutes.
5. Serve immediately.

Per Serving
calories: 150 | fat: 10g | protein: 8g
carbs: 6g | net carbs: 4g | fiber: 2g

Whole Roasted Lemon Cauliflower

Prep time: 5 minutes | Cook time: 15 minutes | Serves 4

1 medium head cauliflower	½ teaspoon garlic powder
2 tablespoons salted butter, melted	1 teaspoon dried parsley
1 medium lemon	

1. Remove the leaves from the head of cauliflower and brush it with melted butter. Cut the lemon in half and zest one half onto the cauliflower. Squeeze the juice of the zested lemon half and pour it over the cauliflower.
2. Sprinkle with garlic powder and parsley. Place cauliflower head into the air fryer basket.
3. Adjust the temperature to 350ºF (177ºC) and air fry for 15 minutes.
4. Check cauliflower every 5 minutes to avoid overcooking. It should be fork tender.
5. To serve, squeeze juice from other lemon half over cauliflower. Serve immediately.

Per Serving
calories: 91 | fat: 6g | protein: 3g
carbs: 8g | net carbs: 5g | fiber: 3g

Cheesy Cauliflower Pizza Crust

Prep time: 15 minutes | Cook time: 11 minutes | Serves 2

1 (12-ounce / 340-g) steamer bag cauliflower	2 tablespoons blanched finely ground almond flour
½ cup shredded sharp Cheddar cheese	1 teaspoon Italian blend seasoning
1 large egg	

1. Cook cauliflower according to package instructions. Remove from bag and place into cheesecloth or paper towel to remove excess water. Place cauliflower into a large bowl.
2. Add cheese, egg, almond flour, and Italian seasoning to the bowl and mix well.
3. Cut a piece of parchment to fit your air fryer basket. Press cauliflower into 6-inch round circle. Place into the air fryer basket.

4. Adjust the temperature to 360ºF (182ºC) and air fry for 11 minutes.
5. After 7 minutes, flip the pizza crust.
6. Add preferred toppings to pizza. Place back into air fryer basket and cook an additional 4 minutes or until fully cooked and golden. Serve immediately.

Per Serving
calories: 230 | fat: 14g | protein: 15g
carbs: 10g | net carbs: 5g | fiber: 5g

Broccoli-Cheese Fritters

Prep time: 5 minutes | Cook time: 20 to 25 minutes | Serves 4

1 cup broccoli florets	1 teaspoon garlic powder
1 cup shredded Mozzarella cheese	Salt and freshly ground black pepper, to taste
¾ cup almond flour	
½ cup flaxseed meal, divided	2 eggs, lightly beaten
2 teaspoons baking powder	½ cup ranch dressing

1. Preheat the air fryer to 400ºF (204ºC).
2. In a food processor fitted with a metal blade, pulse the broccoli until very finely chopped.
3. Transfer the broccoli to a large bowl and add the Mozzarella, almond flour, ¼ cup of the flaxseed meal, baking powder, and garlic powder. Stir until thoroughly combined. Season to taste with salt and black pepper. Add the eggs and stir again to form a sticky dough. Shape the dough into 1¼-inch fritters.
4. Place the remaining ¼ cup flaxseed meal in a shallow bowl and roll the fritters in the meal to form an even coating.
5. Working in batches if necessary, arrange the fritters in a single layer in the basket of the air fryer and spray generously with olive oil. Pausing halfway through the cooking time to shake the basket, air fry for 20 to 25 minutes until the fritters are golden brown and crispy. Serve with the ranch dressing for dipping.

Per Serving
calories: 450 | fat: 36g | protein: 19g
carbs: 16g | net carbs: 10g | fiber: 6g

Crispy Cabbage Steaks

Prep time: 5 minutes | Cook time: 10 minutes | Serves 4

1 small head green cabbage, cored and cut into ½-inch-thick slices
¼ teaspoon salt
¼ teaspoon ground black pepper

2 tablespoons olive oil
1 clove garlic, peeled and finely minced
½ teaspoon dried thyme
½ teaspoon dried parsley

1. Sprinkle each side of cabbage with salt and pepper, then place into ungreased air fryer basket, working in batches if needed.
2. Drizzle each side of cabbage with olive oil, then sprinkle with remaining ingredients on both sides. Adjust the temperature to 350°F (177°C) and air fry for 10 minutes, turning "steaks" halfway through cooking. Cabbage will be browned at the edges and tender when done. Serve warm.

Per Serving
calories: 105 | fat: 7g | protein: 2g
carbs: 11g | net carbs: 6g | fiber: 5g

Spaghetti Squash Alfredo

Prep time: 10 minutes | Cook time: 15 minutes | Serves 2

½ large cooked spaghetti squash
2 tablespoons salted butter, melted
½ cup low-carb Alfredo sauce
¼ cup grated vegetarian Parmesan cheese

½ teaspoon garlic powder
1 teaspoon dried parsley
¼ teaspoon ground peppercorn
½ cup shredded Italian blend cheese

1. Using a fork, remove the strands of spaghetti squash from the shell. Place into a large bowl with butter and Alfredo sauce. Sprinkle with Parmesan, garlic powder, parsley, and peppercorn.
2. Pour into a 4-cup round baking dish and top with shredded cheese. Place dish into the air fryer basket.
3. Adjust the temperature to 320°F (160°C) and bake for 15 minutes.

4. When finished, cheese will be golden and bubbling. Serve immediately.

Per Serving
calories: 375 | fat: 24g | protein: 13g
carbs: 20g | net carbs: 16g | fiber: 4g

Portobello Mini Pizzas

Prep time: 10 minutes | Cook time: 10 minutes | Serves 2

2 large portobello mushrooms
2 tablespoons unsalted butter, melted
½ teaspoon garlic powder
⅔ cup shredded

Mozzarella cheese
4 grape tomatoes, sliced
2 leaves fresh basil, chopped
1 tablespoon balsamic vinegar

1. Scoop out the inside of the mushrooms, leaving just the caps. Brush each cap with butter and sprinkle with garlic powder.
2. Fill each cap with Mozzarella and sliced tomatoes. Place each mini pizza into a round baking pan. Place pan into the air fryer basket.
3. Adjust the temperature to 380°F (193°C) and air fry for 10 minutes.
4. Carefully remove the pizzas from the fryer basket and garnish with basil and a drizzle of vinegar.

Per Serving
calories: 244 | fat: 18g | protein: 10g
carbs: 7g | net carbs: 5g | fiber: 2g

Zucchini-Ricotta Tart

Prep time: 10 minutes | Cook time: 60 minutes | Serves 6

½ cup grated Parmesan cheese, divided
1½ cups almond flour
1 tablespoon coconut flour
½ teaspoon garlic powder
¾ teaspoon salt, divided
¼ cup unsalted butter, melted
1 zucchini, thinly sliced (about 2 cups)
1 cup ricotta cheese
3 eggs
2 tablespoons heavy cream
2 cloves garlic, minced
½ teaspoon dried tarragon

1. Preheat the air fryer to 330ºF (166ºC). Coat a round 6-cup pan with olive oil and set aside.
2. In a large bowl, whisk ¼ cup of the Parmesan with the almond flour, coconut flour, garlic powder, and ¼ teaspoon of the salt. Stir in the melted butter until the dough resembles coarse crumbs. Press the dough firmly into the bottom and up the sides of the prepared pan. Air fry for 12 to 15 minutes until the crust begins to brown. Let cool to room temperature.
3. Meanwhile, place the zucchini in a colander and sprinkle with the remaining ½ teaspoon salt. Toss gently to distribute the salt and let sit for 30 minutes. Use paper towels to pat the zucchini dry.
4. In a large bowl, whisk together the ricotta, eggs, heavy cream, garlic, and tarragon. Gently stir in the zucchini slices. Pour the cheese mixture into the cooled crust and sprinkle with the remaining ¼ cup Parmesan.
5. Increase the air fryer to 350ºF (177ºC). Place the pan in the air fryer basket and air fry for 45 to 50 minutes, or until set and a tester inserted into the center of the tart comes out clean. Serve warm or at room temperature.

Per Serving
calories: 390 | fat: 30g | protein: 19g
carbs: 14g | net carbs: 12g | fiber: 2g

Eggplant Lasagna

Prep time: 10 minutes | Cook time: 46 minutes | Serves 4

1 small eggplant (about ¾ pound / 340 g), sliced into rounds
2 teaspoons salt
1 tablespoon olive oil
1 cup shredded Mozzarella, divided
1 cup ricotta cheese
1 large egg
¼ cup grated Parmesan cheese
½ teaspoon dried oregano
1½ cups no-sugar-added marinara
1 tablespoon chopped fresh parsley

1. Preheat the air fryer to 350ºF (177ºC). Coat a 6-cup casserole dish that fits in your air fryer with olive oil; set aside.
2. Arrange the eggplant slices in a single layer on a baking sheet and sprinkle with the salt. Let sit for 10 minutes. Use a paper towel to remove the excess moisture and salt.
3. Working in batches if necessary, brush the eggplant with the olive oil and arrange in a single layer in the air fryer basket. Pausing halfway through the cooking time to turn the eggplant, air fry for 6 minutes until softened. Transfer the eggplant back to the baking sheet and let cool.
4. In a small bowl, combine ½ cup of the Mozzarella with the ricotta, egg, Parmesan, and oregano. To assemble the lasagna, spread a spoonful of marinara in the bottom of the casserole dish, followed by a layer of eggplant, a layer of the cheese mixture, and a layer of marinara. Repeat the layers until all of the ingredients are used, ending with the remaining ½ cup of Mozzarella. Scatter the parsley on top. Cover the baking dish with foil.
5. Increase the air fryer to 370ºF (188ºC) and air fry for 30 minutes. Uncover the dish and continue baking for 10 minutes longer until the cheese begins to brown. Let the casserole sit for at least 10 minutes before serving.

Per Serving
calories: 350 | fat: 22g | protein: 20g
carbs: 17g | net carbs: 12g | fiber: 5g

Garlic White Zucchini Rolls

Prep time: 20 minutes | Cook time: 20 minutes | Serves 4

2 medium zucchini
2 tablespoons unsalted butter
¼ white onion, peeled and diced
½ teaspoon finely minced roasted garlic
¼ cup heavy cream
2 tablespoons vegetable broth
⅛ teaspoon xanthan gum
½ cup full-fat ricotta cheese
¼ teaspoon salt
½ teaspoon garlic powder
¼ teaspoon dried oregano
2 cups spinach, chopped
½ cup sliced baby portobello mushrooms
¾ cup shredded Mozzarella cheese, divided

1. Using a mandoline or sharp knife, slice zucchini into long strips lengthwise. Place strips between paper towels to absorb moisture. Set aside.
2. In a medium saucepan over medium heat, melt butter. Add onion and sauté until fragrant. Add garlic and sauté 30 seconds.
3. Pour in heavy cream, broth, and xanthan gum. Turn off heat and whisk mixture until it begins to thicken, about 3 minutes.
4. In a medium bowl, add ricotta, salt, garlic powder, and oregano and mix well. Fold in spinach, mushrooms, and ½ cup Mozzarella.
5. Pour half of the sauce into a round baking pan. To assemble the rolls, place two strips of zucchini on a work surface. Spoon 2 tablespoons of ricotta mixture onto the slices and roll up. Place seam side down on top of sauce. Repeat with remaining ingredients.
6. Pour remaining sauce over the rolls and sprinkle with remaining Mozzarella. Cover with foil and place into the air fryer basket.
7. Adjust the temperature to 350°F (177°C) and bake for 20 minutes.
8. In the last 5 minutes, remove the foil to brown the cheese. Serve immediately.

Per Serving
calories: 245 | fat: 19g | protein: 10g
carbs: 7g | net carbs: 5g | fiber: 2g

Buffalo Cauliflower Bites with Blue Cheese

Prep time: 10 minutes | Cook time: 8 to 10 minutes | Serves 4

1 large head cauliflower, chopped into florets
1 tablespoon olive oil
Salt and freshly ground black pepper, to taste
¼ cup unsalted butter, melted
¼ cup hot sauce
Garlic Blue Cheese Dip:
½ cup mayonnaise
¼ cup sour cream
2 tablespoons heavy cream
1 tablespoon fresh lemon juice
1 clove garlic, minced
¼ cup crumbled blue cheese
Salt and freshly ground black pepper, to taste

1. Preheat the air fryer to 400°F (204°C).
2. In a large bowl, combine the cauliflower and olive oil. Season to taste with salt and black pepper. Toss until the vegetables are thoroughly coated.
3. Working in batches, place half of the cauliflower in the air fryer basket. Pausing halfway through the cooking time to shake the basket, air fry for 8 to 10 minutes until the cauliflower is evenly browned. Transfer to a large bowl and repeat with the remaining cauliflower.
4. In a small bowl, whisk together the melted butter and hot sauce.
5. To make the dip: In a small bowl, combine the mayonnaise, sour cream, heavy cream, lemon juice, garlic, and blue cheese. Season to taste with salt and freshly ground black pepper.
6. Just before serving, pour the butter mixture over the cauliflower and toss gently until thoroughly coated. Serve with the dip on the side.

Per Serving
calories: 510 | fat: 50g | protein: 7g
carbs: 13g | net carbs: 8g | fiber: 5g

Chapter 7 Poultry

Greek Chicken Stir-Fry

Prep time: 15 minutes | Cook time: 15 minutes | Serves 2

1 (6-ounce / 170-g) chicken breast, cut into 1-inch cubes
½ medium zucchini, chopped
½ medium red bell pepper, seeded and chopped
¼ medium red onion, peeled and sliced
1 tablespoon coconut oil
1 teaspoon dried oregano
½ teaspoon garlic powder
¼ teaspoon dried thyme

1. Place all ingredients into a large mixing bowl and toss until the coconut oil coats the meat and vegetables. Pour the contents of the bowl into the air fryer basket.
2. Adjust the temperature to 375ºF (191ºC) and air fry for 15 minutes.
3. Shake the fryer basket halfway through the cooking time to redistribute the food. Serve immediately.

Per Serving
calories: 186 | fat: 8g | protein: 20g
carbs: 6g | net carbs: 4g | fiber: 2g

Buffalo Chicken Cheese Sticks

Prep time: 5 minutes | Cook time: 8 minutes | Serves 2

1 cup shredded cooked chicken
¼ cup buffalo sauce
1 cup shredded Mozzarella cheese
1 large egg
¼ cup crumbled feta

1. In a large bowl, mix all ingredients except the feta. Cut a piece of parchment to fit your air fryer basket and press the mixture into a ½-inch-thick circle.
2. Sprinkle the mixture with feta and place into the air fryer basket.
3. Adjust the temperature to 400ºF (204ºC) and air fry for 8 minutes.
4. After 5 minutes, flip over the cheese mixture.
5. Allow to cool 5 minutes before cutting into sticks. Serve warm.

Per Serving
calories: 369 | fat: 21g | protein: 36g
carbs: 2g | net carbs: 2g | fiber: 0g

Italian Chicken Thighs

Prep time: 5 minutes | Cook time: 20 minutes | Serves 2

4 bone-in, skin-on chicken thighs
2 tablespoons unsalted butter, melted
1 teaspoon dried parsley
1 teaspoon dried basil
½ teaspoon garlic powder
¼ teaspoon onion powder
¼ teaspoon dried oregano

1. Brush chicken thighs with butter and sprinkle remaining ingredients over thighs. Place thighs into the air fryer basket.
2. Adjust the temperature to 380ºF (193ºC) and roast for 20 minutes.
3. Halfway through the cooking time, flip the thighs.
4. When fully cooked, internal temperature will be at least 165ºF (74ºC) and skin will be crispy. Serve warm.

Per Serving
calories: 596 | fat: 31g | protein: 68g
carbs: 1g | net carbs: 1g | fiber: 0g

Garlic Dill Wings

Prep time: 5 minutes | Cook time: 25 minutes | Serves 4

2 pounds (907 g) bone-in chicken wings, separated at joints
½ teaspoon salt
½ teaspoon ground black pepper
½ teaspoon onion powder
½ teaspoon garlic powder
1 teaspoon dried dill

1. In a large bowl, toss wings with salt, pepper, onion powder, garlic powder, and dill until evenly coated. Place wings into ungreased air fryer basket in a single layer, working in batches if needed.
2. Adjust the temperature to 400ºF (204ºC) and air fry for 25 minutes, shaking the basket every 7 minutes during cooking. Wings should have an internal temperature of at least 165ºF (74ºC) and be golden brown when done. Serve warm.

Per Serving
calories: 319 | fat: 22g | protein: 29g
carbs: 1g | net carbs: 1g | fiber: 0g

Almond-Crusted Chicken

Prep time: 15 minutes | Cook time: 25 minutes | Serves 4

¼ cup slivered almonds
2 (6-ounce / 170-g) boneless, skinless chicken breasts

2 tablespoons full-fat mayonnaise
1 tablespoon Dijon mustard

1. Pulse the almonds in a food processor or chop until finely chopped. Place almonds evenly on a plate and set aside.
2. Completely slice each chicken breast in half lengthwise.
3. Mix the mayonnaise and mustard in a small bowl and then coat chicken with the mixture.
4. Lay each piece of chicken in the chopped almonds to fully coat. Carefully move the pieces into the air fryer basket.
5. Adjust the temperature to 350°F (177°C) and air fry for 25 minutes.
6. Chicken will be done when it has reached an internal temperature of 165°F (74°C) or more. Serve warm.

Per Serving
calories: 195 | fat: 10g | protein: 21g
carbs: 2g | net carbs: 1g | fiber: 1g

Quick Chicken Fajitas

Prep time: 10 minutes | Cook time: 15 minutes | Serves 2

10 ounces (283 g) boneless, skinless chicken breast, sliced into ¼-inch strips
2 tablespoons coconut oil, melted
1 tablespoon chili powder
½ teaspoon cumin
½ teaspoon paprika

½ teaspoon garlic powder
¼ medium onion, peeled and sliced
½ medium green bell pepper, seeded and sliced
½ medium red bell pepper, seeded and sliced

1. Place chicken and coconut oil into a large bowl and sprinkle with chili powder, cumin, paprika, and garlic powder. Toss chicken until well coated with seasoning. Place chicken into the air fryer basket.
2. Adjust the temperature to 350°F (177°C) and air fry for 15 minutes.

3. Add onion and peppers into the fryer basket when the cooking time has 7 minutes remaining.
4. Toss the chicken two or three times during cooking. Vegetables should be tender and chicken fully cooked to at least 165°F (74°C) internal temperature when finished. Serve warm.

Per Serving
calories: 326 | fat: 16g | protein: 34g
carbs: 8g | net carbs: 5g | fiber: 3g

Thanksgiving Turkey Breast

Prep time: 5 minutes | Cook time: 30 minutes | Serves 4

1½ teaspoons fine sea salt
1 teaspoon ground black pepper
1 teaspoon chopped fresh rosemary leaves
1 teaspoon chopped fresh sage
1 teaspoon chopped fresh tarragon

1 teaspoon chopped fresh thyme leaves
1 (2-pound / 907-g) turkey breast
3 tablespoons ghee or unsalted butter, melted
3 tablespoons Dijon mustard

1. Spray the air fryer with avocado oil. Preheat the air fryer to 390°F (199°C).
2. In a small bowl, stir together the salt, pepper, and herbs until well combined. Season the turkey breast generously on all sides with the seasoning.
3. In another small bowl, stir together the ghee and Dijon. Brush the ghee mixture on all sides of the turkey breast.
4. Place the turkey breast in the air fryer basket and air fry for 30 minutes, or until the internal temperature reaches 165°F (74°C). Transfer the breast to a cutting board and allow it to rest for 10 minutes before cutting it into ½-inch-thick slices.
5. Store leftovers in an airtight container in the refrigerator for up to 4 days or in the freezer for up to a month. Reheat in a preheated 350°F (177°C) air fryer for 4 minutes, or until warmed through.

Per Serving
calories: 388 | fat: 18g | protein: 50g
carbs: 1g | net carbs: 1g | fiber: 0g

Home-Style Rotisserie Chicken

Prep time: 10 minutes | Cook time: 60 minutes | Serves 4

1 (4-pound / 1.8-kg) chicken, giblets removed
Secret Spice Rub:
2 teaspoons salt
1 teaspoon paprika
½ teaspoon onion powder
½ teaspoon garlic powder

½ onion, quartered
1 tablespoon olive oil

½ teaspoon dried thyme
½ teaspoon freshly ground black pepper
¼ teaspoon cayenne

1. Preheat the air fryer to 350ºF (177ºC).
2. Use paper towels to blot the chicken dry. Stuff the chicken with the onion. Rub the chicken with the oil.
3. To make the spice rub: In a small bowl, combine the salt, paprika, onion powder, garlic powder, thyme, black pepper, and cayenne; stir until thoroughly combined. Sprinkle the chicken with the spice rub until thoroughly coated.
4. Place the chicken breast side down in the air fryer basket. Air fry the chicken for 30 minutes. Use tongs to carefully flip the chicken over and air fry for an additional 30 minutes, or until the temperature of a thermometer inserted into the thickest part of the chicken registers 165ºF (74ºC).
5. Let the chicken rest for 10 minutes. Discard the onion and serve.

Per Serving
calories: 500 | fat: 27g | protein: 61g
carbs: 0g | net carbs: 0g | fiber: 0g

Jerk Chicken Thighs

Prep time: 5 minutes | Cook time: 15 to 20 minutes | Serves 6

2 teaspoons ground coriander
1 teaspoon ground allspice
1 teaspoon cayenne pepper
1 teaspoon ground ginger
1 teaspoon salt
1 teaspoon dried

thyme
½ teaspoon ground cinnamon
½ teaspoon ground nutmeg
2 pounds (907 g) boneless chicken thighs, skin on
2 tablespoons olive oil

1. In a small bowl, combine the coriander, allspice, cayenne, ginger, salt, thyme, cinnamon, and nutmeg. Stir until thoroughly combined.
2. Place the chicken in a baking dish and use paper towels to pat dry. Thoroughly coat both sides of the chicken with the spice mixture. Cover and refrigerate for at least 2 hours, preferably overnight.
3. Preheat the air fryer to 360ºF (182ºC).
4. Working in batches if necessary, arrange the chicken in a single layer in the air fryer basket and lightly coat with the olive oil. Pausing halfway through the cooking time to flip the chicken, air fry for 15 to 20 minutes, until a thermometer inserted into the thickest part registers 165ºF (74ºC).

Per Serving
calories: 400 | fat: 27g | protein: 35g
carbs: 1g | net carbs: 1g | fiber: 0g

Lemon Chicken

Prep time: 5 minutes | Cook time: 20 to 25 minutes | Serves 4

8 bone-in chicken thighs, skin on
1 tablespoon olive oil
1½ teaspoons lemon-pepper seasoning
½ teaspoon paprika

½ teaspoon garlic powder
¼ teaspoon freshly ground black pepper
Juice of ½ lemon

1. Preheat the air fryer to 360ºF (182ºC).
2. Place the chicken in a large bowl and drizzle with the olive oil. Top with the lemon-pepper seasoning, paprika, garlic powder, and freshly ground black pepper. Toss until thoroughly coated.
3. Working in batches if necessary, arrange the chicken in a single layer in the basket of the air fryer. Pausing halfway through the cooking time to turn the chicken, air fry for 20 to 25 minutes, until a thermometer inserted into the thickest piece registers 165ºF (74ºC).
4. Transfer the chicken to a serving platter and squeeze the lemon juice over the top.

Per Serving
calories: 335 | fat: 22g | protein: 32g
carbs: 0g | net carbs: 0g | fiber: 0g

Chicken Cordon Bleu Casserole

Prep time: 15 minutes | Cook time: 15 minutes | Serves 4

2 cups cubed cooked chicken thigh meat
½ cup cubed cooked ham
2 ounces (57 g) Swiss cheese, cubed
4 ounces (113 g) full-fat cream cheese, softened

1 tablespoon heavy cream
2 tablespoons unsalted butter, melted
2 teaspoons Dijon mustard
1 ounce (28 g) pork rinds, crushed

1. Place chicken and ham into a round baking pan and toss so meat is evenly mixed. Sprinkle cheese cubes on top of meat.
2. In a large bowl, mix cream cheese, heavy cream, butter, and mustard and then pour the mixture over the meat and cheese. Top with pork rinds. Place pan into the air fryer basket.
3. Adjust the temperature to 350°F (177°C) and bake for 15 minutes.
4. The casserole will be browned and bubbling when done. Serve warm.

Per Serving
calories: 403 | fat: 28g | protein: 31g
carbs: 2g | net carbs: 2g | fiber: 0g

Stuffed Chicken Florentine

Prep time: 10 minutes | Cook time: 20 minutes | Serves 4

3 tablespoons pine nuts
¾ cup frozen spinach, thawed and squeezed dry
⅓ cup ricotta cheese
2 tablespoons grated Parmesan cheese
3 cloves garlic,

minced
Salt and freshly ground black pepper, to taste
4 small boneless, skinless chicken breast halves (about 1½ pounds / 680 g)
8 slices bacon

1. Place the pine nuts in a small pan and set in the air fryer basket. Set the air fryer to 400°F (204°C) and air fry for 2 to 3 minutes until toasted. Remove the pine nuts to a mixing bowl and continue preheating the air fryer.
2. In a large bowl, combine the spinach, ricotta, Parmesan, and garlic. Season to taste with salt and pepper and stir well until thoroughly combined.
3. Using a sharp knife, cut into the chicken breasts, slicing them across and opening them up like a book, but be careful not to cut them all the way through. Sprinkle the chicken with salt and pepper.
4. Spoon equal amounts of the spinach mixture into the chicken, then fold the top of the chicken breast back over the top of the stuffing. Wrap each chicken breast with 2 slices of bacon.
5. Working in batches if necessary, air fry the chicken for 18 to 20 minutes until the bacon is crisp and a thermometer inserted into the thickest part of the chicken registers 165°F (74°C).

Per Serving
calories: 440 | fat: 20g | protein: 63g
carbs: 4g | net carbs: 3g | fiber: 1g

Blackened Cajun Chicken Tenders

Prep time: 10 minutes | Cook time: 17 minutes | Serves 4

2 teaspoons paprika
1 teaspoon chili powder
½ teaspoon garlic powder
½ teaspoon dried thyme
¼ teaspoon onion powder

⅛ teaspoon ground cayenne pepper
2 tablespoons coconut oil
1 pound (454 g) boneless, skinless chicken tenders
¼ cup full-fat ranch dressing

1. In a small bowl, combine all seasonings.
2. Drizzle oil over chicken tenders and then generously coat each tender in the spice mixture. Place tenders into the air fryer basket.
3. Adjust the temperature to 375°F (191°C) and air fry for 17 minutes.
4. Tenders will be 165°F (74°C) internally when fully cooked. Serve with ranch dressing for dipping.

Per Serving
calories: 163 | fat: 7g | protein: 21g
carbs: 2g | net carbs: 1g | fiber: 1g

Fajita-Stuffed Chicken Breast

Prep time: 15 minutes | Cook time: 25 minutes | Serves 4

2 (6-ounce / 170-g) boneless, skinless chicken breasts
¼ medium white onion, peeled and sliced
1 medium green bell pepper, seeded and sliced

1 tablespoon coconut oil
2 teaspoons chili powder
1 teaspoon ground cumin
½ teaspoon garlic powder

1. Slice each chicken breast completely in half lengthwise into two even pieces. Using a meat tenderizer, pound out the chicken until it's about ¼-inch thickness.
2. Lay each slice of chicken out and place three slices of onion and four slices of green pepper on the end closest to you. Begin rolling the peppers and onions tightly into the chicken. Secure the roll with either toothpicks or a couple pieces of butcher's twine.
3. Drizzle coconut oil over chicken. Sprinkle each side with chili powder, cumin, and garlic powder. Place each roll into the air fryer basket.
4. Adjust the temperature to 350ºF (177ºC) and air fry for 25 minutes.
5. Serve warm.

Per Serving
calories: 146 | fat: 5g | protein: 20g
carbs: 3g | net carbs: 2g | fiber: 1g

Jalapeño Popper Hasselback Chicken

Prep time: 20 minutes | Cook time: 20 minutes | Serves 2

4 slices sugar-free bacon, cooked and crumbled
2 ounces (57 g) full-fat cream cheese, softened
½ cup shredded sharp

Cheddar cheese, divided
¼ cup sliced pickled jalapeños
2 (6-ounce / 170-g) boneless, skinless chicken breasts

1. In a medium bowl, place cooked bacon, then fold in cream cheese, half of the Cheddar, and the jalapeño slices.

2. Use a sharp knife to make slits in each of the chicken breasts about ¾ of the way across the chicken, being careful not to cut all the way through. Depending on the size of the chicken breast, you'll likely have 6 to 8 slits per breast.
3. Spoon the cream cheese mixture into the slits of the chicken. Sprinkle remaining shredded cheese over chicken breasts and place into the air fryer basket.
4. Adjust the temperature to 350ºF (177ºC) and roast for 20 minutes.
5. Serve warm.

Per Serving
calories: 501 | fat: 25g | protein: 54g
carbs: 2g | net carbs: 1g | fiber: 1g

Chicken Enchiladas

Prep time: 20 minutes | Cook time: 10 minutes | Serves 4

1½ cups shredded cooked chicken
⅓ cup low-carb enchilada sauce, divided
½ pound (227 g) medium-sliced deli chicken
1 cup shredded

medium Cheddar cheese
½ cup shredded Monterey Jack cheese
½ cup full-fat sour cream
1 medium avocado, peeled, pitted, and sliced

1. In a large bowl, mix shredded chicken and half of the enchilada sauce. Lay slices of deli chicken on a work surface and spoon 2 tablespoons shredded chicken mixture onto each slice.
2. Sprinkle 2 tablespoons of Cheddar onto each roll. Gently roll closed.
3. In a 4-cup round baking dish, place each roll, seam side down. Pour remaining sauce over rolls and top with Monterey jack. Place dish into the air fryer basket.
4. Adjust the temperature to 370ºF (188ºC) and bake for 10 minutes.
5. Enchiladas will be golden on top and bubbling when cooked. Serve warm with sour cream and sliced avocado.

Per Serving
calories: 416 | fat: 25g | protein: 34g
carbs: 6g | net carbs: 4g | fiber: 2g

Cilantro Lime Chicken Thighs

Prep time: 15 minutes | Cook time: 22 minutes | Serves 4

4 bone-in, skin-on chicken thighs
1 teaspoon baking powder
½ teaspoon garlic powder

2 teaspoons chili powder
1 teaspoon cumin
2 medium limes
¼ cup chopped fresh cilantro

1. Pat chicken thighs dry and sprinkle with baking powder.
2. In a small bowl, mix garlic powder, chili powder, and cumin and sprinkle evenly over thighs, gently rubbing on and under chicken skin.
3. Cut one lime in half and squeeze juice over thighs. Place chicken into the air fryer basket.
4. Adjust the temperature to 380ºF (193ºC) and roast for 22 minutes.
5. Cut other lime into four wedges for serving and garnish cooked chicken with wedges and cilantro.

Per Serving
calories: 435 | fat: 29g | protein: 32g
carbs: 3g | net carbs: 2g | fiber: 1g

Turkey Pot Pie

Prep time: 20 minutes | Cook time: 30 to 35 minutes | Serves 8

¼ cup (4 tablespoons) unsalted butter
2 shallots, minced
1 cup mushrooms, chopped
2 celery stalks, chopped
1 teaspoon minced garlic
1 teaspoon sea salt
¼ teaspoon freshly ground black pepper
1¾ cups turkey broth

or chicken broth
²/₃ cup heavy (whipping) cream
2 ounces (57 g) cream cheese
½ teaspoon xanthan gum
3 cups chopped cooked turkey
½ cup frozen baby peas (optional)
1 recipe Fathead Pizza Dough

1. Melt the butter in a large saucepan over medium heat. Add the shallots, mushrooms, and celery. Cook for 5 minutes, stirring frequently. Add the garlic, salt, and pepper and cook for 1 minute more.

2. Stir in the broth, heavy cream, cream cheese, and xanthan gum. Bring to a simmer and cook for 1 minute, stirring constantly. Reduce the heat to low and cook for 5 minutes, stirring often, until thickened.
3. Stir in the turkey and peas (if using).
4. Divide the mixture among 8 individual ramekins.
5. Roll out the pizza dough between two sheets of parchment paper. Cut the dough into pieces large enough to cover each ramekin, and place them over the filling. Using a sharp knife, cut a slit or two in the top of each crust to vent.
6. Set the air fryer to 325ºF (163ºC). Place the ramekins in the air fryer basket and bake for 18 to 23 minutes, until the crusts are golden brown.

Per Serving
calories: 359 | fat: 32g | protein: 17g
carbs: 7g | net carbs: 5g | fiber: 2g

Chipotle Drumsticks

Prep time: 5 minutes | Cook time: 25 minutes | Serves 4

1 tablespoon tomato paste
½ teaspoon chipotle powder
¼ teaspoon apple cider vinegar

¼ teaspoon garlic powder
8 chicken drumsticks
½ teaspoon salt
⅛ teaspoon ground black pepper

1. In a small bowl, combine tomato paste, chipotle powder, vinegar, and garlic powder.
2. Sprinkle drumsticks with salt and pepper, then place into a large bowl and pour in tomato paste mixture. Toss or stir to evenly coat all drumsticks in mixture.
3. Place drumsticks into ungreased air fryer basket. Adjust the temperature to 400ºF (204ºC) and air fry for 25 minutes, turning drumsticks halfway through cooking. Drumsticks will be dark red with an internal temperature of at least 165ºF (74ºC) when done. Serve warm.

Per Serving
calories: 432 | fat: 22g | protein: 48g
carbs: 1g | net carbs: 1g | fiber: 0g

Lemon Pepper Drumsticks

Prep time: 5 minutes | Cook time: 25 minutes | Makes 8 drumsticks

2 teaspoons baking powder
½ teaspoon garlic powder
8 chicken drumsticks
4 tablespoons salted butter, melted
1 tablespoon lemon pepper seasoning

1. Sprinkle baking powder and garlic powder over drumsticks and rub into chicken skin. Place drumsticks into the air fryer basket.
2. Adjust the temperature to 375°F (191°C) and roast for 25 minutes.
3. Use tongs to turn drumsticks halfway through the cooking time.
4. When skin is golden and internal temperature is at least 165°F (74°C), remove from fryer.
5. In a large bowl, mix butter and lemon pepper seasoning. Add drumsticks to the bowl and toss until coated. Serve warm.

Per Serving
calories: 532 | fat: 0g | protein: 48g
carbs: 1g | net carbs: 1g | fiber: 0g

Lemon Thyme Roasted Chicken

Prep time: 10 minutes | Cook time: 60 minutes | Serves 6

1 (4-pound / 1.8-kg) chicken
2 teaspoons dried thyme
1 teaspoon garlic powder
½ teaspoon onion powder
2 teaspoons dried parsley
1 teaspoon baking powder
1 medium lemon
2 tablespoons salted butter, melted

1. Rub chicken with thyme, garlic powder, onion powder, parsley, and baking powder.
2. Slice lemon and place four slices on top of chicken, breast side up, and secure with toothpicks. Place remaining slices inside of the chicken.
3. Place entire chicken into the air fryer basket, breast side down.
4. Adjust the temperature to 350°F (177°C) and air fry for 60 minutes.
5. After 30 minutes, flip chicken so breast side is up.
6. When done, internal temperature should be 165°F (74°C) and the skin golden and crispy. To serve, pour melted butter over entire chicken.

Per Serving
calories: 504 | fat: 37g | protein: 32g
carbs: 1g | net carbs: 1g | fiber: 0g

Buffalo Chicken Tenders

Prep time: 15 minutes | Cook time: 7 to 10 minutes | Serves 4

½ cup finely ground blanched almond flour
½ cup finely grated Parmesan cheese
1 teaspoon smoked paprika
¼ teaspoon cayenne pepper
½ teaspoon sea salt, plus additional for seasoning, divided
Freshly ground black pepper, to taste
2 large eggs
1 pound (454 g)
chicken tenders
Avocado oil spray
⅓ cup hot sauce, such as Frank's RedHot
2 tablespoons unsalted butter
2 tablespoons white vinegar
1 garlic clove, minced
Blue Cheese Dressing, for serving
Blue cheese crumbles, for serving

1. In a shallow bowl, combine the almond flour, Parmesan cheese, smoked paprika, and cayenne pepper and season with salt and pepper to taste. In a separate shallow bowl, beat the eggs.
2. One at a time, dip the chicken tenders in the eggs, then coat them with the almond flour mixture, making sure to press the coating into the chicken gently.
3. Set the air fryer to 400°F (204°C). Place the chicken tenders in a single layer in the air fryer basket and spray them with oil. Air fry for 4 minutes. Flip the tenders and spray them with more oil. Cook for 3 to 6 minutes more or until an instant-read thermometer reads 165°F (74°C).
4. While the chicken is cooking, combine the hot sauce, butter, vinegar, garlic, and ½ teaspoon of salt in a small saucepan over medium-low heat. Heat until the butter is melted, whisking to combine.
5. Toss the chicken tenders with the sauce. Serve warm with Blue Cheese Dressing and blue cheese crumbles.

Per Serving
calories: 337 | fat: 20g | protein: 37g
carbs: 4g | net carbs: 2g | fiber: 2g

Broccoli and Cheese Stuffed Chicken

Prep time: 15 minutes | Cook time: 20 minutes | Serves 4

2 ounces (57 g) cream cheese, softened
1 cup chopped fresh broccoli, steamed
½ cup shredded sharp Cheddar cheese
4 (6-ounce / 170-g) boneless, skinless

chicken breasts
2 tablespoons mayonnaise
¼ teaspoon salt
¼ teaspoon garlic powder
⅛ teaspoon ground black pepper

1. In a medium bowl, combine cream cheese, broccoli, and Cheddar. Cut a 4-inch pocket into each chicken breast. Evenly divide mixture between chicken breasts; stuff the pocket of each chicken breast with the mixture.
2. Spread ¼ tablespoon mayonnaise per side of each chicken breast, then sprinkle both sides of breasts with salt, garlic powder, and pepper.
3. Place stuffed chicken breasts into ungreased air fryer basket so that the open seams face up. Adjust the temperature to 350°F (177°C) and air fry for 20 minutes, turning chicken halfway through cooking. When done, chicken will be golden and have an internal temperature of at least 165°F (74°C). Serve warm.

Per Serving
calories: 364 | fat: 16g | protein: 43g
carbs: 3g | net carbs: 2g | fiber: 1g

Chicken Patties

Prep time: 15 minutes | Cook time: 12 minutes | Serves 4

1 pound (454 g) ground chicken thigh meat
½ cup shredded Mozzarella cheese
1 teaspoon dried parsley

½ teaspoon garlic powder
¼ teaspoon onion powder
1 large egg
2 ounces (57 g) pork rinds, finely ground

1. In a large bowl, mix ground chicken, Mozzarella, parsley, garlic powder, and onion powder. Form into four patties.
2. Place patties in the freezer for 15 to 20 minutes until they begin to firm up.
3. Whisk egg in a medium bowl. Place the ground pork rinds into a large bowl.
4. Dip each chicken patty into the egg and then press into pork rinds to fully coat. Place patties into the air fryer basket.
5. Adjust the temperature to 360°F (182°C) and air fry for 12 minutes.
6. Patties will be firm and cooked to an internal temperature of 165°F (74°C) when done. Serve immediately.

Per Serving
calories: 304 | fat: 17g | protein: 33g
carbs: 1g | net carbs: 1g | fiber: 0g

Jalapeño Popper Chicken

Prep time: 10 minutes | Cook time: 14 to 17 minutes | Serves 8

2 pounds (907 g) boneless, skinless chicken breasts or thighs
Sea salt and freshly ground black pepper, to taste
8 ounces (227 g) cream cheese, at

room temperature
4 ounces (113 g) Cheddar cheese, shredded
2 jalapeños, seeded and diced
1 teaspoon minced garlic
Avocado oil spray

1. Place the chicken in a large zip-top bag or between two pieces of plastic wrap. Using a meat mallet or heavy skillet, pound the chicken until it is about ¼-inch thick. Season both sides of the chicken with salt and pepper.
2. In a medium bowl, combine the cream cheese, Cheddar cheese, jalapeños, and garlic. Divide the mixture among the chicken pieces. Roll up each piece from the long side, tucking in the ends as you go. Secure with toothpicks.
3. Set the air fryer to 350°F (177°C). Spray the outside of the chicken with oil. Place the chicken in a single layer in the air fryer basket, working in batches if necessary, and roast for 7 minutes. Flip the chicken and cook for another 7 to 10 minutes, until an instant-read thermometer reads 160°F (71°C).

Per Serving
calories: 264 | fat: 17g | protein: 28g
carbs: 2g | net carbs: 2g | fiber: 0g

Spinach and Feta-Stuffed Chicken Breast

Prep time: 15 minutes | Cook time: 25 minutes | Serves 2

1 tablespoon unsalted butter
5 ounces (142 g) frozen spinach, thawed and drained
½ teaspoon garlic powder, divided
½ teaspoon salt, divided
¼ cup chopped yellow onion
¼ cup crumbled feta
2 (6-ounce / 170-g) boneless, skinless chicken breasts
1 tablespoon coconut oil

1. In a medium skillet over medium heat, add butter to the pan and sauté spinach 3 minutes. Sprinkle ¼ teaspoon garlic powder and ¼ teaspoon salt onto spinach and add onion to the pan.
2. Continue sautéing 3 more minutes, then remove from heat and place in medium bowl. Fold feta into spinach mixture.
3. Slice a roughly 4-inch slit into the side of each chicken breast, lengthwise. Spoon half of the mixture into each piece and secure closed with a couple toothpicks. Sprinkle outside of chicken with remaining garlic powder and salt. Drizzle with coconut oil. Place chicken breasts into the air fryer basket.
4. Adjust the temperature to 350ºF (177ºC) and air fry for 25 minutes.
5. When completely cooked chicken should be golden brown and have an internal temperature of at least 165ºF (74ºC). Slice and serve warm.

Per Serving
calories: 393 | fat: 18g | protein: 44g
carbs: 6g | net carbs: 4g | fiber: 2g

Garlic Parmesan Drumsticks

Prep time: 5 minutes | Cook time: 25 minutes | Serves 4

8 (4-ounce / 113-g) chicken drumsticks
½ teaspoon salt
⅛ teaspoon ground black pepper
½ teaspoon garlic powder
2 tablespoons salted butter, melted
½ cup grated Parmesan cheese
1 tablespoon dried parsley

1. Sprinkle drumsticks with salt, pepper, and garlic powder. Place drumsticks into ungreased air fryer basket.
2. Adjust the temperature to 400ºF (204ºC) and air fry for 25 minutes, turning drumsticks halfway through cooking. Drumsticks will be golden and have an internal temperature of at least 165ºF (74ºC) when done.
3. Transfer drumsticks to a large serving dish. Pour butter over drumsticks, and sprinkle with Parmesan and parsley. Serve warm.

Per Serving
calories: 533 | fat: 30g | protein: 52g
carbs: 3g | net carbs: 3g | fiber: 0g

Simply Terrific Turkey Meatballs

Prep time: 10 minutes | Cook time: 7 to 10 minutes | Serves 4

1 red bell pepper, seeded and coarsely chopped
2 cloves garlic, coarsely chopped
¼ cup chopped fresh parsley
1½ pounds (680 g)
85% lean ground turkey
1 egg, lightly beaten
½ cup grated Parmesan cheese
1 teaspoon salt
½ teaspoon freshly ground black pepper

1. Preheat the air fryer to 400ºF (204ºC).
2. In a food processor fitted with a metal blade, combine the bell pepper, garlic, and parsley. Pulse until finely chopped. Transfer the vegetables to a large mixing bowl.
3. Add the turkey, egg, Parmesan, salt, and black pepper. Mix gently until thoroughly combined. Shape the mixture into 1¼-inch meatballs.
4. Working in batches if necessary, arrange the meatballs in a single layer in the air fryer basket; coat lightly with olive oil spray. Pausing halfway through the cooking time to shake the basket, air fry for 7 to 10 minutes, until lightly browned and a thermometer inserted into the center of a meatball registers 165ºF (74ºC).

Per Serving
calories: 410 | fat: 27g | protein: 38g
carbs: 4g | net carbs: 3g | fiber: 1g

Pecan-Crusted Chicken Tenders

Prep time: 10 minutes | Cook time: 12 minutes | Serves 4

2 tablespoons mayonnaise
1 teaspoon Dijon mustard
1 pound (454 g) boneless, skinless chicken tenders

½ teaspoon salt
¼ teaspoon ground black pepper
½ cup chopped roasted pecans, finely ground

1. In a small bowl, whisk mayonnaise and mustard until combined. Brush mixture onto chicken tenders on both sides, then sprinkle tenders with salt and pepper.
2. Place pecans in a medium bowl and press each tender into pecans to coat each side.
3. Place tenders into ungreased air fryer basket in a single layer, working in batches if needed. Adjust the temperature to 375ºF (191ºC) and roast for 12 minutes, turning tenders halfway through cooking. Tenders will be golden brown and have an internal temperature of at least 165ºF (74ºC) when done. Serve warm.

Per Serving
calories: 237 | fat: 15g | protein: 22g
carbs: 2g | net carbs: 1g | fiber: 1g

Bacon Lovers' Stuffed Chicken

Prep time: 10 minutes | Cook time: 20 minutes | Serves 4

4 (5-ounce / 142-g) boneless, skinless chicken breasts, pounded to ¼ inch thick
2 (5.2-ounce / 147-g) packages Boursin cheese (or Kite Hill

brand chive cream cheese style spread, softened, for dairy-free)
8 slices thin-cut bacon or beef bacon
Sprig of fresh cilantro, for garnish (optional)

1. Spray the air fryer basket with avocado oil. Preheat the air fryer to 400ºF (204ºC).
2. Place one of the chicken breasts on a cutting board. With a sharp knife held parallel to the cutting board, make a 1-inch-wide incision at the top of the breast. Carefully cut into the breast to form a large pocket, leaving a ½-inch border along the sides and bottom. Repeat with the other 3 chicken breasts.

3. Snip the corner of a large resealable plastic bag to form a ¾-inch hole. Place the Boursin cheese in the bag and pipe the cheese into the pockets in the chicken breasts, dividing the cheese evenly among them.
4. Wrap 2 slices of bacon around each chicken breast and secure the ends with toothpicks. Place the bacon-wrapped chicken in the air fryer basket and air fry until the bacon is crisp and the chicken's internal temperature reaches 165ºF (74ºC), about 18 to 20 minutes, flipping after 10 minutes. Garnish with a sprig of cilantro before serving, if desired.
5. Store leftovers in an airtight container in the refrigerator for up to 4 days. Reheat in a preheated 400ºF (204ºC) air fryer for 5 minutes, or until warmed through.

Per Serving
calories: 686 | fat: 51g | protein: 52g
carbs: 2g | net carbs: 2g | fiber: 0g

Butter and Bacon Chicken

Prep time: 10 minutes | Cook time: 65 minutes | Serves 6

1 (4-pound / 1.8-kg) whole chicken
2 tablespoons salted butter, softened
1 teaspoon dried thyme
½ teaspoon garlic

powder
1 teaspoon salt
½ teaspoon ground black pepper
6 slices sugar-free bacon

1. Pat chicken dry with a paper towel, then rub with butter on all sides. Sprinkle thyme, garlic powder, salt, and pepper over chicken.
2. Place chicken into ungreased air fryer basket, breast side up. Lay strips of bacon over chicken and secure with toothpicks.
3. Adjust the temperature to 350ºF (177ºC) and air fry for 65 minutes. Halfway through cooking, remove and set aside bacon and flip chicken over. Chicken will be done when the skin is golden and crispy and the internal temperature is at least 165ºF (74ºC). Serve warm with bacon.

Per Serving
calories: 416 | fat: 26g | protein: 36g
carbs: 0g | net carbs: 0g | fiber: 0g

Chipotle Aioli Wings

Prep time: 5 minutes | Cook time: 25 minutes | Serves 6

2 pounds (907 g) bone-in chicken wings	mayonnaise
½ teaspoon salt	2 teaspoons chipotle powder
¼ teaspoon ground black pepper	2 tablespoons lemon juice
2 tablespoons	

1. In a large bowl, toss wings in salt and pepper, then place into ungreased air fryer basket. Adjust the temperature to 400ºF (204ºC) and air fry for 25 minutes, shaking the basket twice while cooking. Wings will be done when golden and have an internal temperature of at least 165ºF (74ºC).
2. In a small bowl, whisk together mayonnaise, chipotle powder, and lemon juice. Place cooked wings into a large serving bowl and drizzle with aioli. Toss to coat. Serve warm.

Per Serving
calories: 243 | fat: 18g | protein: 19g
carbs: 0g | net carbs: 0g | fiber: 0g

Cobb Salad

Prep time: 15 minutes | Cook time: 8 minutes | Serves 4

8 slices reduced-sodium bacon	1 cup cherry tomatoes, halved
8 chicken breast tenders (about 1½ pounds / 680 g)	¼ red onion, thinly sliced
8 cups chopped romaine lettuce	2 hard-boiled eggs, peeled and sliced

Avocado-Lime Dressing:

½ cup plain Greek yogurt	2 tablespoons fresh cilantro
¼ cup almond milk	⅛ teaspoon ground cumin
½ avocado	Salt and freshly ground black pepper, to taste
Juice of ½ lime	
3 scallions, coarsely chopped	
1 clove garlic	

1. Preheat the air fryer to 400ºF (204ºC).
2. Wrap a piece of bacon around each piece of chicken and secure with a toothpick.

Working in batches if necessary, arrange the bacon-wrapped chicken in a single layer in the air fryer basket. Air fry for 8 minutes until the bacon is browned and a thermometer inserted into the thickest piece of chicken register 165ºF (74ºC). Let cool for a few minutes, then slice into bite-size pieces.

3. To make the dressing: In a blender or food processor, combine the yogurt, milk, avocado, lime juice, scallions, garlic, cilantro, and cumin. Purée until smooth. Season to taste with salt and freshly ground pepper.
4. To assemble the salad, in a large bowl, combine the lettuce, tomatoes, and onion. Drizzle the dressing over the vegetables and toss gently until thoroughly combined. Arrange the chicken and eggs on top just before serving.

Per Serving
calories: 425 | fat: 18g | protein: 52g
carbs: 11g | net carbs: 7g | fiber: 4g

Spice-Rubbed Chicken Thighs

Prep time: 10 minutes | Cook time: 25 minutes | Serves 4

4 (4-ounce / 113-g) bone-in, skin-on chicken thighs	2 teaspoons chili powder
½ teaspoon salt	1 teaspoon paprika
½ teaspoon garlic powder	1 teaspoon ground cumin
	1 small lime, halved

1. Pat chicken thighs dry and sprinkle with salt, garlic powder, chili powder, paprika, and cumin.
2. Squeeze juice from ½ lime over thighs. Place thighs into ungreased air fryer basket. Adjust the temperature to 380ºF (193ºC) and roast for 25 minutes, turning thighs halfway through cooking. Thighs will be crispy and browned with an internal temperature of at least 165ºF (74ºC) when done.
3. Transfer thighs to a large serving plate and drizzle with remaining lime juice. Serve warm.

Per Serving
calories: 255 | fat: 10g | protein: 34g
carbs: 2g | net carbs: 1g | fiber: 1g

Jerk Chicken Kebabs

Prep time: 10 minutes | Cook time: 14 minutes | Serves 4

8 ounces (227 g) boneless, skinless chicken thighs, cut into 1-inch cubes
2 tablespoons jerk seasoning
2 tablespoons coconut oil

½ medium red bell pepper, seeded and cut into 1-inch pieces
¼ medium red onion, peeled and cut into 1-inch pieces
½ teaspoon salt

1. Place chicken in a medium bowl and sprinkle with jerk seasoning and coconut oil. Toss to coat on all sides.
2. Using eight (6-inch) skewers, build skewers by alternating chicken, pepper, and onion pieces, about three repetitions per skewer.
3. Sprinkle salt over skewers and place into ungreased air fryer basket. Adjust the temperature to 370°F (188°C) and air fry for 14 minutes, turning skewers halfway through cooking. Chicken will be golden and have an internal temperature of at least 165°F (74°C) when done. Serve warm.

Per Serving
calories: 138 | fat: 7g | protein: 10g
carbs: 2g | net carbs: 2g | fiber: 0g

Turkey Meatloaf

Prep time: 10 minutes | Cook time: 50 minutes | Serves 4

8 ounces (227 g) sliced mushrooms
1 small onion, coarsely chopped
2 cloves garlic
1½ pounds (680 g) 85% lean ground turkey
2 eggs, lightly beaten
1 tablespoon tomato paste

¼ cup almond meal
2 tablespoons almond milk
1 tablespoon dried oregano
1 teaspoon salt
½ teaspoon freshly ground black pepper
1 Roma tomato, thinly sliced

1. Preheat the air fryer to 350°F (177°C). Lightly coat a round pan with olive oil and set aside.

2. In a food processor fitted with a metal blade, combine the mushrooms, onion, and garlic. Pulse until finely chopped. Transfer the vegetables to a large mixing bowl.
3. Add the turkey, eggs, tomato paste, almond meal, milk, oregano, salt, and black pepper. Mix gently until thoroughly combined. Transfer the mixture to the prepared pan and shape into a loaf. Arrange the tomato slices on top.
4. Air fry for 50 minutes or until the meatloaf is nicely browned and a thermometer inserted into the thickest part registers 165°F (74°C). Remove from the air fryer and let rest for about 10 minutes before slicing.

Per Serving
calories: 429 | fat: 26g | protein: 40g
carbs: 8g | net carbs: 7g | fiber: 1g

Ginger Turmeric Chicken Thighs

Prep time: 5 minutes | Cook time: 25 minutes | Serves 4

4 (4-ounce / 113-g) boneless, skin-on chicken thighs
2 tablespoons coconut oil, melted
½ teaspoon ground turmeric

½ teaspoon salt
½ teaspoon garlic powder
½ teaspoon ground ginger
¼ teaspoon ground black pepper

1. Place chicken thighs in a large bowl and drizzle with coconut oil. Sprinkle with remaining ingredients and toss to coat both sides of thighs.
2. Place thighs skin side up into ungreased air fryer basket. Adjust the temperature to 400°F (204°C) and air fry for 25 minutes. After 10 minutes, turn thighs. When 5 minutes remain, flip thighs once more. Chicken will be done when skin is golden brown and the internal temperature is at least 165°F (74°C). Serve warm.

Per Serving
calories: 306 | fat: 17g | protein: 34g
carbs: 1g | net carbs: 1g | fiber: 0g

Chicken Pesto Pizzas

Prep time: 10 minutes | Cook time: 12 minutes | Serves 4

1 pound (454 g) ground chicken thighs
¼ teaspoon salt
⅛ teaspoon ground black pepper
¼ cup basil pesto
1 cup shredded Mozzarella cheese
4 grape tomatoes, sliced

1. Cut four squares of parchment paper to fit into your air fryer basket.
2. Place ground chicken in a large bowl and mix with salt and pepper. Divide mixture into four equal sections.
3. Wet your hands with water to prevent sticking, then press each section into a 6-inch circle onto a piece of ungreased parchment. Place each chicken crust into air fryer basket, working in batches if needed.
4. Adjust the temperature to 350°F (177°C) and air fry for 10 minutes, turning crusts halfway through cooking.
5. Spread 1 tablespoon pesto across the top of each crust, then sprinkle with ¼ cup Mozzarella and top with 1 sliced tomato. Continue cooking at 350°F (177°C) for 2 minutes. Cheese will be melted and brown when done. Serve warm.

Per Serving
calories: 318 | fat: 19g | protein: 28g
carbs: 4g | net carbs: 4g | fiber: 0g

Smoky Chicken Leg Quarters

Prep time: 5 minutes | Cook time: 23 to 27 minutes | Serves 6

½ cup avocado oil
2 teaspoons smoked paprika
1 teaspoon sea salt
1 teaspoon garlic powder
½ teaspoon dried rosemary
½ teaspoon dried thyme
½ teaspoon freshly ground black pepper
2 pounds (907 g) bone-in, skin-on chicken leg quarters

1. In a blender or small bowl, combine the avocado oil, smoked paprika, salt, garlic powder, rosemary, thyme, and black pepper.
2. Place the chicken in a shallow dish or large zip-top bag. Pour the marinade over the chicken, making sure all the legs are coated. Cover and marinate for at least 2 hours or overnight.
3. Place the chicken in a single layer in the air fryer basket, working in batches if necessary. Set the air fryer to 400°F (204°C) and air fry for 15 minutes. Flip the chicken legs, then reduce the temperature to 350°F (177°C). Cook for 8 to 12 minutes more, until an instant-read thermometer reads 160°F (71°C) when inserted into the thickest piece of chicken.
4. Allow to rest for 5 to 10 minutes before serving.

Per Serving
calories: 569 | fat: 53g | protein: 23g
carbs: 1g | net carbs: 1g | fiber: 0g

Pork Rind Fried Chicken

Prep time: 10 minutes | Cook time: 20 minutes | Serves 4

¼ cup buffalo sauce
4 (4-ounce / 113-g) boneless, skinless chicken breasts
½ teaspoon paprika
½ teaspoon garlic
powder
¼ teaspoon ground black pepper
2 ounces (57 g) plain pork rinds, finely crushed

1. Pour buffalo sauce into a large sealable bowl or bag. Add chicken and toss to coat. Place sealed bowl or bag into refrigerator and let marinate at least 30 minutes up to overnight.
2. Remove chicken from marinade but do not shake excess sauce off chicken. Sprinkle both sides of thighs with paprika, garlic powder, and pepper.
3. Place pork rinds into a large bowl and press each chicken breast into pork rinds to coat evenly on both sides.
4. Place chicken into ungreased air fryer basket. Adjust the temperature to 400°F (204°C) and roast for 20 minutes, turning chicken halfway through cooking. Chicken will be golden and have an internal temperature of at least 165°F (74°C) when done. Serve warm.

Per Serving
calories: 185 | fat: 7g | protein: 27g
carbs: 1g | net carbs: 1g | fiber: 0g

Chicken Nuggets

Prep time: 10 minutes | Cook time: 15 minutes | Serves 4

1 pound (454 g) ground chicken thighs
½ cup shredded Mozzarella cheese
1 large egg, whisked
½ teaspoon salt
¼ teaspoon dried oregano
¼ teaspoon garlic powder

1. In a large bowl, combine all ingredients. Form mixture into twenty nugget shapes, about 2 tablespoons each.
2. Place nuggets into ungreased air fryer basket, working in batches if needed. Adjust the temperature to 375ºF (191ºC) and air fry for 15 minutes, turning nuggets halfway through cooking. Let cool 5 minutes before serving.

Per Serving
calories: 222 | fat: 12g | protein: 25g
carbs: 1g | net carbs: 1g | fiber: 0g

Buffalo Chicken Wings

Prep time: 10 minutes | Cook time: 20 to 25 minutes | Serves 4

2 tablespoons baking powder
1 teaspoon smoked paprika
Sea salt and freshly ground black pepper, to taste
2 pounds (907 g) chicken wings or chicken drumettes
Avocado oil spray
⅓ cup avocado oil
½ cup Buffalo hot sauce, such as Frank's RedHot
¼ cup (4 tablespoons) unsalted butter
2 tablespoons apple cider vinegar
1 teaspoon minced garlic
Blue Cheese Dressing or Garlic Ranch Dressing, for serving

1. In a large bowl, stir together the baking powder, smoked paprika, and salt and pepper to taste. Add the chicken wings and toss to coat.
2. Set the air fryer to 400ºF (204ºC). Spray the wings with oil.
3. Place the wings in the basket in a single layer, working in batches, and air fry for 20 to 25 minutes. Check with an instant-read thermometer and remove when they reach 155ºF (68ºC). Let rest until they reach 165ºF (74ºC).
4. While the wings are cooking, whisk together the avocado oil, hot sauce, butter, vinegar, and garlic in a small saucepan over medium-low heat until warm.
5. When the wings are done cooking, toss them with the Buffalo sauce. Serve warm with the dressing.

Per Serving
calories: 750 | fat: 64g | protein: 34g
carbs: 2g | net carbs: 1g | fiber: 1g

Tandoori Chicken

Prep time: 10 minutes | Cook time: 15 to 20 minutes | Serves 6

¼ cup plain Greek yogurt
2 cloves garlic, minced
1 tablespoon grated fresh ginger
½ teaspoon ground cayenne
½ teaspoon ground turmeric
½ teaspoon garam masala
1 teaspoon ground cumin
1 teaspoon salt
2 pounds (907 g) boneless chicken thighs, skin on
2 tablespoons chopped fresh cilantro
1 lemon, cut into 6 wedges
½ sweet onion, sliced

1. In a small bowl, combine the yogurt, garlic, ginger, cayenne, turmeric, garam masala, cumin, and salt. Whisk until thoroughly combined.
2. Transfer the yogurt mixture to a large resealable bag. Add the chicken, seal the bag, and massage the bag to ensure chicken is evenly coated. Refrigerate for 1 hour (or up to 8 hours).
3. Preheat the air fryer to 360ºF (182ºC).
4. Remove the chicken from the marinade (discard the marinade) and arrange in a single layer in the air fryer basket. Pausing halfway through the cooking time to flip the chicken, air fry for 15 to 20 minutes, until a thermometer inserted into the thickest part registers 165ºF (74ºC).
5. Transfer the chicken to a serving platter. Top with the cilantro and serve with the lemon wedges and sliced onion.

Per Serving
calories: 350 | fat: 22g | protein: 35g
carbs: 1g | net carbs: 1g | fiber: 0g

Cajun-Breaded Chicken Bites

Prep time: 10 minutes | Cook time: 12 minutes | Serves 4

1 pound (454 g) boneless, skinless chicken breasts, cut into 1-inch cubes
½ cup heavy whipping cream
½ teaspoon salt
¼ teaspoon ground

black pepper
1 ounce (28 g) plain pork rinds, finely crushed
¼ cup unflavored whey protein powder
½ teaspoon Cajun seasoning

1. Place chicken in a medium bowl and pour in cream. Stir to coat. Sprinkle with salt and pepper.
2. In a separate large bowl, combine pork rinds, protein powder, and Cajun seasoning. Remove chicken from cream, shaking off any excess, and toss in dry mix until fully coated.
3. Place bites into ungreased air fryer basket. Adjust the temperature to 400ºF (204ºC) and air fry for 12 minutes, shaking the basket twice during cooking. Bites will be done when golden brown and have an internal temperature of at least 165ºF (74ºC). Serve warm.

Per Serving
calories: 285 | fat: 16g | protein: 34g
carbs: 1g | net carbs: 1g | fiber: 0g

Fried Chicken Breasts

Prep time: 10 minutes | Cook time: 12 to 14 minutes | Serves 4

1 pound (454 g) boneless, skinless chicken breasts
¾ cup dill pickle juice
¾ cup finely ground blanched almond flour
¾ cup finely grated

Parmesan cheese
½ teaspoon sea salt
½ teaspoon freshly ground black pepper
2 large eggs
Avocado oil spray

1. Place the chicken breasts in a zip-top bag or between two pieces of plastic wrap. Using a meat mallet or heavy skillet, pound the chicken to a uniform ½-inch thickness.
2. Place the chicken in a large bowl with the pickle juice. Cover and allow to brine in the refrigerator for up to 2 hours.
3. In a shallow dish, combine the almond flour, Parmesan cheese, salt, and pepper. In a separate, shallow bowl, beat the eggs.
4. Drain the chicken and pat it dry with paper towels. Dip in the eggs and then in the flour mixture, making sure to press the coating into the chicken. Spray both sides of the coated breasts with oil.
5. Spray the air fryer basket with oil and put the chicken inside. Set the temperature to 400ºF (204ºC) and air fry for 6 to 7 minutes.
6. Carefully flip the breasts with a spatula. Spray the breasts again with oil and continue cooking for 6 to 7 minutes more, until golden and crispy.

Per Serving
calories: 345 | fat: 18g | protein: 39g
carbs: 8g | net carbs: 6g | fiber: 2g

Spice-Rubbed Turkey Breast

Prep time: 5 minutes | Cook time: 45 to 55 minutes | Serves 10

1 tablespoon sea salt
1 teaspoon paprika
1 teaspoon onion powder
1 teaspoon garlic powder
½ teaspoon freshly

ground black pepper
4 pounds (1.8 kg) bone-in, skin-on turkey breast
2 tablespoons unsalted butter, melted

1. In a small bowl, combine the salt, paprika, onion powder, garlic powder, and pepper.
2. Sprinkle the seasonings all over the turkey. Brush the turkey with some of the melted butter.
3. Set the air fryer to 350ºF (177ºC). Place the turkey in the air fryer basket, skin-side down, and roast for 25 minutes.
4. Flip the turkey and brush it with the remaining butter. Continue cooking for another 20 to 30 minutes, until an instant-read thermometer reads 160ºF (71ºC).
5. Remove the turkey breast from the air fryer. Tent a piece of aluminum foil over the turkey, and allow it to rest for about 5 minutes before serving.

Per Serving
calories: 278 | fat: 14g | protein: 34g
carbs: 1g | net carbs: 0g | fiber: 1g

Chicken Kiev

Prep time: 15 minutes | Cook time: 25 minutes | Serves 4

1 cup (2 sticks) unsalted butter, softened (or butter-flavored coconut oil for dairy-free)
2 tablespoons lemon juice
2 tablespoons plus 1 teaspoon chopped fresh parsley leaves, divided, plus more for garnish
2 tablespoons chopped fresh tarragon leaves

3 cloves garlic, minced
1 teaspoon fine sea salt, divided
4 (4-ounce / 113-g) boneless, skinless chicken breasts
2 large eggs
2 cups pork dust
1 teaspoon ground black pepper
Sprig of fresh parsley, for garnish
Lemon slices, for serving

1. Spray the air fryer basket with avocado oil. Preheat the air fryer to 350°F (177°C).
2. In a medium-sized bowl, combine the butter, lemon juice, 2 tablespoons of the parsley, the tarragon, garlic, and ¼ teaspoon of the salt. Cover and place in the fridge to harden for 7 minutes.
3. While the butter mixture chills, place one of the chicken breasts on a cutting board. With a sharp knife held parallel to the cutting board, make a 1-inch-wide incision at the top of the breast. Carefully cut into the breast to form a large pocket, leaving a ½-inch border along the sides and bottom. Repeat with the other 3 breasts.
4. Stuff one-quarter of the butter mixture into each chicken breast and secure the openings with toothpicks.
5. Beat the eggs in a small shallow dish. In another shallow dish, combine the pork dust, the remaining 1 teaspoon of parsley, the remaining ¾ teaspoon of salt, and the pepper.
6. One at a time, dip the chicken breasts in the egg, shake off the excess egg, and dredge the breasts in the pork dust mixture. Use your hands to press the pork dust onto each breast to form a nice crust. If you desire a thicker coating, dip it again in the egg and pork dust. As you finish, spray each coated chicken breast with avocado oil and place it in the air fryer basket.
7. Roast the chicken in the air fryer for 15 minutes, flip the breasts, and cook for another 10 minutes, or until the internal temperature of the chicken is 165°F (74°C) and the crust is golden brown.
8. Serve garnished with chopped fresh parsley and a parsley sprig, with lemon slices on the side.
9. Store leftovers in an airtight container in the refrigerator for up to 4 days or in the freezer for up to a month. Reheat in a preheated 350°F (177°C) air fryer for 5 minutes, or until heated through.

Per Serving
calories: 801 | fat: 64g | protein: 51g
carbs: 3g | net carbs: 2g | fiber: 1g

Lemon-Dijon Boneless Chicken

Prep time: 5 minutes | Cook time: 13 to 16 minutes | Serves 6

½ cup sugar-free mayonnaise
1 tablespoon Dijon mustard
1 tablespoon freshly squeezed lemon juice (optional)
1 tablespoon coconut aminos
1 teaspoon Italian

seasoning
1 teaspoon sea salt
½ teaspoon freshly ground black pepper
¼ teaspoon cayenne pepper
1½ pounds (680 g) boneless, skinless chicken breasts or thighs

1. In a small bowl, combine the mayonnaise, mustard, lemon juice (if using), coconut aminos, Italian seasoning, salt, black pepper, and cayenne pepper.
2. Place the chicken in a shallow dish or large zip-top plastic bag. Add the marinade, making sure all the pieces are coated. Cover and refrigerate for at least 30 minutes or up to 4 hours.
3. Set the air fryer to 400°F (204°C). Arrange the chicken in a single layer in the air fryer basket, working in batches if necessary. Air fry for 7 minutes. Flip the chicken and continue cooking for 6 to 9 minutes more, until an instant-read thermometer reads 160°F (71°C).

Per Serving
calories: 236 | fat: 17g | protein: 23g
carbs: 1g | net carbs: 1g | fiber: 0g

Porchetta-Style Chicken Breasts

Prep time: 10 minutes | Cook time: 15 minutes | Serves 4

½ cup fresh parsley leaves

¼ cup roughly chopped fresh chives

4 cloves garlic, peeled

2 tablespoons lemon juice

3 teaspoons fine sea salt

1 teaspoon dried rubbed sage

1 teaspoon fresh rosemary leaves

1 teaspoon ground fennel

½ teaspoon red pepper flakes

4 (4-ounce / 113-g) boneless, skinless chicken breasts, pounded to ¼ inch thick

8 slices bacon

Sprigs of fresh rosemary, for garnish (optional)

1. Spray the air fryer basket with avocado oil. Preheat the air fryer to 340ºF (171ºC).
2. Place the parsley, chives, garlic, lemon juice, salt, sage, rosemary, fennel, and red pepper flakes in a food processor and purée until a smooth paste forms.
3. Place the chicken breasts on a cutting board and rub the paste all over the tops. With a short end facing you, roll each breast up like a jelly roll to make a log and secure it with toothpicks.
4. Wrap 2 slices of bacon around each chicken breast log to cover the entire breast. Secure the bacon with toothpicks.
5. Place the chicken breast logs in the air fryer basket and air fry for 5 minutes, flip the logs over, and cook for another 5 minutes. Increase the heat to 390ºF (199ºC) and cook until the bacon is crisp, about 5 minutes more.
6. Remove the toothpicks and garnish with fresh rosemary sprigs, if desired, before serving. Store leftovers in an airtight container in the refrigerator for up to 4 days or in the freezer for up to a month. Reheat in a preheated 350ºF (177ºC) air fryer for 5 minutes, then increase the heat to 390ºF (199ºC) and cook for 2 minutes to crisp the bacon.

Per Serving

calories: 468 | fat: 25g | protein: 56g
carbs: 3g | net carbs: 2g | fiber: 1g

Chicken Paillard

Prep time: 10 minutes | Cook time: 10 minutes | Serves 2

2 large eggs, room temperature

1 tablespoon water

½ cup powdered Parmesan cheese (about 1½ ounces / 43 g) or pork dust

2 teaspoons dried

Lemon Butter Sauce:

2 tablespoons unsalted butter, melted

2 teaspoons lemon juice

¼ teaspoon finely chopped fresh thyme

thyme leaves

1 teaspoon ground black pepper

2 (5-ounce / 142-g) boneless, skinless chicken breasts, pounded to ½ inch thick

leaves, plus more for garnish

⅛ teaspoon fine sea salt

Lemon slices, for serving

1. Spray the air fryer basket with avocado oil. Preheat the air fryer to 390ºF (199ºC).
2. Beat the eggs in a shallow dish, then add the water and stir well.
3. In a separate shallow dish, mix together the Parmesan, thyme, and pepper until well combined.
4. One at a time, dip the chicken breasts in the eggs and let any excess drip off, then dredge both sides of the chicken in the Parmesan mixture. As you finish, set the coated chicken in the air fryer basket.
5. Roast the chicken in the air fryer for 5 minutes, then flip the chicken and cook for another 5 minutes, or until cooked through and the internal temperature reaches 165ºF (74ºC).
6. While the chicken cooks, make the lemon butter sauce: In a small bowl, mix together all the sauce ingredients until well combined.
7. Plate the chicken and pour the sauce over it. Garnish with chopped fresh thyme and serve with lemon slices.
8. Store leftovers in an airtight container in the refrigerator for up to 4 days. Reheat in a preheated 390ºF (199ºC) air fryer for 5 minutes, or until heated through.

Per Serving

calories: 526 | fat: 33g | protein: 53g
carbs: 3g | net carbs: 2g | fiber: 1g

Chicken Strips with Satay Sauce

Prep time: 5 minutes | Cook time: 10 minutes | Serves 4

4 (6-ounce / 170-g) boneless, skinless chicken breasts, sliced into 16 (1-inch) strips

Sauce:
¼ cup creamy almond butter (or sunflower seed butter for nut-free)
2 tablespoons chicken broth
1½ tablespoons coconut vinegar or unseasoned rice vinegar
1 teaspoon fine sea salt
1 teaspoon paprika
1 clove garlic, minced
1 teaspoon peeled and minced fresh ginger
½ teaspoon hot sauce
⅛ teaspoon stevia glycerite, or 2 to 3 drops liquid stevia

For Garnish/Serving (Optional):
¼ cup chopped cilantro leaves
Red pepper flakes
Sea salt flakes
Thinly sliced red, orange, and yellow bell peppers

Special Equipment:
16 wooden or bamboo skewers, soaked in water for 15 minutes

1. Spray the air fryer basket with avocado oil. Preheat the air fryer to 400°F (204°C).
2. Thread the chicken strips onto the skewers. Season on all sides with the salt and paprika. Place the chicken skewers in the air fryer basket and air fry for 5 minutes, flip, and cook for another 5 minutes, until the chicken is cooked through and the internal temperature reaches 165°F (74°C).
3. While the chicken skewers cook, make the sauce: In a medium-sized bowl, stir together all the sauce ingredients until well combined. Taste and adjust the sweetness and heat to your liking.
4. Garnish the chicken with cilantro, red pepper flakes, and salt flakes, if desired, and serve with sliced bell peppers, if desired. Serve the sauce on the side.
5. Store leftovers in an airtight container in the fridge for up to 4 days or in the freezer for up to a month. Reheat in a preheated 350°F (177°C) air fryer for 3 minutes per side, or until heated through.

Per Serving
calories: 359 | fat: 16g | protein: 49g
carbs: 2g | net carbs: 1g | fiber: 1g

Chicken Pesto Parmigiana

Prep time: 10 minutes | Cook time: 23 minutes | Serves 4

2 large eggs
1 tablespoon water
Fine sea salt and ground black pepper, to taste
1 cup powdered Parmesan cheese (about 3 ounces / 85 g)
2 teaspoons Italian seasoning
4 (5-ounce / 142-g) boneless, skinless chicken breasts or thighs, pounded to ¼ inch thick
1 cup pesto
1 cup shredded Mozzarella cheese (about 4 ounces / 113 g)
Finely chopped fresh basil, for garnish (optional)
Grape tomatoes, halved, for serving (optional)

1. Spray the air fryer basket with avocado oil. Preheat the air fryer to 400°F (204°C).
2. Crack the eggs into a shallow baking dish, add the water and a pinch each of salt and pepper, and whisk to combine. In another shallow baking dish, stir together the Parmesan and Italian seasoning until well combined.
3. Season the chicken breasts well on both sides with salt and pepper. Dip one chicken breast in the eggs and let any excess drip off, then dredge both sides of the breast in the Parmesan mixture. Spray the breast with avocado oil and place it in the air fryer basket. Repeat with the remaining 3 chicken breasts.
4. Air fry the chicken in the air fryer for 20 minutes, or until the internal temperature reaches 165°F (74°C) and the breading is golden brown, flipping halfway through.
5. Dollop each chicken breast with ¼ cup of the pesto and top with the Mozzarella. Return the breasts to the air fryer and cook for 3 minutes, or until the cheese is melted. Garnish with basil and serve with halved grape tomatoes on the side, if desired.
6. Store leftovers in an airtight container in the refrigerator for up to 4 days. Reheat in a preheated 400°F (204°C) air fryer for 5 minutes, or until warmed through.

Per Serving (with breasts)
calories: 558 | fat: 43g | protein: 40g
carbs: 4g | net carbs: 3g | fiber: 1g

Thai Tacos with Peanut Sauce

Prep time: 10 minutes | Cook time: 6 minutes | Serves 4

1 pound (454 g) ground chicken

¼ cup diced onions (about 1 small onion)

2 cloves garlic, minced

¼ teaspoon fine sea salt

Sauce:

¼ cup creamy peanut butter, room temperature

2 tablespoons chicken broth, plus more if needed

2 tablespoons lime juice

2 tablespoons grated

fresh ginger

2 tablespoons wheat-free tamari or coconut aminos

1½ teaspoons hot sauce

5 drops liquid stevia (optional)

For Serving:

2 small heads butter lettuce, leaves

separated

Lime slices (optional)

For Garnish (Optional):

Cilantro leaves

Shredded purple

cabbage

Sliced green onions

1. Preheat the air fryer to 350ºF (177ºC).
2. Place the ground chicken, onions, garlic, and salt in a pie pan or a dish that will fit in your air fryer. Break up the chicken with a spatula. Place in the air fryer and bake for 5 minutes, or until the chicken is browned and cooked through. Break up the chicken again into small crumbles.
3. Make the sauce: In a medium-sized bowl, stir together the peanut butter, broth, lime juice, ginger, tamari, hot sauce, and stevia (if using) until well combined. If the sauce is too thick, add another tablespoon or two of broth. Taste and add more hot sauce if desired.
4. Add half of the sauce to the pan with the chicken. Cook for another minute, until heated through, and stir well to combine.
5. Assemble the tacos: Place several lettuce leaves on a serving plate. Place a few tablespoons of the chicken mixture in each lettuce leaf and garnish with cilantro leaves, purple cabbage, and sliced green onions, if desired. Serve the remaining sauce on the side. Serve with lime slices, if desired.
6. Store leftover meat mixture in an airtight container in the refrigerator for up to 4 days; store leftover sauce, lettuce leaves, and garnishes separately. Reheat the meat mixture in a lightly greased pie pan in a preheated 350ºF (177ºC) air fryer for 3 minutes, or until heated through.

Per Serving

calories: 350 | fat: 17g | protein: 39g
carbs: 11g | net carbs: 8g | fiber: 3g

Chicken and Broccoli Casserole

Prep time: 5 minutes | Cook time: 20 to 25 minutes | Serves 4

½ pound (227 g) broccoli, chopped into florets

2 cups shredded cooked chicken

4 ounces (113 g) cream cheese

⅓ cup heavy cream

1½ teaspoons Dijon mustard

½ teaspoon garlic powder

Salt and freshly ground black pepper, to taste

2 tablespoons chopped fresh basil

1 cup shredded Cheddar cheese

1. Preheat the air fryer to 390ºF (199ºC). Lightly coat a 6-cup casserole dish that will fit in air fryer, with olive oil and set aside.
2. Place the broccoli in a large glass bowl with 1 tablespoon of water and cover with a microwavable plate. Microwave on high for 2 to 3 minutes until the broccoli is bright green but not mushy. Drain if necessary and add to another large bowl along with the shredded chicken.
3. In the same glass bowl used to microwave the broccoli, combine the cream cheese and cream. Microwave for 30 seconds to 1 minute on high and stir until smooth. Add the mustard and garlic powder and season to taste with salt and freshly ground black pepper. Whisk until the sauce is smooth.
4. Pour the warm sauce over the broccoli and chicken mixture and then add the basil. Using a silicone spatula, gently fold the mixture until thoroughly combined.
5. Transfer the chicken mixture to the prepared casserole dish and top with the cheese. Air fry for 20 to 25 minutes until warmed through and the cheese has browned.

Per Serving

calories: 430 | fat: 32g | protein: 29g
carbs: 6g | net carbs: 5g | fiber: 1g

Personal Cauliflower Pizzas

Prep time: 10 minutes | Cook time: 25 minutes | Serves 2

1 (12-ounce / 340-g) bag frozen riced cauliflower
1/3 cup shredded Mozzarella cheese
¼ cup almond flour
¼ grated Parmesan cheese
1 large egg
½ teaspoon salt
1 teaspoon garlic powder
1 teaspoon dried oregano

4 tablespoons no-sugar-added marinara sauce, divided
4 ounces (113 g) fresh Mozzarella, chopped, divided
1 cup cooked chicken breast, chopped, divided
½ cup chopped cherry tomatoes, divided
¼ cup fresh baby arugula, divided

1. Preheat the air fryer to 400ºF (204ºC). Cut 4 sheets of parchment paper to fit the basket of the air fryer. Brush with olive oil and set aside.
2. In a large glass bowl, microwave the cauliflower according to package directions. Place the cauliflower on a clean towel, draw up the sides, and squeeze tightly over a sink to remove the excess moisture. Return the cauliflower to the bowl and add the shredded Mozzarella along with the almond flour, Parmesan, egg, salt, garlic powder, and oregano. Stir until thoroughly combined.
3. Divide the dough into two equal portions. Place one piece of dough on the prepared parchment paper and pat gently into a thin, flat disk 7 to 8 inches in diameter. Air fry for 15 minutes until the crust begins to brown. Let cool for 5 minutes.
4. Transfer the parchment paper with the crust on top to a baking sheet. Place a second sheet of parchment paper over the crust. While holding the edges of both sheets together, carefully lift the crust off the baking sheet, flip it, and place it back in the air fryer basket. The new sheet of parchment paper is now on the bottom. Remove the top piece of paper and air fry the crust for another 15 minutes until the top begins to brown. Remove the basket from the air fryer.
5. Spread 2 tablespoons of the marinara sauce on top of the crust, followed by half the fresh Mozzarella, chicken, cherry tomatoes, and arugula. Air fry for 5 to 10 minutes longer, until the cheese is melted and beginning to brown. Remove the pizza from the oven and let it sit for 10 minutes before serving. Repeat with the remaining ingredients to make a second pizza.

Per Serving
calories: 550 | fat: 19g | protein: 53g
carbs: 20g | net carbs: 14g | fiber: 6g

Tex-Mex Chicken Roll-Ups

Prep time: 10 minutes | Cook time: 14 to 17 minutes | Serves 8

2 pounds (907 g) boneless, skinless chicken breasts or thighs
1 teaspoon chili powder
½ teaspoon smoked paprika
½ teaspoon ground cumin

Sea salt and freshly ground black pepper, to taste
6 ounces (170 g) Monterey Jack cheese, shredded
4 ounces (113 g) canned diced green chiles
Avocado oil spray

1. Place the chicken in a large zip-top bag or between two pieces of plastic wrap. Using a meat mallet or heavy skillet, pound the chicken until it is about ¼ inch thick.
2. In a small bowl, combine the chili powder, smoked paprika, cumin, and salt and pepper to taste. Sprinkle both sides of the chicken with the seasonings.
3. Sprinkle the chicken with the Monterey Jack cheese, then the diced green chiles.
4. Roll up each piece of chicken from the long side, tucking in the ends as you go. Secure the roll-up with a toothpick.
5. Set the air fryer to 350ºF (177ºC). Spray the outside of the chicken with avocado oil. Place the chicken in a single layer in the basket, working in batches if necessary, and roast for 7 minutes. Flip and cook for another 7 to 10 minutes, until an instant-read thermometer reads 160ºF (71ºC).
6. Remove the chicken from the air fryer and allow it to rest for about 5 minutes before serving.

Per Serving
calories: 192 | fat: 9g | protein: 28g
carbs: 1g | net carbs: 0g | fiber: 1g

Taco Chicken

Prep time: 10 minutes | Cook time: 23 minutes | Serves 4

2 large eggs
1 tablespoon water
Fine sea salt and ground black pepper, to taste
1 cup pork dust
1 teaspoon ground cumin
1 teaspoon smoked paprika
4 (5-ounce / 142-g) boneless, skinless

chicken breasts or thighs, pounded to ¼ inch thick
1 cup salsa
1 cup shredded Monterey Jack cheese (about 4 ounces / 113 g) (omit for dairy-free)
Sprig of fresh cilantro, for garnish (optional)

1. Spray the air fryer basket with avocado oil. Preheat the air fryer to 400ºF (204ºC).
2. Crack the eggs into a shallow baking dish, add the water and a pinch each of salt and pepper, and whisk to combine. In another shallow baking dish, stir together the pork dust, cumin, and paprika until well combined.
3. Season the chicken breasts well on both sides with salt and pepper. Dip 1 chicken breast in the eggs and let any excess drip off, then dredge both sides of the chicken breast in the pork dust mixture. Spray the breast with avocado oil and place it in the air fryer basket. Repeat with the remaining 3 chicken breasts.
4. Air fry the chicken in the air fryer for 20 minutes, or until the internal temperature reaches 165ºF (74ºC) and the breading is golden brown, flipping halfway through.
5. Dollop each chicken breast with ¼ cup of the salsa and top with ¼ cup of the cheese. Return the breasts to the air fryer and cook for 3 minutes, or until the cheese is melted. Garnish with cilantro before serving, if desired.
6. Store leftovers in an airtight container in the refrigerator for up to 4 days. Reheat in a preheated 400ºF (204ºC) air fryer for 5 minutes, or until warmed through.

Per Serving (with breasts)
calories: 486 | fat: 29g | protein: 54g
carbs: 3g | net carbs: 3g | fiber: 0g

Mediterranean Stuffed Chicken Breasts

Prep time: 5 minutes | Cook time: 20 to 25 minutes | Serves 4

4 small boneless, skinless chicken breast halves (about 1½ pounds / 680 g)
Salt and freshly ground black pepper, to taste
4 ounces (113 g) goat cheese
6 pitted Kalamata olives, coarsely

chopped
Zest of ½ lemon
1 teaspoon minced fresh rosemary or ½ teaspoon ground dried rosemary
½ cup almond meal
¼ cup balsamic vinegar
6 tablespoons unsalted butter

1. Preheat the air fryer to 360ºF (182ºC).
2. With a boning knife, cut a wide pocket into the thickest part of each chicken breast half, taking care not to cut all the way through. Season the chicken evenly on both sides with salt and freshly ground black pepper.
3. In a small bowl, mix the cheese, olives, lemon zest, and rosemary. Stuff the pockets with the cheese mixture and secure with toothpicks.
4. Place the almond meal in a shallow bowl and dredge the chicken, shaking off the excess. Coat lightly with olive oil spray.
5. Working in batches if necessary, arrange the chicken breasts in a single layer in the air fryer basket. Pausing halfway through the cooking time to flip the chicken, air fry for 20 to 25 minutes, until a thermometer inserted into the thickest part registers 165ºF (74ºC).
6. While the chicken is baking, prepare the sauce. In a small pan over medium heat, simmer the balsamic vinegar until thick and syrupy, about 5 minutes. Set aside until the chicken is done. When ready to serve, warm the sauce over medium heat and whisk in the butter, 1 tablespoon at a time, until melted and smooth. Season to taste with salt and pepper.
7. Serve the chicken breasts with the sauce drizzled on top.

Per Serving
calories: 510 | fat: 32g | protein: 50g
carbs: 7g | net carbs: 7g | fiber: g0

Nashville Hot Chicken

Prep time: 20 minutes | Cook time: 24 to 28 minutes | Serves 8

3 pounds (1.4 kg) bone-in, skin-on chicken pieces, breasts halved crosswise
1 tablespoon sea salt
1 tablespoon freshly ground black pepper
1½ cups finely ground blanched almond flour
1½ cups grated Parmesan cheese
1 tablespoon baking powder
2 teaspoons garlic powder, divided
½ cup heavy (whipping) cream
2 large eggs, beaten
1 tablespoon vinegar-based hot sauce
Avocado oil spray
½ cup (1 stick) unsalted butter
½ cup avocado oil
1 tablespoon cayenne pepper (more or less to taste)
2 tablespoons Swerve

1. Sprinkle the chicken with the salt and pepper.
2. In a large shallow bowl, whisk together the almond flour, Parmesan cheese, baking powder, and 1 teaspoon of the garlic powder.
3. In a separate bowl, whisk together the heavy cream, eggs, and hot sauce.
4. Dip the chicken pieces in the egg, then coat each with the almond flour mixture, pressing the mixture into the chicken to adhere. Allow to sit for 15 minutes to let the breading set.
5. Set the air fryer to 400ºF (204ºC). Place the chicken in a single layer in the air fryer basket, being careful not to overcrowd the pieces, working in batches if necessary. Spray the chicken with oil and roast for 13 minutes.
6. Carefully flip the chicken and spray it with more oil. Reduce the air fryer temperature to 350ºF (177ºC). Roast for another 11 to 15 minutes, until an instant-read thermometer reads 160ºF (71ºC).
7. While the chicken cooks, heat the butter, avocado oil, cayenne pepper, Swerve, and remaining 1 teaspoon of garlic powder in a saucepan over medium-low heat. Cook until the butter is melted and the sugar substitute has dissolved.
8. Remove the chicken from the air fryer. Use tongs to dip the chicken in the sauce. Place the coated chicken on a rack over a baking sheet, and allow it to rest for 5 minutes before serving.

Per Serving
calories: 677 | fat: 50g | protein: 52g
carbs: 10g | net carbs: 4g | fiber: 6g

Chicken Parmesan

Prep time: 25 minutes | Cook time: 18 to 20 minutes | Serves 8

2 pounds (907 g) boneless, skinless chicken breasts or thighs
1 cup finely ground blanched almond flour
1 cup grated Parmesan cheese
1 teaspoon Italian seasoning
Sea salt and freshly
ground black pepper, to taste
2 large eggs
Avocado oil spray
⅓ cup sugar-free marinara sauce
4 ounces (113 g) fresh Mozzarella cheese, sliced or shredded

1. Place the chicken in a zip-top bag or between two pieces of plastic wrap. Use a meat mallet or heavy skillet to pound the chicken to a uniform ½-inch thickness.
2. Place the almond flour, Parmesan cheese, Italian seasoning, and salt and pepper to taste in a large shallow bowl.
3. In a separate shallow bowl, beat the eggs.
4. Dip a chicken breast in the egg, then coat it in the almond flour mixture, making sure to press the coating onto the chicken gently. Repeat with the remaining chicken.
5. Set the air fryer to 400ºF (204ºC). Spray both sides of the chicken well with oil and place the pieces in a single layer in the air fryer basket, working in batches if necessary. Roast for 10 minutes.
6. Flip the chicken with a spatula. Spray each piece with more oil and continue cooking for 5 minutes more.
7. Top each chicken piece with the marinara sauce and Mozzarella. Return to the air fryer and cook for 3 to 5 minutes, until the cheese is melted and an instant-read thermometer reads 160ºF (71ºC).
8. Allow the chicken to rest for 5 minutes, then serve.

Per Serving
calories: 306 | fat: 17g | protein: 36g
carbs: 5g | net carbs: 3g | fiber: 2g

Chapter 8 Beef, Pork, and Lamb

Buttery Pork Chops

Prep time: 5 minutes | Cook time: 12 minutes | Serves 4

4 (4-ounce / 113-g) boneless pork chops
½ teaspoon salt
¼ teaspoon ground

black pepper
2 tablespoons salted butter, softened

1. Sprinkle pork chops on all sides with salt and pepper. Place chops into ungreased air fryer basket in a single layer. Adjust the temperature to 400ºF (204ºC) and air fry for 12 minutes. Pork chops will be golden and have an internal temperature of at least 145ºF (63ºC) when done.
2. Use tongs to remove cooked pork chops from air fryer and place onto a large plate. Top each chop with ½ tablespoon butter and let sit 2 minutes to melt. Serve warm.

Per Serving
calories: 78 | fat: 19g | protein: 24g
carbs: 0g | net carbs: 0g | fiber: 0g

Baby Back Ribs

Prep time: 5 minutes | Cook time: 25 minutes | Serves 4

2 pounds (907 g) baby back ribs
2 teaspoons chili powder
1 teaspoon paprika
½ teaspoon onion powder

½ teaspoon garlic powder
¼ teaspoon ground cayenne pepper
½ cup low-carb, sugar-free barbecue sauce

1. Rub ribs with all ingredients except barbecue sauce. Place into the air fryer basket.
2. Adjust the temperature to 400ºF (204ºC) and roast for 25 minutes.
3. When done, ribs will be dark and charred with an internal temperature of at least 185ºF (85ºC). Brush ribs with barbecue sauce and serve warm.

Per Serving
calories: 650 | fat: 51g | protein: 40g
carbs: 4g | net carbs: 3g | fiber: 1g

Bacon and Cheese Stuffed Pork Chops

Prep time: 10 minutes | Cook time: 12 minutes | Serves 4

½ ounce (14 g) plain pork rinds, finely crushed
½ cup shredded sharp Cheddar cheese
4 slices cooked sugar-

free bacon, crumbled
4 (4-ounce / 113-g) boneless pork chops
½ teaspoon salt
¼ teaspoon ground black pepper

1. In a small bowl, mix pork rinds, Cheddar, and bacon.
2. Make a 3-inch slit in the side of each pork chop and stuff with ¼ pork rind mixture. Sprinkle each side of pork chops with salt and pepper.
3. Place pork chops into ungreased air fryer basket, stuffed side up. Adjust the temperature to 400ºF (204ºC) and air fry for 12 minutes. Pork chops will be browned and have an internal temperature of at least 145ºF (63ºC) when done. Serve warm.

Per Serving
calories: 348 | fat: 22g | protein: 33g
carbs: 0g | net carbs: 0g | fiber: 0g

Chorizo and Beef Burger

Prep time: 10 minutes | Cook time: 15 minutes | Serves 4

¾ pound (340 g) 80/20 ground beef
¼ pound (113 g) Mexican-style ground chorizo
¼ cup chopped onion
5 slices pickled

jalapeños, chopped
2 teaspoons chili powder
1 teaspoon minced garlic
¼ teaspoon cumin

1. In a large bowl, mix all ingredients. Divide the mixture into four sections and form them into burger patties.
2. Place burger patties into the air fryer basket, working in batches if necessary.
3. Adjust the temperature to 375ºF (191ºC) and air fry for 15 minutes.
4. Flip the patties halfway through the cooking time. Serve warm.

Per Serving
calories: 291 | fat: 18g | protein: 21g
carbs: 5g | net carbs: 4g | fiber: 1g

Parmesan-Crusted Pork Chops

Prep time: 5 minutes | Cook time: 12 minutes | Serves 4

1 large egg
½ cup grated Parmesan cheese
4 (4-ounce / 113-g)
boneless pork chops
½ teaspoon salt
¼ teaspoon ground black pepper

1. Whisk egg in a medium bowl and place Parmesan in a separate medium bowl.
2. Sprinkle pork chops on both sides with salt and pepper. Dip each pork chop into egg, then press both sides into Parmesan.
3. Place pork chops into ungreased air fryer basket. Adjust the temperature to 400°F (204°C) and air fry for 12 minutes, turning chops halfway through cooking. Pork chops will be golden and have an internal temperature of at least 145°F (63°C) when done. Serve warm.

Per Serving
calories: 298 | fat: 17g | protein: 29g
carbs: 2g | net carbs: 2g | fiber: 0g

Peppercorn-Crusted Beef Tenderloin

Prep time: 10 minutes | Cook time: 25 minutes | Serves 6

2 tablespoons salted butter, melted
2 teaspoons minced roasted garlic
3 tablespoons ground
4-peppercorn blend
1 (2-pound / 907-g) beef tenderloin, trimmed of visible fat

1. In a small bowl, mix the butter and roasted garlic. Brush it over the beef tenderloin.
2. Place the ground peppercorns onto a plate and roll the tenderloin through them, creating a crust. Place tenderloin into the air fryer basket.
3. Adjust the temperature to 400°F (204°C) and roast for 25 minutes.
4. Turn the tenderloin halfway through the cooking time.
5. Allow meat to rest 10 minutes before slicing.

Per Serving
calories: 289 | fat: 14g | protein: 35g
carbs: 3g | net carbs: 2g | fiber: 1g

Mexican-Style Shredded Beef

Prep time: 5 minutes | Cook time: 35 minutes | Serves 6

1 (2-pound / 907-g) beef chuck roast, cut into 2-inch cubes
1 teaspoon salt
½ teaspoon ground black pepper
½ cup no-sugar-added chipotle sauce

1. In a large bowl, sprinkle beef cubes with salt and pepper and toss to coat. Place beef into ungreased air fryer basket. Adjust the temperature to 400°F (204°C) and air fry for 30 minutes, shaking the basket halfway through cooking. Beef will be done when internal temperature is at least 160°F (71°C).
2. Place cooked beef into a large bowl and shred with two forks. Pour in chipotle sauce and toss to coat.
3. Return beef to air fryer basket for an additional 5 minutes at 400°F (204°C) to crisp with sauce. Serve warm.

Per Serving
calories: 217 | fat: 6g | protein: 37g
carbs: 0g | net carbs: 0g | fiber: 0g

Pork Meatballs

Prep time: 10 minutes | Cook time: 12 minutes | Makes 18 meatballs

1 pound (454 g) ground pork
1 large egg, whisked
½ teaspoon garlic powder
½ teaspoon salt
½ teaspoon ground ginger
¼ teaspoon crushed red pepper flakes
1 medium scallion, trimmed and sliced

1. Combine all ingredients in a large bowl. Spoon out 2 tablespoons mixture and roll into a ball. Repeat to form eighteen meatballs total.
2. Place meatballs into ungreased air fryer basket. Adjust the temperature to 400°F (204°C) and air fry for 12 minutes, shaking the basket three times throughout cooking. Meatballs will be browned and have an internal temperature of at least 145°F (63°C) when done. Serve warm.

Per Serving (3 meatballs)
calories: 164 | fat: 10g | protein: 15g
carbs: 1g | net carbs: 1g | fiber: 0g

Sausage-Stuffed Peppers

Prep time: 15 minutes | Cook time: 28 to 30 minutes | Serves 6

Avocado oil spray
8 ounces (227 g) Italian sausage, casings removed
½ cup chopped mushrooms
¼ cup diced onion
1 teaspoon Italian seasoning
Sea salt and freshly

ground black pepper, to taste
1 cup keto-friendly marinara sauce
3 bell peppers, halved and seeded
3 ounces (85 g) provolone cheese, shredded

1. Spray a large skillet with oil and place it over medium-high heat. Add the sausage and cook for 5 minutes, breaking up the meat with a wooden spoon. Add the mushrooms, onion, and Italian seasoning, and season with salt and pepper. Cook for 5 minutes more. Stir in the marinara sauce and cook until heated through.
2. Scoop the sausage filling into the bell pepper halves.
3. Set the air fryer to 350ºF (177ºC). Arrange the peppers in a single layer in the air fryer basket, working in batches if necessary. Air fry for 15 minutes.
4. Top the stuffed peppers with the cheese and air fry for 3 to 5 minutes more, until the cheese is melted and the peppers are tender.

Per Serving
calories: 186 | fat: 12g | protein: 11g
carbs: 8g | net carbs: 6g | fiber: 2g

Greek Beef Kebabs with Tzatziki

Prep time: 15 minutes | Cook time: 8 to 10 minutes | Serves 6

1 pound (454 g) boneless sirloin steak, cut into 2-inch chunks
¼ cup avocado oil
2 teaspoons minced garlic
2 teaspoons dried oregano
Sea salt and freshly

ground black pepper, to taste
1 small red onion, cut into wedges
½ cup cherry tomatoes
Tzatziki Sauce
4 ounces (113 g) feta cheese, crumbled

1. Place the steak in a shallow dish.

2. In a blender, combine the avocado oil, garlic, oregano, and salt and pepper to taste. Blend until smooth, then pour over the steak. Cover the dish with plastic wrap and allow to marinate in the refrigerator for at least 4 hours or overnight.
3. Thread the steak, onion, and cherry tomatoes onto 6 skewers, alternating as you go. (If using wooden skewers, first soak them in water for 30 minutes.)
4. Set the air fryer to 400ºF (204ºC). Place the skewers in the basket and air fry for 5 minutes. Flip and cook for 3 to 5 minutes more.
5. Transfer the kebabs to serving plates. Drizzle with Tzatziki Sauce and sprinkle with the crumbled feta cheese.

Per Serving
calories: 307 | fat: 25g | protein: 18g
carbs: 3g | net carbs: 2g | fiber: 1g

Bacon Wedge Salad

Prep time: 10 minutes | Cook time: 10 to 13 minutes | Serves 4

8 ounces (227 g) bacon, sliced
1 head iceberg lettuce
6 ounces (170 g) blue cheese crumbles
½ cup pecans,

chopped
8 cherry tomatoes, halved
1 recipe Blue Cheese Dressing

1. Set the air fryer to 400ºF (204ºC). Arrange the bacon strips in a single layer in the air fryer basket (some overlapping is okay because the bacon will shrink as it cooks, but work in batches if necessary). Air fry for 8 minutes. Flip the bacon and cook for 2 to 5 minutes more, until the bacon is crisp. The total cooking time will depend on the thickness of your bacon.
2. Cut the iceberg lettuce into 8 wedges and place 2 wedges on each of 4 serving plates.
3. Crumble the bacon and scatter it and the blue cheese crumbles, chopped pecans, and cherry tomatoes over the lettuce.
4. Spoon the desired amount of dressing onto each wedge so it drips down the sides.

Per Serving
calories: 900 | fat: 85g | protein: 27g
carbs: 12g | net carbs: 8g | fiber: 3g

Mustard Herb Pork Tenderloin

Prep time: 5 minutes | Cook time: 20 minutes | Serves 6

¼ cup mayonnaise
2 tablespoons Dijon mustard
½ teaspoon dried thyme
¼ teaspoon dried

rosemary
1 (1-pound / 454-g) pork tenderloin
½ teaspoon salt
¼ teaspoon ground black pepper

1. In a small bowl, mix mayonnaise, mustard, thyme, and rosemary. Brush tenderloin with mixture on all sides, then sprinkle with salt and pepper on all sides.
2. Place tenderloin into ungreased air fryer basket. Adjust the temperature to 400ºF (204ºC) and air fry for 20 minutes, turning tenderloin halfway through cooking. Tenderloin will be golden and have an internal temperature of at least 145ºF (63ºC) when done. Serve warm.

Per Serving
calories: 158 | fat: 9g | protein: 16g
carbs: 1g | net carbs: 1g | fiber: 0g

Smoky Pork Tenderloin

Prep time: 5 minutes | Cook time: 19 to 22 minutes | Serves 6

1½ pounds (680 g) pork tenderloin
1 tablespoon avocado oil
1 teaspoon chili powder
1 teaspoon smoked

paprika
1 teaspoon garlic powder
1 teaspoon sea salt
1 teaspoon freshly ground black pepper

1. Pierce the tenderloin all over with a fork and rub the oil all over the meat.
2. In a small dish, stir together the chili powder, smoked paprika, garlic powder, salt, and pepper.
3. Rub the spice mixture all over the tenderloin.
4. Set the air fryer to 400ºF (204ºC). Place the pork in the air fryer basket and air fry for 10 minutes. Flip the tenderloin and cook for 9 to 12 minutes more, until an instant-read thermometer reads at least 145ºF (63ºC).

5. Allow the tenderloin to rest for 5 minutes, then slice and serve.

Per Serving
calories: 255 | fat: 12g | protein: 34g
carbs: 1g | net carbs: 1g | fiber: 0g

Sausage and Spinach Calzones

Prep time: 20 minutes | Cook time: 18 to 24 minutes | Serves 4

Avocado oil spray
5 ounces (142 g) Italian sausage, casings removed
1 teaspoon minced garlic
3 ounces (85 g) baby spinach, chopped
½ cup ricotta cheese
½ cup shredded Mozzarella cheese
¼ cup grated

Parmesan cheese
½ teaspoon red pepper flakes
Sea salt and freshly ground black pepper, to taste
1 recipe Fathead Pizza Dough
Keto-friendly marinara sauce, for serving

1. Spray a skillet with oil and heat it over medium-high heat. Put the sausage in the skillet and cook for 5 minutes, breaking up the meat with a spoon. Add the garlic and spinach and cook until the spinach wilts, 2 to 3 minutes. Remove the skillet from the heat.
2. Stir together the ricotta, Mozzarella, Parmesan, red pepper flakes, and the sausage-spinach mixture in a large bowl. Season with salt and pepper.
3. Divide the pizza dough into 4 equal pieces and roll each into a 6-inch round. Spoon one-fourth of the filling onto the center of each round. Fold the dough over the filling and use the back of a fork to seal the edges closed.
4. Set the air fryer to 325ºF (163ºC). Place the calzones in a single layer in the basket, working in batches if necessary. Air fry for 11 to 15 minutes, until golden brown. Serve warm with marinara sauce.

Per Serving
calories: 564 | fat: 46g | protein: 35g
carbs: 11g | net carbs: 6g | fiber: 5g

Marinated Steak Tips with Mushrooms

Prep time: 10 minutes | Cook time: 10 minutes | Serves 4

1½ pounds (680 g) sirloin, trimmed and cut into 1-inch pieces
8 ounces (227 g) brown mushrooms, halved
¼ cup Worcestershire sauce
1 tablespoon Dijon

mustard
1 tablespoon olive oil
1 teaspoon paprika
1 teaspoon crushed red pepper flakes
2 tablespoons chopped fresh parsley (optional)

1. Place the beef and mushrooms in a gallon-size resealable bag. In a small bowl, whisk together the Worcestershire, mustard, olive oil, paprika, and red pepper flakes. Pour the marinade into the bag and massage gently to ensure the beef and mushrooms are evenly coated. Seal the bag and refrigerate for at least 4 hours, preferably overnight. Remove from the refrigerator 30 minutes before cooking.
2. Preheat the air fryer to 400ºF (204ºC).
3. Drain and discard the marinade. Arrange the steak and mushrooms in the air fryer basket. Air fry for 10 minutes, pausing halfway through the baking time to shake the basket. Transfer to a serving plate and top with the parsley, if desired.

Per Serving
calories: 330 | fat: 17g | protein: 41g
carbs: 2g | net carbs: 2g | fiber: 0g

Beef and Broccoli Stir-Fry

Prep time: 10 minutes | Cook time: 20 minutes | Serves 2

½ pound (227 g) sirloin steak, thinly sliced
2 tablespoons coconut aminos
¼ teaspoon grated ginger
¼ teaspoon finely minced garlic

1 tablespoon coconut oil
2 cups broccoli florets
¼ teaspoon crushed red pepper
⅛ teaspoon xanthan gum
½ teaspoon sesame seeds

1. To marinate beef, place it into a large bowl or storage bag and add coconut aminos, ginger, garlic, and coconut oil. Allow to marinate for 1 hour in refrigerator.
2. Remove beef from marinade, reserving marinade, and place beef into the air fryer basket.
3. Adjust the temperature to 320ºF (160ºC) and air fry for 20 minutes.
4. After 10 minutes, add broccoli and sprinkle red pepper into the fryer basket and shake.
5. Pour the marinade into a skillet over medium heat and bring to a boil, then reduce to simmer. Stir in xanthan gum and allow to thicken.
6. When done, quickly empty fryer basket into skillet and toss. Sprinkle with sesame seeds. Serve immediately.

Per Serving
calories: 342 | fat: 19g | protein: 27g
carbs: 10g | net carbs: 7g | fiber: 3g

Bacon-Wrapped Vegetable Kebabs

Prep time: 10 minutes | Cook time: 10 to 12 minutes | Serves 4

4 ounces (113 g) mushrooms, sliced
1 small zucchini, sliced
12 grape tomatoes
4 ounces (113 g) sliced bacon, halved

Avocado oil spray
Sea salt and freshly ground black pepper, to taste
Garlic Ranch Dressing, for serving

1. Stack 3 mushroom slices, 1 zucchini slice, and 1 grape tomato. Wrap a bacon strip around the vegetables and thread them onto a skewer. Repeat with the remaining vegetables and bacon. Spray with oil and sprinkle with salt and pepper.
2. Set the air fryer to 400ºF (204ºC). Place the skewers in the air fryer basket in a single layer, working in batches if necessary, and air fry for 5 minutes. Flip the skewers and cook for 5 to 7 minutes more, until the bacon is crispy and the vegetables are tender.
3. Serve with Garlic Ranch Dressing.

Per Serving
calories: 73 | fat: 4g | protein: 6g
carbs: 4g | net carbs: 3g | fiber: 1g

Spinach and Provolone Steak Rolls

Prep time: 10 minutes | Cook time: 12 minutes | Makes 8 rolls

1 (1-pound / 454-g) flank steak, butterflied
8 (1-ounce / 28-g, ¼-inch-thick) deli slices provolone cheese
1 cup fresh spinach leaves
½ teaspoon salt
¼ teaspoon ground black pepper

1. Place steak on a large plate. Place provolone slices to cover steak, leaving 1-inch at the edges. Lay spinach leaves over cheese. Gently roll steak and tie with kitchen twine or secure with toothpicks. Carefully slice into eight pieces. Sprinkle each with salt and pepper.
2. Place rolls into ungreased air fryer basket, cut side up. Adjust the temperature to 400ºF (204ºC) and air fry for 12 minutes. Steak rolls will be browned and cheese will be melted when done and have an internal temperature of at least 150ºF (66ºC) for medium steak and 180ºF (82ºC) for well-done steak. Serve warm.

Per Serving (2 rolls)
calories: 376 | fat: 21g | protein: 40g
carbs: 2g | net carbs: 2g | fiber: 0g

Pigs in a Blanket

Prep time: 10 minutes | Cook time: 7 minutes | Serves 2

½ cup shredded Mozzarella cheese
2 tablespoons blanched finely ground almond flour
1 ounce (28 g) full-fat cream cheese
2 (2-ounce / 57-g) beef smoked sausages
½ teaspoon sesame seeds

1. Place Mozzarella, almond flour, and cream cheese in a large microwave-safe bowl. Microwave for 45 seconds and stir until smooth. Roll dough into a ball and cut in half.
2. Press each half out into a 4 × 5-inch rectangle. Roll one sausage up in each dough half and press seams closed. Sprinkle the top with sesame seeds.
3. Place each wrapped sausage into the air fryer basket.

4. Adjust the temperature to 400ºF (204ºC) and air fry for 7 minutes.
5. The outside will be golden when completely cooked. Serve immediately.

Per Serving
calories: 405 | fat: 32g | protein: 17g
carbs: 3g | net carbs: 2g | fiber: 1g

Scotch Eggs

Prep time: 10 minutes | Cook time: 15 minutes | Makes 8 eggs

2 pounds (907 g) ground pork or ground beef
2 teaspoons fine sea salt
½ teaspoon ground black pepper, plus
more for garnish
8 large hard-boiled eggs, peeled
2 cups pork dust
Dijon mustard, for serving (optional)

1. Spray the air fryer basket with avocado oil. Preheat the air fryer to 400ºF (204ºC).
2. Place the ground pork in a large bowl, add the salt and pepper, and use your hands to mix until seasoned throughout. Flatten about ¼ pound (113 g) of ground pork in the palm of your hand and place a peeled egg in the center. Fold the pork completely around the egg. Repeat with the remaining eggs.
3. Place the pork dust in a medium-sized bowl. One at a time, roll the ground pork-covered eggs in the pork dust and use your hands to press it into the eggs to form a nice crust. Place the eggs in the air fryer basket and spray them with avocado oil.
4. Air fry the eggs for 15 minutes, or until the internal temperature of the pork reaches 145ºF (63ºC) and the outside is golden brown. Garnish with ground black pepper and serve with Dijon mustard, if desired.
5. Store leftovers in an airtight container in the fridge for up to 7 days or in the freezer for up to a month. Reheat in a preheated 400ºF (204ºC) air fryer for 3 minutes, or until heated through.

Per Serving
calories: 447 | fat: 34g | protein: 43g
carbs: 1g | net carbs: 0g | fiber: 1g

Pork Spare Ribs

Prep time: 10 minutes | Cook time: 30 minutes | Serves 4

1 (4-pound / 1.8-kg) rack pork spare ribs
1 teaspoon ground cumin
2 teaspoons salt
1 teaspoon ground black pepper
1 teaspoon garlic powder
½ teaspoon dry ground mustard
½ cup low-carb barbecue sauce

1. Place ribs on ungreased aluminum foil sheet. Carefully use a knife to remove membrane and sprinkle meat evenly on both sides with cumin, salt, pepper, garlic powder, and ground mustard.
2. Cut rack into portions that will fit in your air fryer, and wrap each portion in one layer of aluminum foil, working in batches if needed.
3. Place ribs into ungreased air fryer basket. Adjust the temperature to 400ºF (204ºC) and air fry for 25 minutes.
4. Carefully remove ribs from foil and brush with barbecue sauce. Return to air fryer and cook at 400ºF (204ºC) for an additional 5 minutes to brown. Ribs will be done when no pink remains and internal temperature is at least 180ºF (82ºC). Serve warm.

Per Serving
calories: 192 | fat: 12g | protein: 13g
carbs: 3g | net carbs: 3g | fiber: 0g

Bone-in Pork Chops

Prep time: 5 minutes | Cook time: 10 to 12 minutes | Serves 2

1 pound (454 g) bone-in pork chops
1 tablespoon avocado oil
1 teaspoon smoked paprika
½ teaspoon onion powder
¼ teaspoon cayenne pepper
Sea salt and freshly ground black pepper, to taste

1. Brush the pork chops with the avocado oil. In a small dish, mix together the smoked paprika, onion powder, cayenne pepper, and salt and black pepper to taste. Sprinkle the seasonings over both sides of the pork chops.
2. Set the air fryer to 400ºF (204ºC). Place the chops in the air fryer basket in a single layer, working in batches if necessary. Air fry for 10 to 12 minutes, until an instant-read thermometer reads 145ºF (63ºC) at the chops' thickest point.
3. Remove the chops from the air fryer and allow them to rest for 5 minutes before serving.

Per Serving
calories: 344 | fat: 21g | protein: 33g
carbs: 2g | net carbs: 2g | fiber: 0g

Jalapeño Popper Pork Chops

Prep time: 15 minutes | Cook time: 6 to 8 minutes | Serves 4

1¾ pounds (794 g) bone-in, center-cut loin pork chops
Sea salt and freshly ground black pepper, to taste
6 ounces (170 g) cream cheese, at room temperature
4 ounces (113 g)
sliced bacon, cooked and crumbled
4 ounces (113 g) Cheddar cheese, shredded
1 jalapeño, seeded and diced
1 teaspoon garlic powder

1. Cut a pocket into each pork chop, lengthwise along the side, making sure not to cut it all the way through. Season the outside of the chops with salt and pepper.
2. In a small bowl, combine the cream cheese, bacon, Cheddar cheese, jalapeño, and garlic powder. Divide this mixture among the pork chops, stuffing it into the pocket of each chop.
3. Set the air fryer to 400ºF (204ºC). Place the pork chops in the air fryer basket in a single layer, working in batches if necessary. Air fry for 3 minutes. Flip the chops and cook for 3 to 5 minutes more, until an instant-read thermometer reads 145ºF (63ºC).
4. Allow the chops to rest for 5 minutes, then serve warm.

Per Serving
calories: 656 | fat: 40g | protein: 14g
carbs: 4g | net carbs: 3g | fiber: 1g

Pork Taco Bowls

Prep time: 15 minutes | Cook time: 13 to 16 minutes | Serves 4

2 tablespoons avocado oil
2 tablespoons freshly squeezed lime juice
1 pound (454 g) boneless pork shoulder
2 tablespoons Taco Seasoning
½ small head cabbage, cored and

thinly sliced
Sea salt and freshly ground black pepper, to taste
1 cup shredded Cheddar cheese
¼ cup diced red onion
¼ cup diced tomatoes
1 avocado, sliced
1 lime, cut into wedges

1. In a small dish, whisk together the avocado oil and lime juice.
2. Pierce the pork all over with a fork and spread half of the oil mixture over it. Sprinkle with the taco seasoning and allow to sit at room temperature for 30 minutes.
3. Place the cabbage in a large bowl and toss with the remaining oil mixture. Season with salt and pepper.
4. Set the air fryer to 400°F (204°C). Place the pork in the air fryer basket and air fry for 13 to 16 minutes, until an instant-read thermometer reads 145°F (63°C).
5. Allow the pork to rest for 10 minutes, then chop or shred the meat.
6. Place the cabbage in serving bowls. Top each serving with some pork, Cheddar cheese, red onion, tomatoes, and avocado. Serve with lime wedges.

Per Serving
calories: 521 | fat: 41g | protein: 25g
carbs: 17g | net carbs: 10g | fiber: 7g

Blackened Steak Nuggets

Prep time: 10 minutes | Cook time: 7 minutes | Serves 2

1 pound (454 g) rib eye steak, cut into 1-inch cubes
2 tablespoons salted butter, melted
½ teaspoon paprika
½ teaspoon salt
¼ teaspoon garlic

powder
¼ teaspoon onion powder
¼ teaspoon ground black pepper
⅛ teaspoon cayenne pepper

1. Place steak into a large bowl and pour in butter. Toss to coat. Sprinkle with remaining ingredients.
2. Place bites into ungreased air fryer basket. Adjust the temperature to 400°F (204°C) and air fry for 7 minutes, shaking the basket three times during cooking. Steak will be crispy on the outside and browned when done and internal temperature is at least 150°F (66°C) for medium and 180°F (82°C) for well-done. Serve warm.

Per Serving
calories: 466 | fat: 28g | protein: 49g
carbs: 1g | net carbs: 1g | fiber: 0g

Deconstructed Chicago Dogs

Prep time: 10 minutes | Cook time: 7 minutes | Serves 4

4 hot dogs
2 large dill pickles
¼ cup diced onions
1 tomato, cut into
For Garnish (Optional):
Brown mustard
Celery salt

½-inch dice
4 pickled sport peppers, diced

Poppy seeds

1. Spray the air fryer basket with avocado oil. Preheat the air fryer to 400°F (204°C).
2. Place the hot dogs in the air fryer basket and air fry for 5 to 7 minutes, until hot and slightly crispy.
3. While the hot dogs cook, quarter one of the dill pickles lengthwise, so that you have 4 pickle spears. Finely dice the other pickle.
4. When the hot dogs are done, transfer them to a serving platter and arrange them in a row, alternating with the pickle spears. Top with the diced pickles, onions, tomato, and sport peppers. Drizzle brown mustard on top and garnish with celery salt and poppy seeds, if desired.
5. Best served fresh. Store leftover hot dogs in an airtight container in the refrigerator for up to 3 days. Reheat in a preheated 390°F (199°C) air fryer for 2 minutes, or until warmed through.

Per Serving
calories: 123 | fat: 8g | protein: 8g
carbs: 3g | net carbs: 2g | fiber: 1g

Spice-Rubbed Pork Loin

Prep time: 5 minutes | Cook time: 20 minutes | Serves 6

1 teaspoon paprika
½ teaspoon ground cumin
½ teaspoon chili powder
½ teaspoon garlic powder

2 tablespoons coconut oil
1 (1½-pound / 680-g) boneless pork loin
½ teaspoon salt
¼ teaspoon ground black pepper

1. In a small bowl, mix paprika, cumin, chili powder, and garlic powder.
2. Drizzle coconut oil over pork. Sprinkle pork loin with salt and pepper, then rub spice mixture evenly on all sides.
3. Place pork loin into ungreased air fryer basket. Adjust the temperature to 400°F (204°C) and air fry for 20 minutes, turning pork halfway through cooking. Pork loin will be browned and have an internal temperature of at least 145°F (63°C) when done. Serve warm.

Per Serving
calories: 249 | fat: 16g | protein: 24g
carbs: 1g | net carbs: 1g | fiber: 0g

Rosemary Roast Beef

Prep time: 5 minutes | Cook time: 30 to 35 minutes | Serves 8

1 (2-pound / 907-g) top round beef roast, tied with kitchen string
Sea salt and freshly ground black pepper, to taste

2 teaspoons minced garlic
2 tablespoons finely chopped fresh rosemary
¼ cup avocado oil

1. Season the roast generously with salt and pepper.
2. In a small bowl, whisk together the garlic, rosemary, and avocado oil. Rub this all over the roast. Cover loosely with aluminum foil or plastic wrap and refrigerate for at least 12 hours or up to 2 days.
3. Remove the roast from the refrigerator and allow to sit at room temperature for about 1 hour.

4. Set the air fryer to 325°F (163°C). Place the roast in the air fryer basket and roast for 15 minutes. Flip the roast and cook for 15 to 20 minutes more, until the meat is browned and an instant-read thermometer reads 120°F (49°C) at the thickest part (for medium-rare).
5. Transfer the meat to a cutting board, and let it rest for 15 minutes before thinly slicing and serving.

Per Serving
calories: 213 | fat: 10g | protein: 25g
carbs: 2g | net carbs: 1g | fiber: 1g

Sausage and Pork Meatballs

Prep time: 15 minutes | Cook time: 8 to 12 minutes | Serves 8

1 large egg
1 teaspoon gelatin
1 pound (454 g) ground pork
½ pound (227 g) Italian sausage, casings removed, crumbled
⅓ cup Parmesan cheese
¼ cup finely diced onion
1 tablespoon tomato

paste
1 teaspoon minced garlic
1 teaspoon dried oregano
¼ teaspoon red pepper flakes
Sea salt and freshly ground black pepper, to taste
Keto-friendly marinara sauce, for serving

1. Beat the egg in a small bowl and sprinkle with the gelatin. Allow to sit for 5 minutes.
2. In a large bowl, combine the ground pork, sausage, Parmesan, onion, tomato paste, garlic, oregano, and red pepper flakes. Season with salt and black pepper.
3. Stir the gelatin mixture, then add it to the other ingredients and, using clean hands, mix to ensure that everything is well combined. Form into 1½-inch round meatballs.
4. Set the air fryer to 400°F (204°C). Place the meatballs in the air fryer basket in a single layer, cooking in batches as needed. Air fry for 5 minutes. Flip and cook for 3 to 7 minutes more, or until an instant-read thermometer reads 160°F (71°C).

Per Serving
calories: 254 | fat: 20g | protein: 17g
carbs: 1g | net carbs: 1g | fiber: 0g

Tenderloin with Crispy Shallots

Prep time: 5 minutes | Cook time: 18 to 20 minutes | Serves 6

1½ pounds (680 g) beef tenderloin steaks	to taste
Sea salt and freshly ground black pepper,	4 medium shallots
	1 teaspoon olive oil or avocado oil

1. Season both sides of the steaks with salt and pepper, and let them sit at room temperature for 45 minutes.
2. Set the air fryer to 400°F (204°C) and let it preheat for 5 minutes.
3. Working in batches if necessary, place the steaks in the air fryer basket in a single layer and air fry for 5 minutes. Flip and cook for 5 minutes longer, until an instant-read thermometer inserted in the center of the steaks registers 120°F (49°C) for medium-rare (or as desired). Remove the steaks and tent with aluminum foil to rest.
4. Set the air fryer to 300°F (149°C). In a medium bowl, toss the shallots with the oil. Place the shallots in the basket and air fry for 5 minutes, then give them a toss and cook for 3 to 5 minutes more, until crispy and golden brown.
5. Place the steaks on serving plates and arrange the shallots on top.

Per Serving
calories: 186 | fat: 5g | protein: 30g
carbs: 5g | net carbs: 5g | fiber: 0g

Italian-Style Pork Chops

Prep time: 5 minutes | Cook time: 20 to 25 minutes | Serves 4

4 thick center-cut boneless pork chops (about 1½ pounds / 680 g)	1 tablespoon Italian seasoning
1 tablespoon olive oil	2 cloves garlic, minced
1 teaspoon salt	¼ cup chopped kalamata olives
1 (15-ounce / 425-g) can crushed tomatoes	2 tablespoons chopped fresh parsley

1. Preheat the air fryer to 400°F (204°C).
2. Arrange the pork chops in a round baking dish. Drizzle with the olive oil and season both sides with the salt.
3. In a bowl, combine the tomatoes, Italian seasoning, and garlic. Pour the tomato mixture over the pork chops.
4. Pausing halfway through the cooking time to turn the chops, air fry for 20 to 25 minutes, until a thermometer inserted into the thickest piece registers 145°F (63°C). Remove the chops from the sauce and let rest for 5 minutes. Stir the olives and parsley into the sauce before serving with the pork chops.

Per Serving
calories: 350 | fat: 17g | protein: 40g
carbs: 9g | net carbs: 7g | fiber: 2g

Ricotta and Sausage Pizzas

Prep time: 15 minutes | Cook time: 30 to 42 minutes | Serves 6

1 recipe Fathead Pizza Dough	3 ounces (85 g) low-moisture Mozzarella cheese, shredded
6 ounces (170 g) Italian sausage, casings removed	½ small red onion, thinly sliced
1/3 cup sugar-free marinara sauce	3 tablespoons ricotta cheese

1. Divide the dough into 3 equal pieces. Working with one at a time, place a dough piece between 2 sheets of parchment paper and roll it into a 7-inch round. Place the dough in a cake pan or pizza pan.
2. Set the air fryer to 375°F (191°C). Place the pan in the air fryer basket and air fry for 6 minutes. Repeat with the remaining dough rounds.
3. While the crusts cook, place a medium skillet over medium-high heat. Once the skillet is hot, put the sausage in the skillet and cook, breaking it up with the back of a spoon, for 8 to 10 minutes, until the meat is browned and cooked through.
4. Spread the marinara sauce on the pizza crusts. Top with the Mozzarella, cooked sausage, and onion slices. Dollop with the ricotta cheese.
5. Set the air fryer to 375°F (191°C). Cooking one at a time, place the pizzas in the air fryer basket and air fry for 4 to 8 more minutes, until the cheese melts.

Per Serving
calories: 365 | fat: 29g | protein: 22g
carbs: 8g | net carbs: 5g | fiber: 3g

Kielbasa and Cabbage

Prep time: 10 minutes | Cook time: 20 to 25 minutes | Serves 4

1 pound (454 g) smoked kielbasa sausage, sliced into ½-inch pieces
1 head cabbage, very coarsely chopped
½ yellow onion, chopped
2 cloves garlic, chopped
2 tablespoons olive oil
½ teaspoon salt
½ teaspoon freshly ground black pepper
¼ cup water

1. Preheat the air fryer to 400ºF (204ºC).
2. In a large bowl, combine the sausage, cabbage, onion, garlic, olive oil, salt, and black pepper. Toss until thoroughly combined.
3. Transfer the mixture to the basket of the air fryer and pour the water over the top. Pausing two or three times during the cooking time to shake the basket, air fry for 20 to 25 minutes, until the sausage is browned and the vegetables are tender.

Per Serving
calories: 410 | fat: 32g | protein: 14g
carbs: 19g | net carbs: 13g | fiber: 6g

Garlic-Marinated Flank Steak

Prep time: 5 minutes | Cook time: 8 to 10 minutes | Serves 6

½ cup avocado oil
¼ cup coconut aminos
1 shallot, minced
1 tablespoon minced garlic
2 tablespoons chopped fresh oregano, or 2
teaspoons dried
1½ teaspoons sea salt
1 teaspoon freshly ground black pepper
¼ teaspoon red pepper flakes
2 pounds (907 g) flank steak

1. In a blender, combine the avocado oil, coconut aminos, shallot, garlic, oregano, salt, black pepper, and red pepper flakes. Process until smooth.
2. Place the steak in a zip-top plastic bag or shallow dish with the marinade. Seal the bag or cover the dish and marinate in the refrigerator for at least 2 hours or overnight.
3. Remove the steak from the bag and discard the marinade.
4. Set the air fryer to 400ºF (204ºC). Place the steak in the air fryer basket (if needed, cut into sections and work in batches). Air fry for 4 to 6 minutes, flip the steak, and cook for another 4 minutes or until the internal temperature reaches 120ºF (49ºC) in the thickest part for medium-rare (or as desired).

Per Serving
calories: 304 | fat: 23g | protein: 16g
carbs: 4g | net carbs: 4g | fiber: 0g

Goat Cheese-Stuffed Flank Steak

Prep time: 10 minutes | Cook time: 14 minutes | Serves 6

1 pound (454 g) flank steak
1 tablespoon avocado oil
½ teaspoon sea salt
½ teaspoon garlic powder
¼ teaspoon freshly ground black pepper
2 ounces goat cheese, crumbled
1 cup baby spinach, chopped

1. Place the steak in a large zip-top bag or between two pieces of plastic wrap. Using a meat mallet or heavy-bottomed skillet, pound the steak to an even ¼-inch thickness.
2. Brush both sides of the steak with the avocado oil.
3. Mix the salt, garlic powder, and pepper in a small dish. Sprinkle this mixture over both sides of the steak.
4. Sprinkle the goat cheese over top, and top that with the spinach.
5. Starting at one of the long sides, roll the steak up tightly. Tie the rolled steak with kitchen string at 3-inch intervals.
6. Set the air fryer to 400ºF (204ºC). Place the steak roll-up in the air fryer basket. Air fry for 7 minutes. Flip the steak and cook for an additional 7 minutes, until an instant-read thermometer reads 120ºF (49ºC) for medium-rare (adjust the cooking time for your desired doneness).

Per Serving
calories: 165 | fat: 9g | protein: 18g
carbs: 1g | net carbs: 0g | fiber: 1g

Sausage and Zucchini Lasagna

Prep time: 25 minutes | Cook time: 56 minutes | Serves 4

1 zucchini
Avocado oil spray
6 ounces (170 g) hot Italian sausage, casings removed
2 ounces (57 g) mushrooms, stemmed and sliced
1 teaspoon minced garlic
1 cup keto-friendly marinara sauce
¾ cup ricotta cheese
1 cup shredded fontina cheese, divided
½ cup finely grated Parmesan cheese
Sea salt and freshly ground black pepper, to taste
Fresh basil, for garnish

1. Cut the zucchini into long thin slices using a mandoline slicer or sharp knife. Spray both sides of the slices with oil.
2. Place the slices in a single layer in the air fryer basket, working in batches if necessary. Set the air fryer to 325ºF (163ºC) and air fry for 4 to 6 minutes, until most of the moisture has been released from the zucchini.
3. Place a large skillet over medium-high heat. Crumble the sausage into the hot skillet and cook for 6 minutes, breaking apart the meat with the back of a spoon. Remove the sausage from the skillet, leaving any fats that remain. Add the mushrooms to the skillet and cook for 10 minutes, until the liquid nearly evaporates. Add the garlic and cook for 1 minute more. Stir in the marinara and cook for 2 more minutes.
4. In a medium bowl, combine the ricotta cheese, ½ cup of fontina cheese, Parmesan cheese, and salt and pepper to taste.
5. Spread ¼ cup of the meat sauce in the bottom of a deep pan (or other pan that fits inside your air fryer). Top with half of the zucchini slices. Add half of the cheese mixture. Top the cheese with half of the remaining meat sauce. Layer the remaining zucchini over the meat sauce and top with the remaining cheese mixture. Top the lasagna with the remaining ½ cup of fontina cheese.
6. Cover the lasagna with aluminum foil or parchment paper and place it in the air fryer. Bake for 25 minutes. Remove the foil and cook for 8 to 10 minutes more.
7. Allow the lasagna to rest for 15 minutes before cutting and serving. Garnish with basil.

Per Serving
calories: 454 | fat: 31g | protein: 33g
carbs: 11g | net carbs: 9g | fiber: 2g

Fajita Meatball Lettuce Wraps

Prep time: 10 minutes | Cook time: 10 minutes | Serves 4

1 pound (454 g) ground beef (85% lean)
½ cup salsa, plus more for serving if desired
¼ cup chopped onions
¼ cup diced green or red bell peppers
1 large egg, beaten
1 teaspoon fine sea salt
½ teaspoon chili powder
½ teaspoon ground cumin
1 clove garlic, minced

For Serving (Optional):
8 leaves Boston lettuce
Pico de gallo or salsa
Lime slices

1. Spray the air fryer basket with avocado oil. Preheat the air fryer to 350ºF (177ºC).
2. In a large bowl, mix together all the ingredients until well combined.
3. Shape the meat mixture into eight 1-inch balls. Place the meatballs in the air fryer basket, leaving a little space between them. Air fry for 10 minutes, or until cooked through and no longer pink inside and the internal temperature reaches 145ºF (63ºC).
4. Serve each meatball on a lettuce leaf, topped with pico de gallo or salsa, if desired. Serve with lime slices if desired.
5. Store leftovers in an airtight container in the fridge for 3 days or in the freezer for up to a month. Reheat in a preheated 350ºF (177ºC) air fryer for 4 minutes, or until heated through.

Per Serving
calories: 272 | fat: 18g | protein: 23g
carbs: 3g | net carbs: 2g | fiber: 1g

Savory Sausage Cobbler

Prep time: 15 minutes | Cook time: 34 minutes | Serves 4

Filling:

1 pound (454 g) ground Italian sausage	1 teaspoon fine sea salt
1 cup sliced mushrooms	2 cups marinara sauce

Biscuits:

3 large egg whites	salt
¾ cup blanched almond flour	2½ tablespoons very cold unsalted butter, cut into ¼-inch pieces
1 teaspoon baking powder	Fresh basil leaves, for garnish
¼ teaspoon fine sea	

1. Preheat the air fryer to 400°F (204°C).
2. Place the sausage in a pie pan (or a pan that fits into your air fryer). Use your hands to break up the sausage and spread it evenly on the bottom of the pan. Place the pan in the air fryer and air fry for 5 minutes.
3. Remove the pan from the air fryer and use a fork or metal spatula to crumble the sausage more. Season the mushrooms with the salt and add them to the pie pan. Stir to combine the mushrooms and sausage, then return the pan to the air fryer and air fry for 4 minutes, or until the mushrooms are soft and the sausage is cooked through.
4. Remove the pan from the air fryer. Add the marinara sauce and stir well. Set aside.
5. Make the biscuits: Place the egg whites in a large mixing bowl or the bowl of a stand mixer. Using a hand mixer or stand mixer, whip the egg whites until stiff peaks form.
6. In a medium-sized bowl, whisk together the almond flour, baking powder, and salt, then cut in the butter. Gently fold the flour mixture into the egg whites with a rubber spatula.
7. Using a large spoon or ice cream scoop, spoon one-quarter of the dough on top of the sausage mixture, making sure the butter stays in separate clumps. Repeat with the remaining dough, spacing the biscuits about 1 inch apart.
8. Place the pan in the air fryer and cook for 5 minutes, then lower the heat to 325°F (163°C) and bake for another 15 to 20 minutes, until the biscuits are golden brown. Serve garnished with fresh basil leaves.
9. Store leftovers in an airtight container in the refrigerator for up to 3 days. Reheat in a preheated 350°F (177°C) air fryer for 5 minutes, or until warmed through.

Per Serving
calories: 588 | fat: 48g | protein: 28g
carbs: 9g | net carbs: 6g | fiber: 3g

Roast Beef with Horseradish Cream

Prep time: 5 minutes | Cook time: 35 to 45 minutes | Serves 6

2 pounds (907 g) beef roast top round or eye of round	powder
	1 teaspoon freshly ground black pepper
1 tablespoon salt	1 teaspoon dried thyme
2 teaspoons garlic	

Horseradish Cream:

⅓ cup heavy cream	lemon juice
⅓ cup sour cream	Salt and freshly ground black pepper, to taste
⅓ cup prepared horseradish	
2 teaspoons fresh	

1. Preheat the air fryer to 400°F (204°C).
2. Season the beef with the salt, garlic powder, black pepper, and thyme. Place the beef fat-side down in the basket of the air fryer and lightly coat with olive oil. Pausing halfway through the cooking time to turn the meat, air fry for 35 to 45 minutes, until a thermometer inserted into the thickest part indicates the desired doneness, 125°F (52°C) (rare) to 150°F (66°C) (medium). Let the beef rest for 10 minutes before slicing.
3. To make the horseradish cream: In a small bowl, combine the heavy cream, sour cream, horseradish, and lemon juice. Whisk until thoroughly combined. Season to taste with salt and freshly ground black pepper. Serve alongside the beef.

Per Serving
calories: 280 | fat: 13g | protein: 34g
carbs: 3g | net carbs: 2g | fiber: 1g

Pork Tenderloin with Avocado Lime Sauce

Prep time: 10 minutes | Cook time: 15 minutes | Serves 4

Marinade:

½ cup lime juice
Grated zest of 1 lime
2 teaspoons stevia glycerite, or ¼ teaspoon liquid stevia
3 cloves garlic, minced
1½ teaspoons fine

sea salt
1 teaspoon chili powder, or more for more heat
1 teaspoon smoked paprika
1 pound (454 g) pork tenderloin

Avocado Lime Sauce:

1 medium-sized ripe avocado, roughly chopped
½ cup full-fat sour cream (or coconut cream for dairy-free)
Grated zest of 1 lime
Juice of 1 lime
2 cloves garlic, roughly chopped
½ teaspoon fine sea

salt
¼ teaspoon ground black pepper
Chopped fresh cilantro leaves, for garnish
Lime slices, for serving
Pico de gallo, for serving

1. In a medium-sized casserole dish, stir together all the marinade ingredients until well combined. Add the tenderloin and coat it well in the marinade. Cover and place in the fridge to marinate for 2 hours or overnight.
2. Spray the air fryer basket with avocado oil. Preheat the air fryer to 400ºF (204ºC).
3. Remove the pork from the marinade and place it in the air fryer basket. Air fry for 13 to 15 minutes, until the internal temperature of the pork is 145ºF (63ºC), flipping after 7 minutes. Remove the pork from the air fryer and place it on a cutting board. Allow it to rest for 8 to 10 minutes, then cut it into ½-inch-thick slices.
4. While the pork cooks, make the avocado lime sauce: Place all the sauce ingredients in a food processor and purée until smooth. Taste and adjust the seasoning to your liking.
5. Place the pork slices on a serving platter and spoon the avocado lime sauce on top. Garnish with cilantro leaves and serve with lime slices and pico de gallo.

6. Store leftovers in an airtight container in the fridge for up to 4 days. Reheat in a preheated 400ºF (204ºC) air fryer for 5 minutes, or until heated through.

Per Serving
calories: 326 | fat: 19g | protein: 26g
carbs: 15g | net carbs: 9g | fiber: 6g

Pork Milanese

Prep time: 10 minutes | Cook time: 12 minutes | Serves 4

4 (1-inch) boneless pork chops
Fine sea salt and ground black pepper, to taste
2 large eggs

¾ cup powdered Parmesan cheese
Chopped fresh parsley, for garnish
Lemon slices, for serving

1. Spray the air fryer basket with avocado oil. Preheat the air fryer to 400ºF (204ºC).
2. Place the pork chops between 2 sheets of plastic wrap and pound them with the flat side of a meat tenderizer until they're ¼ inch thick. Lightly season both sides of the chops with salt and pepper.
3. Lightly beat the eggs in a shallow bowl. Divide the Parmesan cheese evenly between 2 bowls and set the bowls in this order: Parmesan, eggs, Parmesan. Dredge a chop in the first bowl of Parmesan, then dip it in the eggs, and then dredge it again in the second bowl of Parmesan, making sure both sides and all edges are well coated. Repeat with the remaining chops.
4. Place the chops in the air fryer basket and air fry for 12 minutes, or until the internal temperature reaches 145ºF (63ºC), flipping halfway through.
5. Garnish with fresh parsley and serve immediately with lemon slices. Store leftovers in an airtight container in the refrigerator for up to 3 days. Reheat in a preheated 390ºF (199ºC) air fryer for 5 minutes, or until warmed through.

Per Serving
calories: 351 | fat: 18g | protein: 42g
carbs: 3g | net carbs: 2g | fiber: 1g

Sausage and Cauliflower Arancini

Prep time: 20 minutes | Cook time: 28 to 32 minutes | Serves 6

Avocado oil spray
6 ounces (170 g) Italian sausage, casings removed
¼ cup diced onion
1 teaspoon minced garlic
1 teaspoon dried thyme
Sea salt and freshly ground black pepper, to taste
2½ cups cauliflower rice
3 ounces (85 g) cream cheese
4 ounces (113 g) Cheddar cheese, shredded
1 large egg
½ cup finely ground blanched almond flour
¼ cup finely grated Parmesan cheese
Keto-friendly marinara sauce, for serving

1. Spray a large skillet with oil and place it over medium-high heat. Once the skillet is hot, put the sausage in the skillet and cook for 7 minutes, breaking up the meat with the back of a spoon.
2. Reduce the heat to medium and add the onion. Cook for 5 minutes, then add the garlic, thyme, and salt and pepper to taste. Cook for 1 minute more.
3. Add the cauliflower rice and cream cheese to the skillet. Cook for 7 minutes, stirring frequently, until the cream cheese melts and the cauliflower is tender.
4. Remove the skillet from the heat and stir in the Cheddar cheese. Using a cookie scoop, form the mixture into 1½-inch balls. Place the balls on a parchment paper-lined baking sheet. Freeze for 30 minutes.
5. Place the egg in a shallow bowl and beat it with a fork. In a separate bowl, stir together the almond flour and Parmesan cheese.
6. Dip the cauliflower balls into the egg, then coat them with the almond flour mixture, gently pressing the mixture to the balls to adhere.
7. Set the air fryer to 400ºF (204ºC). Spray the cauliflower rice balls with oil, and arrange them in a single layer in the air fryer basket, working in batches if necessary. Air fry for 5 minutes. Flip the rice balls and spray them with more oil. Air fry for 3 to 7 minutes longer, until the balls are golden brown.
8. Serve warm with marinara sauce.

Per Serving
calories: 290 | fat: 23g | protein: 15g
carbs: 6g | net carbs: 4g | fiber: 2g

Steaks with Walnut-Blue Cheese Butter

Prep time: 15 minutes | Cook time: 10 minutes | Serves 6

½ cup unsalted butter, at room temperature
½ cup crumbled blue cheese
2 tablespoons finely chopped walnuts
1 tablespoon minced fresh rosemary
1 teaspoon minced
garlic
¼ teaspoon cayenne pepper
Sea salt and freshly ground black pepper, to taste
1½ pounds (680 g) New York strip steaks, at room temperature

1. In a medium bowl, combine the butter, blue cheese, walnuts, rosemary, garlic, and cayenne pepper and salt and black pepper to taste. Use clean hands to ensure that everything is well combined. Place the mixture on a sheet of parchment paper and form it into a log. Wrap it tightly in plastic wrap. Refrigerate for at least 2 hours or freeze for 30 minutes.
2. Season the steaks generously with salt and pepper.
3. Place the air fryer basket or grill pan in the air fryer. Set the air fryer to 400ºF (204ºC) and let it preheat for 5 minutes.
4. Place the steaks in the basket in a single layer and air fry for 5 minutes. Flip the steaks, and cook for 5 minutes more, until an instant-read thermometer reads 120ºF (49ºC) for medium-rare (or as desired).
5. Transfer the steaks to a plate. Cut the butter into pieces and place the desired amount on top of the steaks. Tent a piece of aluminum foil over the steaks and allow to sit for 10 minutes before serving.
6. Store any remaining butter in a sealed container in the refrigerator for up to 2 weeks.

Per Serving
calories: 418 | fat: 34g | protein: 28g
carbs: 1g | net carbs: 1g | fiber: 0g

Swedish Meatloaf

Prep time: 10 minutes | Cook time: 35 minutes | Serves 8

1½ pounds (680 g) ground beef (85% lean)
¼ pound (113 g) ground pork
1 large egg (omit for egg-free)
½ cup minced onions
¼ cup tomato sauce
Sauce:
½ cup (1 stick) unsalted butter
½ cup shredded Swiss or mild Cheddar cheese (about 2 ounces / 57 g)
2 ounces (57 g) cream cheese (¼

2 tablespoons dry mustard
2 cloves garlic, minced
2 teaspoons fine sea salt
1 teaspoon ground black pepper, plus more for garnish

cup), softened
⅓ cup beef broth
⅛ teaspoon ground nutmeg
Halved cherry tomatoes, for serving (optional)

1. Preheat the air fryer to 390ºF (199ºC).
2. In a large bowl, combine the ground beef, ground pork, egg, onions, tomato sauce, dry mustard, garlic, salt, and pepper. Using your hands, mix until well combined.
3. Place the meatloaf mixture in a loaf pan and place it in the air fryer. Bake for 35 minutes, or until cooked through and the internal temperature reaches 145ºF (63ºC). Check the meatloaf after 25 minutes; if it's getting too brown on the top, cover it loosely with foil to prevent burning.
4. While the meatloaf cooks, make the sauce: Heat the butter in a saucepan over medium-high heat until it sizzles and brown flecks appear, stirring constantly to keep the butter from burning. Turn the heat down to low and whisk in the Swiss cheese, cream cheese, broth, and nutmeg. Simmer for at least 10 minutes. The longer it simmers, the more the flavors open up.
5. When the meatloaf is done, transfer it to a serving tray and pour the sauce over it. Garnish with ground black pepper and serve with cherry tomatoes, if desired. Allow the meatloaf to rest for 10 minutes before slicing so it doesn't crumble apart.
6. Store leftovers in an airtight container in the fridge for 3 days or in the freezer for up to a month. Reheat in a preheated 350ºF (177ºC) air fryer for 4 minutes, or until heated through.

Per Serving
calories: 395 | fat: 32g | protein: 23g
carbs: 3g | net carbs: 2g | fiber: 1g

Grilled Steaks with Horseradish Cream

Prep time: 5 minutes | Cook time: 10 minutes | Serves 8

2 pounds (907 g) rib eye steaks
Sea salt and freshly ground black pepper, to taste
Unsalted butter, for serving
1 cup sour cream
⅓ cup heavy

(whipping) cream
4 tablespoons prepared horseradish
1 teaspoon Dijon mustard
1 teaspoon apple cider vinegar
¼ teaspoon Swerve

1. Pat the steaks dry. Season with salt and pepper and let sit at room temperature for about 45 minutes.
2. Place the grill pan in the air fryer and set the air fryer to 400ºF (204ºC). Let preheat for 5 minutes.
3. Working in batches, place the steaks in a single layer on the grill pan and air fry for 5 minutes. Flip the steaks and air fry for 5 minutes more, until an instant-read thermometer reads 120ºF (49ºC) (or to your desired doneness).
4. Transfer the steaks to a plate and top each with a pat of butter. Tent with foil and let rest for 10 minutes.
5. Combine the sour cream, heavy cream, horseradish, Dijon mustard, vinegar, and Swerve in a bowl. Stir until smooth.
6. Serve the steaks with the horseradish cream.

Per Serving
calories: 322 | fat: 22g | protein: 23g
carbs: 6g | net carbs: 6g | fiber: 0g

Mojito Lamb Chops

Prep time: 5 minutes | Cook time: 5 minutes | Serves 2

Marinade:

2 teaspoons grated lime zest
½ cup lime juice
¼ cup avocado oil
¼ cup chopped fresh mint leaves

4 cloves garlic, roughly chopped
2 teaspoons fine sea salt
½ teaspoon ground black pepper

4 (1-inch-thick) lamb chops
Sprigs of fresh mint, for garnish (optional)
Lime slices, for serving (optional)

1. Make the marinade: Place all the ingredients for the marinade in a food processor or blender and purée until mostly smooth with a few small chunks. Transfer half of the marinade to a shallow dish and set the other half aside for serving. Add the lamb to the shallow dish, cover, and place in the refrigerator to marinate for at least 2 hours or overnight.
2. Spray the air fryer basket with avocado oil. Preheat the air fryer to 390ºF (199ºC).
3. Remove the chops from the marinade and place them in the air fryer basket. Air fry for 5 minutes, or until the internal temperature reaches 145ºF (63ºC) for medium doneness.
4. Allow the chops to rest for 10 minutes before serving with the rest of the marinade as a sauce. Garnish with fresh mint leaves and serve with lime slices, if desired. Best served fresh.

Per Serving
calories: 692 | fat: 53g | protein: 48g
carbs: 5g | net carbs: 4g | fiber: 1g

Italian Sausages with Peppers and Onions

Prep time: 5 minutes | Cook time: 28 minutes | Serves 3

1 medium onion, thinly sliced
1 yellow or orange bell pepper, thinly sliced
1 red bell pepper, thinly sliced

¼ cup avocado oil or melted coconut oil
1 teaspoon fine sea salt
6 Italian sausages
Dijon mustard, for serving (optional)

1. Preheat the air fryer to 400ºF (204ºC).
2. Place the onion and peppers in a large bowl. Drizzle with the oil and toss well to coat the veggies. Season with the salt.
3. Place the onion and peppers in a pie pan and cook in the air fryer for 8 minutes, stirring halfway through. Remove from the air fryer and set aside.
4. Spray the air fryer basket with avocado oil. Place the sausages in the air fryer basket and air fry for 20 minutes, or until crispy and golden brown. During the last minute or two of cooking, add the onion and peppers to the basket with the sausages to warm them through.
5. Place the onion and peppers on a serving platter and arrange the sausages on top. Serve Dijon mustard on the side, if desired.
6. Store leftovers in an airtight container in the fridge for up to 7 days or in the freezer for up to a month. Reheat in a preheated 390ºF (199ºC) air fryer for 3 minutes, or until heated through.

Per Serving
calories: 576 | fat: 49g | protein: 25g
carbs: 8g | net carbs: 6g | fiber: 2g

Poblano Pepper Cheeseburgers

Prep time: 5 minutes | Cook time: 30 minutes | Serves 4

2 poblano chile peppers
1½ pounds (680 g) 85% lean ground beef
1 clove garlic, minced
1 teaspoon salt
½ teaspoon freshly ground black pepper
4 slices Cheddar cheese (about 3 ounces / 85 g)
4 large lettuce leaves

1. Preheat the air fryer to 400ºF (204ºC).
2. Arrange the poblano peppers in the basket of the air fryer. Pausing halfway through the cooking time to turn the peppers, air fry for 20 minutes, or until they are softened and beginning to char. Transfer the peppers to a large bowl and cover with a plate. When cool enough to handle, peel off the skin, remove the seeds and stems, and slice into strips. Set aside.
3. Meanwhile, in a large bowl, combine the ground beef with the garlic, salt, and pepper. Shape the beef into 4 patties.
4. Lower the heat on the air fryer to 360ºF (182ºC). Arrange the burgers in a single layer in the basket of the air fryer. Pausing halfway through the cooking time to turn the burgers, air fry for 10 minutes, or until a thermometer inserted into the thickest part registers 160ºF (71ºC).
5. Top the burgers with the cheese slices and continue baking for a minute or two, just until the cheese has melted. Serve the burgers on a lettuce leaf topped with the roasted poblano peppers.

Per Serving
calories: 310 | fat: 20g | protein: 28g
carbs: 2g | net carbs: 1g | fiber: 1g

London Broil with Herb Butter

Prep time: 5 minutes | Cook time: 20 to 25 minutes | Serves 4

1½ pounds (680 g) London broil top round steak
¼ cup olive oil
2 tablespoons
balsamic vinegar
1 tablespoon Worcestershire sauce
4 cloves garlic, minced

Herb Butter:
6 tablespoons unsalted butter, softened
1 tablespoon chopped fresh parsley
¼ teaspoon salt
¼ teaspoon dried
ground rosemary or thyme
¼ teaspoon garlic powder
Pinch of red pepper flakes

1. Place the beef in a gallon-size resealable bag. In a small bowl, whisk together the olive oil, balsamic vinegar, Worcestershire sauce, and garlic. Pour the marinade over the beef, massaging gently to coat, and seal the bag. Let sit at room temperature for an hour or refrigerate overnight.
2. To make the herb butter: In a small bowl, mix the butter with the parsley, salt, rosemary, garlic powder, and red pepper flakes until smooth. Cover and refrigerate until ready to use.
3. Preheat the air fryer to 400ºF (204ºC).
4. Remove the beef from the marinade (discard the marinade) and place the beef in the air fryer basket. Pausing halfway through the cooking time to turn the meat, air fry for 20 to 25 minutes, until a thermometer inserted into the thickest part indicates the desired doneness, 125ºF (52ºC) (rare) to 150ºF (66ºC) (medium). Let the beef rest for 10 minutes before slicing. Serve topped with the herb butter.

Per Serving
calories: 420 | fat: 28g | protein: 41g
carbs: 1g | net carbs: 1g | fiber: 0g

Tomato and Bacon Zoodles

Prep time: 10 minutes | Cook time: 15 to 22 minutes | Serves 2

8 ounces (227 g) sliced bacon
½ cup grape tomatoes
1 large zucchini, spiralized
½ cup ricotta cheese
¼ cup heavy (whipping) cream
$^1/_3$ cup finely grated Parmesan cheese, plus more for serving
Sea salt and freshly ground black pepper, to taste

1. Set the air fryer to 400ºF (204ºC). Arrange the bacon strips in a single layer in the air fryer basket—some overlapping is okay because the bacon will shrink, but cook in batches if needed. Air fry for 8 minutes. Flip the bacon strips and air fry for 2 to 5 minutes more, until the bacon is crisp. Remove the bacon from the air fryer.
2. Put the tomatoes in the air fryer basket and air fry for 3 to 5 minutes, until they are just starting to burst. Remove the tomatoes from the air fryer.
3. Put the zucchini noodles in the air fryer and air fry for 2 to 4 minutes, to the desired doneness.
4. Meanwhile, combine the ricotta, heavy cream, and Parmesan in a saucepan over medium-low heat. Cook, stirring often, until warm and combined.
5. Crumble the bacon. Place the zucchini, bacon, and tomatoes in a bowl. Toss with the ricotta sauce. Season with salt and pepper, and sprinkle with additional Parmesan.

Per Serving
calories: 535 | fat: 40g | protein: 35g
carbs: 11g | net carbs: 9g | fiber: 2g

Short Ribs with Chimichurri

Prep time: 15 minutes | Cook time: 13 minutes | Serves 4

1 pound (454 g) boneless short ribs
1½ teaspoons sea salt, divided
½ teaspoon freshly ground black pepper, divided
½ cup fresh parsley leaves
½ cup fresh cilantro leaves
1 teaspoon minced garlic
1 tablespoon freshly squeezed lemon juice
½ teaspoon ground cumin
¼ teaspoon red pepper flakes
2 tablespoons extra-virgin olive oil
Avocado oil spray

1. Pat the short ribs dry with paper towels. Sprinkle the ribs all over with 1 teaspoon salt and ¼ teaspoon black pepper. Let sit at room temperature for 45 minutes.
2. Meanwhile, place the parsley, cilantro, garlic, lemon juice, cumin, red pepper flakes, the remaining ½ teaspoon salt, and the remaining ¼ teaspoon black pepper in a blender or food processor. With the blender running, slowly drizzle in the olive oil. Blend for about 1 minute, until the mixture is smooth and well combined.
3. Set the air fryer to 400ºF (204ºC). Spray both sides of the ribs with oil. Place in the basket and air fry for 8 minutes. Flip and cook for another 5 minutes, until an instant-read thermometer reads 125ºF (52ºC) for medium-rare (or to your desired doneness).
4. Allow the meat to rest for 5 to 10 minutes, then slice. Serve warm with the chimichurri sauce.

Per Serving
calories: 329 | fat: 24g | protein: 21g
carbs: 7g | net carbs: 6g | fiber: 1g

Steak Gyro Platter

Prep time: 15 minutes | Cook time: 8 to 10 minutes | Serves 4

1 pound (454 g) flank steak
1 teaspoon garlic powder
1 teaspoon ground cumin
½ teaspoon sea salt
½ teaspoon freshly ground black pepper
5 ounces (142 g) shredded romaine lettuce
½ cup crumbled feta cheese
½ cup peeled and diced cucumber
⅓ cup sliced red onion
¼ cup seeded and diced tomato
2 tablespoons pitted and sliced black olives
Tzatziki Sauce, for serving

1. Pat the steak dry with paper towels. In a small bowl, combine the garlic powder, cumin, salt, and pepper. Sprinkle this mixture all over the steak, and allow the steak to rest at room temperature for 45 minutes.
2. Preheat the air fryer to 400ºF (204ºC). Place the steak in the air fryer basket and air fry for 4 minutes. Flip the steak and cook 4 to 6 minutes more, until an instant-read thermometer reads 120ºF (49ºC) at the thickest point for medium-rare (or as desired). Remove the steak from the air fryer and let it rest for 5 minutes.
3. Divide the romaine among plates. Top with the feta, cucumber, red onion, tomato, and olives.
4. Thinly slice the steak diagonally. Add the steak to the plates and drizzle with tzatziki sauce before serving.

Per Serving
calories: 244 | fat: 12g | protein: 28g
carbs: 5g | net carbs: 4g | fiber: 1g

Ground Beef Taco Rolls

Prep time: 20 minutes | Cook time: 10 minutes | Serves 4

½ pound (227 g) 80/20 ground beef
⅓ cup water
1 tablespoon chili powder
2 teaspoons cumin
½ teaspoon garlic powder
¼ teaspoon dried oregano
¼ cup canned diced
tomatoes and chiles, drained
2 tablespoons chopped cilantro
1½ cups shredded Mozzarella cheese
½ cup blanched finely ground almond flour
2 ounces (57 g) full-fat cream cheese
1 large egg

1. In a medium skillet over medium heat, brown the ground beef about 7 to 10 minutes. When meat is fully cooked, drain.
2. Add water to skillet and stir in chili powder, cumin, garlic powder, oregano, and tomatoes with chiles. Add cilantro. Bring to a boil, then reduce heat to simmer for 3 minutes.
3. In a large microwave-safe bowl, place Mozzarella, almond flour, cream cheese, and egg. Microwave for 1 minute. Stir the mixture quickly until smooth ball of dough forms.
4. Cut a piece of parchment for your work surface. Press the dough into a large rectangle on the parchment, wetting your hands to prevent the dough from sticking as necessary. Cut the dough into eight rectangles.
5. On each rectangle place a few spoons of the meat mixture. Fold the short ends of each roll toward the center and roll the length as you would a burrito.
6. Cut a piece of parchment to fit your air fryer basket. Place taco rolls onto the parchment and place into the air fryer basket.
7. Adjust the temperature to 360ºF (182ºC) and air fry for 10 minutes.
8. Flip halfway through the cooking time.
9. Allow to cool 10 minutes before serving.

Per Serving
calories: 380 | fat: 26g | protein: 25g
carbs: 7g | net carbs: 5g | fiber: 2g

Beefy Poppers

Prep time: 15 minutes | Cook time: 15 minutes | Makes 8 poppers

8 medium jalapeño peppers, stemmed, halved, and seeded
1 (8-ounce / 227-g) package cream cheese (or Kite Hill brand cream cheese style spread for dairy-free), softened
2 pounds (907 g) ground beef (85% lean)
1 teaspoon fine sea salt
½ teaspoon ground black pepper
8 slices thin-cut bacon
Fresh cilantro leaves, for garnish

1. Spray the air fryer basket with avocado oil. Preheat the air fryer to 400ºF (204ºC).
2. Stuff each jalapeño half with a few tablespoons of cream cheese. Place the halves back together again to form 8 jalapeños.
3. Season the ground beef with the salt and pepper and mix with your hands to incorporate. Flatten about ¼ pound (113 g) of ground beef in the palm of your hand and place a stuffed jalapeño in the center. Fold the beef around the jalapeño, forming an egg shape. Wrap the beef-covered jalapeño with a slice of bacon and secure it with a toothpick.
4. Place the jalapeños in the air fryer basket, leaving space between them (if you're using a smaller air fryer, work in batches if necessary), and air fry for 15 minutes, or until the beef is cooked through and the bacon is crispy. Garnish with cilantro before serving.
5. Store leftovers in an airtight container in the fridge for 3 days or in the freezer for up to a month. Reheat in a preheated 350ºF (177ºC) air fryer for 4 minutes, or until heated through and the bacon is crispy.

Per Serving
calories: 679 | fat: 53g | protein: 42g
carbs: 3g | net carbs: 2g | fiber: 1g

Bacon Guacamole Burgers

Prep time: 15 minutes | Cook time: 9 minutes | Serves 8

2 pounds (907 g) ground beef
2 teaspoons Taco Seasoning
Sea salt and freshly ground black pepper, to taste
Avocado oil spray
2 large ripe avocados, peeled and pits removed
1 tablespoon freshly squeezed lime juice
½ teaspoon ground cumin
8 ounces (227 g) sliced bacon, cooked and crumbled
¼ cup chopped red onion
1 tablespoon minced garlic
1 canned chipotle chile in adobo sauce, seeded and chopped with sauce removed
1 small tomato, seeded and diced
¼ cup fresh cilantro, chopped
Lettuce leaves or keto-friendly buns, for serving

1. In a large bowl, combine the ground beef and taco seasoning. Season with salt and pepper. Mix with your hands until well-combined. Form the mixture into 8 patties, making them thinner in the center for even cooking. Spray the patties with oil.
2. Set the air fryer to 350ºF (177ºC). Working in batches if necessary, place the patties in the air fryer basket. Air fry the burgers for 5 minutes. Flip and air fry for 4 minutes more, until the patties are cooked through and an instant-read thermometer reads 160ºF (71ºC). Allow the burgers to rest for 5 minutes before serving.
3. Meanwhile, mash the avocados in a medium bowl. Add the lime juice and cumin. Season with salt and pepper. Stir to combine. Gently stir in the bacon, onion, garlic, chipotle chile, tomato, and cilantro. Cover with plastic wrap, gently pressing it directly on the surface of the guacamole. Refrigerate until ready to serve.
4. Top each burger with a dollop of guacamole and serve in lettuce wraps or on keto-friendly buns.

Per Serving
calories: 321 | fat: 26g | protein: 15g
carbs: 6g | net carbs: 3g | fiber: 3g

Beef Empanadas

Prep time: 20 minutes | Cook time: 24 to 27 minutes | Serves 10

1 tablespoon unsalted butter
½ medium onion, chopped
2 teaspoons minced garlic
½ pound (227 g) ground beef
2 teaspoons ground cumin
1 teaspoon smoked paprika
⅛ teaspoon cayenne pepper (more or less to taste)
Sea salt and freshly ground black pepper, to taste
½ cup keto-friendly tomato sauce
1 recipe Fathead Pizza Dough
½ cup shredded sharp Cheddar cheese

1. Heat the butter over medium-high heat in a large skillet. Once the butter is melted and hot, add the onion and cook, stirring occasionally, for about 6 minutes or until soft. Stir in the garlic and sauté for 1 minute.
2. Add the ground beef and cook, breaking the meat up with a spoon, until browned, about 5 minutes. Stir in the cumin, paprika, cayenne pepper, and salt and black pepper to taste, and cook for 2 minutes. Stir in the tomato sauce. Bring to a boil and then reduce the heat to a simmer. Cook for 3 minutes, then remove the skillet from the heat.
3. Line a baking sheet with parchment paper.
4. On another sheet of parchment paper, roll out the dough to about the size of your baking sheet. Use a 3½- or 3¾-inch round cookie cutter to cut the dough into rounds. Ball up the scraps, roll them out again, and cut more rounds until all the dough has been used.
5. Transfer the rounds to a clean sheet of parchment paper. Place about ½ tablespoon of ground beef filling in the center of each round. Top with a sprinkle of Cheddar cheese. Fold the dough in half over the filling, using a fork to seal the edges together.
6. Set the air fryer to 400ºF (204ºC). Working in batches if needed, place the empanadas in the air fryer basket in a single layer. Air fry for 7 to 10 minutes, until golden brown.

Per Serving
calories: 250 | fat: 21g | protein: 13g
carbs: 5g | net carbs: 3g | fiber: 2g

Cheeseburger Casserole

Prep time: 5 minutes | Cook time: 50 minutes | Serves 4

¼ pound (113 g) reduced-sodium bacon
1 pound (454 g) 85% lean ground beef
1 clove garlic, minced
¼ teaspoon onion powder
4 eggs
¼ cup heavy cream
¼ cup tomato paste
2 tablespoons dill pickle relish
¼ teaspoon salt
¼ teaspoon freshly ground black pepper
1½ cups grated Cheddar cheese, divided

1. Lightly coat a 6-cup casserole dish that will fit in air fryer, with olive oil and set aside.
2. Arrange the bacon in a single layer in the air fryer basket (it's OK if the bacon sits a bit on the sides). Set the air fryer to 350ºF (177ºC) and air fry for 10 minutes. Check for crispiness and air fry for 2 to 3 minutes longer if needed. Transfer the bacon to a plate lined with paper towels and let cool. Drain the grease.
3. Set the air fryer to 400ºF (204ºC). Crumble the beef into a single layer in the air fryer basket. Scatter the garlic on top and sprinkle with the onion powder. Air fry for 15 to 20 minutes until the beef is browned and cooked through.
4. While the beef is baking, in a bowl whisk together the eggs, cream, tomato paste, pickle relish, salt, and pepper. Stir in 1 cup of the cheese. Set aside.
5. When the beef is done, transfer it to the prepared pan. Use the side of a spoon to break up any large pieces of beef.
6. Drain the grease and, when cool enough to handle, wash the air fryer basket. Set the air fryer to 350ºF (177ºC).
7. Crumble the bacon and add it to the beef, spreading the meats into an even layer. Pour the egg mixture over the beef mixture and top with the remaining ½ cup of cheese. Air fry for 20 to 25 minutes until the eggs are set and the top is golden brown.

Per Serving
calories: 660 | fat: 47g | protein: 50g
carbs: 8g | net carbs: 7g | fiber: 1g

Sesame Beef Lettuce Tacos

Prep time: 15 minutes | Cook time: 8 to 10 minutes | Serves 4

¼ cup coconut aminos
¼ cup avocado oil
2 tablespoons cooking sherry
1 tablespoon Swerve
1 tablespoon ground cumin
1 teaspoon minced garlic
Sea salt and freshly ground black pepper, to taste
1 pound (454 g) flank steak
8 butter lettuce leaves
2 scallions, sliced
1 tablespoon toasted sesame seeds
Hot sauce, for serving
Lime wedges, for serving
Flaky sea salt (optional)

1. In a small bowl, whisk together the coconut aminos, avocado oil, cooking sherry, Swerve, cumin, garlic, and salt and pepper to taste.
2. Place the steak in a shallow dish. Pour the marinade over the beef. Cover the dish with plastic wrap and let it marinate in the refrigerator for at least 2 hours or overnight.
3. Remove the flank steak from the dish and discard the marinade.
4. Set the air fryer to 400ºF (204ºC). Place the steak in the air fryer basket and air fry for 4 to 6 minutes. Flip the steak and cook for 4 minutes more, until an instant-read thermometer reads 120ºF (49ºC) at the thickest part (or cook it to your desired doneness). Allow the steak to rest for 10 minutes, then slice it thinly against the grain.
5. Stack 2 lettuce leaves on top of each other and add some sliced meat. Top with scallions and sesame seeds. Drizzle with hot sauce and lime juice, and finish with a little flaky salt (if using). Repeat with the remaining lettuce leaves and fillings.

Per Serving
calories: 349 | fat: 22g | protein: 25g
carbs: 10g | net carbs: 5g | fiber: 5g

Chipotle Taco Pizzas

Prep time: 25 minutes | Cook time: 36 minutes | Serves 6

1 recipe Fathead Pizza Dough
1 pound (454 g) ground beef
2 tablespoons Taco Seasoning
1 canned chipotle chile in adobo sauce, diced and sauce removed
⅓ cup plus 1 tablespoon sugar-free salsa, divided
6 ounces (170 g) Cheddar cheese, grated
3 scallions, chopped
¼ cup sour cream

1. Divide the dough into three equal pieces. Place each piece between two sheets of parchment paper, and roll it into a 7-inch round. Place one dough round in a cake pan or air fryer pizza pan (or a similar pan that fits inside your air fryer). Place the pan in the air fryer basket.
2. Set your air fryer to 375ºF (191ºC). Bake the dough for 6 minutes. Remove from the air fryer and repeat with the remaining dough.
3. While the crusts are cooking, heat a large skillet over medium-high heat. Add the ground beef and cook, breaking the meat up with a spoon, for 5 minutes. Stir in the taco seasoning and chipotle chile, and cook until the meat is browned. Remove the skillet from the heat and stir in ⅓ cup of salsa.
4. Divide the meat among the pizza crusts. Top with the cheese and scallions. Return one pizza to the air fryer and bake for 6 minutes, until the cheese is melted. Repeat with the remaining pizzas.
5. Combine the sour cream and remaining 1 tablespoon of salsa in a small bowl. Drizzle this over the finished pizzas.
6. If desired, top the pizzas with additional desired toppings, such as shredded romaine lettuce, pickled jalapeño slices, diced tomatoes, cilantro, and lime juice. Serve warm.

Per Serving
calories: 614 | fat: 52g | protein: 34g
carbs: 10g | net carbs: 6g | fiber: 4g

Greek Stuffed Tenderloin

Prep time: 10 minutes | Cook time: 10 minutes | Serves 4

1½ pounds (680 g) venison or beef tenderloin, pounded to ¼ inch thick
3 teaspoons fine sea salt
1 teaspoon ground black pepper
2 ounces (57 g) creamy goat cheese
½ cup crumbled feta cheese (about 2 ounces / 57 g)
¼ cup finely chopped onions
2 cloves garlic, minced

For Garnish/Serving (Optional):
Prepared yellow mustard
Halved cherry tomatoes
Extra-virgin olive oil
Sprigs of fresh rosemary
Lavender flowers

1. Spray the air fryer basket with avocado oil. Preheat the air fryer to 400ºF (204ºC).
2. Season the tenderloin on all sides with the salt and pepper.
3. In a medium-sized mixing bowl, combine the goat cheese, feta, onions, and garlic. Place the mixture in the center of the tenderloin. Starting at the end closest to you, tightly roll the tenderloin like a jelly roll. Tie the rolled tenderloin tightly with kitchen twine.
4. Place the meat in the air fryer basket and air fry for 5 minutes. Flip the meat over and cook for another 5 minutes, or until the internal temperature reaches 135ºF (57ºC) for medium-rare.
5. To serve, smear a line of prepared yellow mustard on a platter, then place the meat next to it and add halved cherry tomatoes on the side, if desired. Drizzle with olive oil and garnish with rosemary sprigs and lavender flowers, if desired.
6. Best served fresh. Store leftovers in an airtight container in the fridge for 3 days. Reheat in a preheated 350ºF (177ºC) air fryer for 4 minutes, or until heated through.

Per Serving
calories: 415 | fat: 16g | protein: 62g
carbs: 4g | net carbs: 3g | fiber: 1g

Herb-Crusted Lamb Chops

Prep time: 10 minutes | Cook time: 5 minutes | Serves 2

1 large egg
2 cloves garlic, minced
¼ cup pork dust
¼ cup powdered Parmesan cheese
1 tablespoon chopped fresh oregano leaves
1 tablespoon chopped fresh rosemary leaves
1 teaspoon chopped fresh thyme leaves
½ teaspoon ground black pepper
4 (1-inch-thick) lamb chops

For Garnish/Serving (Optional):
Sprigs of fresh oregano
Sprigs of fresh rosemary
Sprigs of fresh thyme
Lavender flowers
Lemon slices

1. Spray the air fryer basket with avocado oil. Preheat the air fryer to 400ºF (204ºC).
2. Beat the egg in a shallow bowl, add the garlic, and stir well to combine. In another shallow bowl, mix together the pork dust, Parmesan, herbs, and pepper.
3. One at a time, dip the lamb chops into the egg mixture, shake off the excess egg, and then dredge them in the Parmesan mixture. Use your hands to coat the chops well in the Parmesan mixture and form a nice crust on all sides; if necessary, dip the chops again in both the egg and the Parmesan mixture.
4. Place the lamb chops in the air fryer basket, leaving space between them, and air fry for 5 minutes, or until the internal temperature reaches 145ºF (63ºC) for medium doneness. Allow to rest for 10 minutes before serving.
5. Garnish with sprigs of oregano, rosemary, and thyme, and lavender flowers, if desired. Serve with lemon slices, if desired.
6. Best served fresh. Store leftovers in an airtight container in the fridge for up to 4 days. Serve chilled over a salad, or reheat in a 350ºF (177ºC) air fryer for 3 minutes, or until heated through.

Per Serving
calories: 790 | fat: 60g | protein: 57g
carbs: 2g | net carbs: 1g | fiber: 1g

Chicken Fried Steak with Cream Gravy

Prep time: 5 minutes | Cook time: 10 minutes | Serves 4

4 small thin cube steaks (about 1 pound / 454 g)
½ teaspoon salt
½ teaspoon freshly ground black pepper
Cream Gravy:
½ cup heavy cream
2 ounces (57 g) cream cheese
¼ cup bacon grease
2 to 3 tablespoons water

¼ teaspoon garlic powder
1 egg, lightly beaten
1 cup crushed pork rinds (about 3 ounces / 85 g)

2 to 3 dashes Worcestershire sauce
Salt and freshly ground black pepper, to taste

1. Preheat the air fryer to 400ºF (204ºC).
2. Working one at a time, place the steak between two sheets of parchment paper and use a meat mallet to pound to an even thickness.
3. In a small bowl, combine the salt, pepper, and garlic power. Season both sides of each steak with the mixture.
4. Place the egg in a small shallow dish and the pork rinds in another small shallow dish. Dip each steak first in the egg wash, followed by the pork rinds, pressing lightly to form an even coating. Working in batches if necessary, arrange the steaks in a single layer in the air fryer basket. Air fry for 10 minutes until crispy and cooked through.
5. To make the cream gravy: In a heavy-bottomed pot, warm the cream, cream cheese, and bacon grease over medium heat, whisking until smooth. Lower the heat if the mixture begins to boil. Continue whisking as you slowly add the water, 1 tablespoon at a time, until the sauce reaches the desired consistency. Season with the Worcestershire sauce and salt and pepper to taste. Serve over the chicken fried steaks.

Per Serving
calories: 560 | fat: 42g | protein: 43g
carbs: 2g | net carbs: 2g | fiber: 0g

Spaghetti Zoodles and Meatballs

Prep time: 15 minutes | Cook time: 11 to 13 minutes | Serves 6

1 pound (454 g) ground beef
1½ teaspoons sea salt, plus more for seasoning
1 large egg, beaten
1 teaspoon gelatin
¾ cup Parmesan cheese
2 teaspoons minced garlic
1 teaspoon Italian

seasoning
Freshly ground black pepper, to taste
Avocado oil spray
Keto-friendly marinara sauce, for serving
6 ounces (170 g) zucchini noodles, made using a spiralizer or store-bought

1. Place the ground beef in a large bowl, and season with the salt.
2. Place the egg in a separate bowl and sprinkle with the gelatin. Allow to sit for 5 minutes.
3. Stir the gelatin mixture, then pour it over the ground beef. Add the Parmesan, garlic, and Italian seasoning. Season with salt and pepper.
4. Form the mixture into 1½-inch meatballs and place them on a plate; cover with plastic wrap and refrigerate for at least 1 hour or overnight.
5. Spray the meatballs with oil. Set the air fryer to 400ºF (204ºC) and arrange the meatballs in a single layer in the air fryer basket. Air fry for 4 minutes. Flip the meatballs and spray them with more oil. Air fry for 4 minutes more, until an instant-read thermometer reads 160ºF (71ºC). Transfer the meatballs to a plate and allow them to rest.
6. While the meatballs are resting, heat the marinara in a saucepan on the stove over medium heat.
7. Place the zucchini noodles in the air fryer, and cook at 400ºF (204ºC) for 3 to 5 minutes.
8. To serve, place the zucchini noodles in serving bowls. Top with meatballs and warm marinara.

Per Serving
calories: 312 | fat: 25g | protein: 20g
carbs: 2g | net carbs: 1g | fiber: 1g

Blue Cheese Steak Salad

Prep time: 15 minutes | Cook time: 22 minutes | Serves 4

2 tablespoons balsamic vinegar
2 tablespoons red wine vinegar
1 tablespoon Dijon mustard
1 tablespoon Swerve
1 teaspoon minced garlic
Sea salt and freshly ground black pepper, to taste
¾ cup extra-virgin olive oil
1 pound (454 g) boneless sirloin steak
Avocado oil spray
1 small red onion, cut into ¼-inch-thick rounds
6 ounces (170 g) baby spinach
½ cup cherry tomatoes, halved
3 ounces (85 g) blue cheese, crumbled

1. In a blender, combine the balsamic vinegar, red wine vinegar, Dijon mustard, Swerve, and garlic. Season with salt and pepper and process until smooth. With the blender running, drizzle in the olive oil. Process until well combined. Transfer to a jar with a tight-fitting lid, and refrigerate until ready to serve (it will keep for up to 2 weeks).
2. Season the steak with salt and pepper and let sit at room temperature for at least 45 minutes, time permitting.
3. Set the air fryer to 400ºF (204ºC). Spray the steak with oil and place it in the air fryer basket. Air fry for 6 minutes. Flip the steak and spray it with more oil. Air fry for 6 minutes more for medium-rare or until the steak is done to your liking.
4. Transfer the steak to a plate, tent with a piece of aluminum foil, and allow it to rest.
5. Spray the onion slices with oil and place them in the air fryer basket. Cook at 400ºF (204ºC) for 5 minutes. Flip the onion slices and spray them with more oil. Air fry for 5 minutes more.
6. Slice the steak diagonally into thin strips. Place the spinach, cherry tomatoes, onion slices, and steak in a large bowl. Toss with the desired amount of dressing. Sprinkle with crumbled blue cheese and serve.

Per Serving
calories: 670 | fat: 53g | protein: 41g
carbs: 9g | net carbs: 4g | fiber: 5g

Parmesan-Crusted Steak

Prep time: 7 minutes | Cook time: 12 minutes | Serves 6

½ cup (1 stick) unsalted butter, at room temperature
1 cup finely grated Parmesan cheese
¼ cup finely ground blanched almond flour
1½ pounds (680 g) New York strip steak
Sea salt and freshly ground black pepper, to taste

1. Place the butter, Parmesan cheese, and almond flour in a food processor. Process until smooth. Transfer to a sheet of parchment paper and form into a log. Wrap tightly in plastic wrap. Freeze for 45 minutes or refrigerate for at least 4 hours.
2. While the butter is chilling, season the steak liberally with salt and pepper. Let the steak rest at room temperature for about 45 minutes.
3. Place the grill pan or basket in your air fryer, set it to 400ºF (204ºC), and let it preheat for 5 minutes.
4. Working in batches, if necessary, place the steak on the grill pan and air fry for 4 minutes. Flip and cook for 3 minutes more, until the steak is brown on both sides.
5. Remove the steak from the air fryer and arrange an equal amount of the Parmesan butter on top of each steak. Return the steak to the air fryer and continue cooking for another 5 minutes, until an instant-read thermometer reads 120ºF (49ºC) for medium-rare and the crust is golden brown (or to your desired doneness).
6. Transfer the cooked steak to a plate; let rest for 10 minutes before serving.

Per Serving
calories: 463 | fat: 37g | protein: 33g
carbs: 2g | net carbs: 1g | fiber: 1g

Chapter 9 Fish and Seafood

Lemon Garlic Shrimp

Prep time: 5 minutes | Cook time: 6 minutes | Serves 2

1 medium lemon
8 ounces (227 g) medium shelled and deveined shrimp
2 tablespoons unsalted butter,
melted
½ teaspoon Old Bay seasoning
½ teaspoon minced garlic

1. Zest lemon and then cut in half. Place shrimp in a large bowl and squeeze juice from ½ lemon on top of them.
2. Add lemon zest to bowl along with remaining ingredients. Toss shrimp until fully coated.
3. Pour bowl contents into a round baking dish. Place into the air fryer basket.
4. Adjust the temperature to 400ºF (204ºC) and bake for 6 minutes.
5. Shrimp will be bright pink when fully cooked. Serve warm with pan sauce.

Per Serving
calories: 190 | fat: 12g | protein: 16g
carbs: 3g | net carbs: 2g | fiber: 1g

Cajun Salmon

Prep time: 5 minutes | Cook time: 7 minutes | Serves 2

2 (4-ounce / 113-g) salmon fillets, skin removed
2 tablespoons unsalted butter, melted
⅛ teaspoon ground
cayenne pepper
½ teaspoon garlic powder
1 teaspoon paprika
¼ teaspoon ground black pepper

1. Brush each fillet with butter.
2. Combine remaining ingredients in a small bowl and then rub onto fish. Place fillets into the air fryer basket.
3. Adjust the temperature to 390ºF (199ºC) and air fry for 7 minutes.
4. When fully cooked, internal temperature will be 145ºF (63ºC). Serve immediately.

Per Serving
calories: 253 | fat: 16g | protein: 21g
carbs: 2g | net carbs: 1g | fiber: 1g

Coconut Shrimp

Prep time: 5 minutes | Cook time: 6 minutes | Serves 2

8 ounces (227 g) medium shelled and deveined shrimp
2 tablespoons salted butter, melted
½ teaspoon Old Bay seasoning
¼ cup unsweetened shredded coconut

1. In a large bowl, toss the shrimp in butter and Old Bay seasoning.
2. Place shredded coconut in bowl. Coat each piece of shrimp in the coconut and place into the air fryer basket.
3. Adjust the temperature to 400ºF (204ºC) and air fry for 6 minutes.
4. Gently turn the shrimp halfway through the cooking time. Serve immediately.

Per Serving
calories: 252 | fat: 18g | protein: 17g
carbs: 4g | net carbs: 3g | fiber: 1g

Snow Crab Legs

Prep time: 5 minutes | Cook time: 15 minutes | Serves 4

8 pounds (3.6 kg) fresh shell-on snow crab legs
2 tablespoons coconut oil
2 teaspoons Old Bay
seasoning
4 tablespoons salted butter, melted
2 teaspoons lemon juice

1. Place crab legs into ungreased air fryer basket, working in batches if needed. Drizzle legs with coconut oil and sprinkle with Old Bay seasoning.
2. Adjust the temperature to 400ºF (204ºC) and air fry for 15 minutes, shaking the basket three times during cooking. Legs will turn a bright red-orange when done. Serve warm.
3. In a separate small bowl, whisk butter and lemon juice for dipping. Serve on the side.

Per Serving
calories: 284 | fat: 13g | protein: 38g
carbs: 0g | net carbs: 0g | fiber: 0g

Crispy Fish Sticks

Prep time: 15 minutes | Cook time: 10 minutes | Serves 4

1 ounce (28 g) pork rinds, finely ground
¼ cup blanched finely ground almond flour
½ teaspoon Old Bay seasoning
1 tablespoon coconut oil
1 large egg
1 pound (454 g) cod fillet, cut into ¾-inch strips

1. Place ground pork rinds, almond flour, Old Bay seasoning, and coconut oil into a large bowl and mix together. In a medium bowl, whisk egg.
2. Dip each fish stick into the egg and then gently press into the flour mixture, coating as fully and evenly as possible. Place fish sticks into the air fryer basket.
3. Adjust the temperature to 400ºF (204ºC) and air fry for 10 minutes or until golden.
4. Serve immediately.

Per Serving
calories: 205 | fat: 10g | protein: 24g
carbs: 2g | net carbs: 1g | fiber: 1g

Crab Cakes

Prep time: 10 minutes | Cook time: 10 minutes | Serves 4

2 (6-ounce / 170-g) cans lump crab meat
¼ cup blanched finely ground almond flour
1 large egg
2 tablespoons full-fat mayonnaise
½ teaspoon Dijon mustard
½ tablespoon lemon juice
½ medium green bell pepper, seeded and chopped
¼ cup chopped green onion
½ teaspoon Old Bay seasoning

1. In a large bowl, combine all ingredients. Form into four balls and flatten into patties. Place patties into the air fryer basket.
2. Adjust the temperature to 350ºF (177ºC) and air fry for 10 minutes.
3. Flip patties halfway through the cooking time. Serve warm.

Per Serving
calories: 151 | fat: 1g | protein: 13g
carbs: 3g | net carbs: 2g | fiber: 1g

Crab Legs

Prep time: 5 minutes | Cook time: 15 minutes | Serves 4

¼ cup salted butter, melted and divided
3 pounds (1.4 kg) crab legs
¼ teaspoon garlic powder
Juice of ½ medium lemon

1. In a large bowl, drizzle 2 tablespoons butter over crab legs. Place crab legs into the air fryer basket.
2. Adjust the temperature to 400ºF (204ºC) and air fry for 15 minutes.
3. Shake the air fryer basket to toss the crab legs halfway through the cooking time.
4. In a small bowl, mix remaining butter, garlic powder, and lemon juice.
5. To serve, crack open crab legs and remove meat. Dip in lemon butter.

Per Serving
calories: 123 | fat: 6g | protein: 16g
carbs: 0g | net carbs: 0g | fiber: 0g

Sesame-Crusted Tuna Steak

Prep time: 5 minutes | Cook time: 8 minutes | Serves 2

2 (6-ounce / 170-g) tuna steaks
1 tablespoon coconut oil, melted
½ teaspoon garlic
powder
2 teaspoons white sesame seeds
2 teaspoons black sesame seeds

1. Brush each tuna steak with coconut oil and sprinkle with garlic powder.
2. In a large bowl, mix sesame seeds and then press each tuna steak into them, covering the steak as completely as possible. Place tuna steaks into the air fryer basket.
3. Adjust the temperature to 400ºF (204ºC) and air fry for 8 minutes.
4. Flip the steaks halfway through the cooking time. Steaks will be well-done at 145ºF (63ºC) internal temperature. Serve warm.

Per Serving
calories: 280 | fat: 10g | protein: 42g
carbs: 2g | net carbs: 1g | fiber: 1g

Foil-Packet Lobster Tail

Prep time: 15 minutes | Cook time: 12 minutes | Serves 2

2 (6-ounce / 170-g) lobster tails, halved
2 tablespoons salted butter, melted
½ teaspoon Old Bay seasoning
Juice of ½ medium lemon
1 teaspoon dried parsley

1. Place the two halved tails on a sheet of aluminum foil. Drizzle with butter, Old Bay seasoning, and lemon juice.
2. Seal the foil packets, completely covering tails. Place into the air fryer basket.
3. Adjust the temperature to 375ºF (191ºC) and air fry for 12 minutes.
4. Once done, sprinkle with dried parsley and serve immediately.

Per Serving
calories: 234 | fat: 12g | protein: 28g
carbs: 1g | net carbs: 1g | fiber: 0g

Mediterranean-Style Cod

Prep time: 5 minutes | Cook time: 12 minutes | Serves 4

4 (6-ounce / 170-g) cod fillets
3 tablespoons fresh lemon juice
1 tablespoon olive oil
¼ teaspoon salt
6 cherry tomatoes, halved
¼ cup pitted and sliced kalamata olives

1. Place cod into an ungreased round nonstick baking dish. Pour lemon juice into dish and drizzle cod with olive oil. Sprinkle with salt. Place tomatoes and olives around baking dish in between fillets.
2. Place dish into air fryer basket. Adjust the temperature to 350ºF (177ºC) and bake for 12 minutes, carefully turning cod halfway through cooking. Fillets will be lightly browned, easily flake, and have an internal temperature of at least 145ºF (63ºC) when done. Serve warm.

Per Serving
calories: 189 | fat: 8g | protein: 26g
carbs: 2g | net carbs: 2g | fiber: 0g

Garlic Lemon Scallops

Prep time: 5 minutes | Cook time: 10 minutes | Serves 4

4 tablespoons salted butter, melted
4 teaspoons peeled and finely minced garlic
½ small lemon, zested and juiced
8 (1-ounce / 28-g) sea scallops, cleaned and patted dry
¼ teaspoon salt
¼ teaspoon ground black pepper

1. In a small bowl, mix butter, garlic, lemon zest, and lemon juice. Place scallops in an ungreased round nonstick baking dish. Pour butter mixture over scallops, then sprinkle with salt and pepper.
2. Place dish into air fryer basket. Adjust the temperature to 360ºF (182ºC) and bake for 10 minutes. Scallops will be opaque and firm, and have an internal temperature of 135ºF (57ºC) when done. Serve warm.

Per Serving
calories: 145 | fat: 11g | protein: 7g
carbs: 3g | net carbs: 3g | fiber: 0g

Simple Buttery Cod

Prep time: 5 minutes | Cook time: 8 minutes | Serves 2

2 (4-ounce / 113-g) cod fillets
2 tablespoons salted butter, melted
1 teaspoon Old Bay seasoning
½ medium lemon, sliced

1. Place cod fillets into a round baking dish. Brush each fillet with butter and sprinkle with Old Bay seasoning. Lay two lemon slices on each fillet. Cover the dish with foil and place into the air fryer basket.
2. Adjust the temperature to 350ºF (177ºC) and bake for 8 minutes.
3. Flip halfway through the cooking time. When cooked, internal temperature should be at least 145ºF (63ºC). Serve warm.

Per Serving
calories: 179 | fat: 11g | protein: 17g
carbs: 0g | net carbs: 0g | fiber: 0g

Shrimp Scampi

Prep time: 10 minutes | Cook time: 8 minutes | Serves 4

4 tablespoons salted butter	gum
½ medium lemon	¼ teaspoon red pepper flakes
1 teaspoon minced roasted garlic	1 pound (454 g) medium peeled and deveined shrimp
¼ cup heavy whipping cream	1 tablespoon chopped fresh parsley
¼ teaspoon xanthan	

1. In a medium saucepan over medium heat, melt butter. Zest the lemon, then squeeze juice into the pan. Add garlic.
2. Pour in the cream, xanthan gum, and red pepper flakes. Whisk until the mixture begins to thicken, about 2 to 3 minutes.
3. Place shrimp into a 4-cup round baking dish. Pour the cream sauce over the shrimp and cover with foil. Place the dish into the air fryer basket.
4. Adjust the temperature to 400ºF (204ºC) and bake for 8 minutes.
5. Stir twice during cooking.
6. When done, garnish with parsley and serve warm.

Per Serving
calories: 240 | fat: 17g | protein: 17g
carbs: 2g | net carbs: 2g | fiber: 0g

Tuna Cakes

Prep time: 10 minutes | Cook time: 10 minutes | Serves 4

4 (3-ounce / 85-g) pouches tuna, drained	and chopped white onion
1 large egg, whisked	½ teaspoon Old Bay seasoning
2 tablespoons peeled	

1. In a large bowl, mix all ingredients together and form into four patties.
2. Place patties into ungreased air fryer basket. Adjust the temperature to 400ºF (204ºC) and air fry for 10 minutes. Patties will be browned and crispy when done. Let cool 5 minutes before serving.

Per Serving
calories: 100 | fat: 2g | protein: 21g
carbs: 1g | net carbs: 1g | fiber: 0g

Cilantro Lime Baked Salmon

Prep time: 10 minutes | Cook time: 12 minutes | Serves 2

2 (3-ounce / 85-g) salmon fillets, skin removed	minced garlic
	¼ cup sliced pickled jalapeños
1 tablespoon salted butter, melted	½ medium lime, juiced
1 teaspoon chili powder	2 tablespoons chopped cilantro
½ teaspoon finely	

1. Place salmon fillets into a round baking pan. Brush each with butter and sprinkle with chili powder and garlic.
2. Place jalapeño slices on top and around salmon. Pour half of the lime juice over the salmon and cover with foil. Place pan into the air fryer basket.
3. Adjust the temperature to 370ºF (188ºC) and bake for 12 minutes.
4. When fully cooked, salmon should flake easily with a fork and reach an internal temperature of at least 145ºF (63ºC).
5. To serve, spritz with remaining lime juice and garnish with cilantro.

Per Serving
calories: 167 | fat: 10g | protein: 16g
carbs: 2g | net carbs: 1g | fiber: 1g

Ahi Tuna Steaks

Prep time: 5 minutes | Cook time: 14 minutes | Serves 2

2 (6-ounce / 170-g) ahi tuna steaks	3 tablespoons everything bagel seasoning
2 tablespoons olive oil	

1. Drizzle both sides of each steak with olive oil. Place seasoning on a medium plate and press each side of tuna steaks into seasoning to form a thick layer.
2. Place steaks into ungreased air fryer basket. Adjust the temperature to 400ºF (204ºC) and air fry for 14 minutes, turning steaks halfway through cooking. Steaks will be done when internal temperature is at least 145ºF (63ºC) for well-done. Serve warm.

Per Serving
calories: 385 | fat: 14g | protein: 0g
carbs: 0g | net carbs: 0g | fiber: 0g

Shrimp Kebabs

Prep time: 10 minutes | Cook time: 7 minutes | Serves 2

18 medium shelled and deveined shrimp
1 medium zucchini, cut into 1-inch cubes
½ medium red bell pepper, cut into 1-inch-thick squares
¼ medium red onion, cut into 1-inch-thick

squares
1½ tablespoons coconut oil, melted
2 teaspoons chili powder
½ teaspoon paprika
¼ teaspoon ground black pepper

1. Soak four (6-inch) bamboo skewers in water for 30 minutes. Place a shrimp on the skewer, then a zucchini, a pepper, and an onion. Repeat until all ingredients are utilized.
2. Brush each kebab with coconut oil. Sprinkle with chili powder, paprika, and black pepper. Place kebabs into the air fryer basket.
3. Adjust the temperature to 400ºF (204ºC) and air fry for 7 minutes or until shrimp is fully cooked and veggies are tender.
4. Flip kebabs halfway through the cooking time. Serve warm.

Per Serving
calories: 166 | fat: 11g | protein: 9g
carbs: 8g | net carbs: 5g | fiber: 3g

Bacon-Wrapped Scallops

Prep time: 5 minutes | Cook time: 10 minutes | Serves 4

8 (1-ounce / 28-g) sea scallops, cleaned and patted dry
8 slices sugar-free

bacon
¼ teaspoon salt
¼ teaspoon ground black pepper

1. Wrap each scallop in 1 slice bacon and secure with a toothpick. Sprinkle with salt and pepper.
2. Place scallops into ungreased air fryer basket. Adjust the temperature to 360ºF (182ºC) and air fry for 10 minutes. Scallops will be opaque and firm, and have an internal temperature of 135ºF (57ºC) when done. Serve warm.

Per Serving
calories: 125 | fat: 6g | protein: 14g
carbs: 2g | net carbs: 2g | fiber: 0g

Italian Baked Cod

Prep time: 5 minutes | Cook time: 12 minutes | Serves 4

4 (6-ounce / 170-g) cod fillets
2 tablespoons salted butter, melted
1 teaspoon Italian

seasoning
¼ teaspoon salt
½ cup low-carb marinara sauce

1. Place cod into an ungreased round nonstick baking dish. Pour butter over cod and sprinkle with Italian seasoning and salt. Top with marinara.
2. Place dish into air fryer basket. Adjust the temperature to 350ºF (177ºC) and bake for 12 minutes. Fillets will be lightly browned, easily flake, and have an internal temperature of at least 145ºF (63ºC) when done. Serve warm.

Per Serving
calories: 193 | fat: 8g | protein: 27g
carbs: 3g | net carbs: 1g | fiber: 1g

Crab-Stuffed Avocado Boats

Prep time: 5 minutes | Cook time: 7 minutes | Serves 4

2 medium avocados, halved and pitted
8 ounces (227 g) cooked crab meat
¼ teaspoon Old Bay seasoning

2 tablespoons peeled and diced yellow onion
2 tablespoons mayonnaise

1. Scoop out avocado flesh in each avocado half, leaving ½ inch around edges to form a shell. Chop scooped-out avocado.
2. In a medium bowl, combine crab meat, Old Bay seasoning, onion, mayonnaise, and chopped avocado. Place ¼ mixture into each avocado shell.
3. Place avocado boats into ungreased air fryer basket. Adjust the temperature to 350ºF (177ºC) and air fry for 7 minutes. Avocado will be browned on the top and mixture will be bubbling when done. Serve warm.

Per Serving
calories: 209 | fat: 15g | protein: 12g
carbs: 6g | net carbs: 1g | fiber: 2g

Rainbow Salmon Kebabs

Prep time: 10 minutes | Cook time: 8 minutes | Serves 2

6 ounces (170 g) boneless, skinless salmon, cut into 1-inch cubes
¼ medium red onion, peeled and cut into 1-inch pieces
½ medium yellow bell pepper, seeded and
cut into 1-inch pieces
½ medium zucchini, trimmed and cut into ½-inch slices
1 tablespoon olive oil
½ teaspoon salt
¼ teaspoon ground black pepper

1. Using one (6-inch) skewer, skewer 1 piece salmon, then 1 piece onion, 1 piece bell pepper, and finally 1 piece zucchini. Repeat this pattern with additional skewers to make four kebabs total. Drizzle with olive oil and sprinkle with salt and black pepper.
2. Place kebabs into ungreased air fryer basket. Adjust the temperature to 400°F (204°C) and air fry for 8 minutes, turning kebabs halfway through cooking. Salmon will easily flake and have an internal temperature of at least 145°F (63°C) when done; vegetables will be tender. Serve warm.

Per Serving
calories: 183 | fat: 9g | protein: 17g
carbs: 6g | net carbs: 5g | fiber: 1g

Breaded Shrimp Tacos

Prep time: 10 minutes | Cook time: 9 minutes | Makes 8 tacos

2 large eggs
1 teaspoon prepared yellow mustard
1 pound (454 g) small shrimp, peeled, deveined, and tails
removed
½ cup finely shredded Gouda or Parmesan cheese
½ cup pork dust

For Serving:
8 large Boston lettuce leaves
¼ cup pico de gallo
¼ cup shredded
purple cabbage
1 lemon, sliced
Guacamole (optional)

1. Preheat the air fryer to 400°F (204°C).
2. Crack the eggs into a large bowl, add the mustard, and whisk until well combined. Add the shrimp and stir well to coat.
3. In a medium-sized bowl, mix together the cheese and pork dust until well combined.
4. One at a time, roll the coated shrimp in the pork dust mixture and use your hands to press it onto each shrimp. Spray the coated shrimp with avocado oil and place them in the air fryer basket, leaving space between them.
5. Air fry the shrimp for 9 minutes, or until cooked through and no longer translucent, flipping after 4 minutes.
6. To serve, place a lettuce leaf on a serving plate, place several shrimp on top, and top with 1½ teaspoons each of pico de gallo and purple cabbage. Squeeze some lemon juice on top and serve with guacamole, if desired.
7. Store leftover shrimp in an airtight container in the refrigerator for up to 3 days. Reheat in a preheated 400°F (204°C) air fryer for 5 minutes, or until warmed through.

Per Serving
calories: 194 | fat: 8g | protein: 28g
carbs: 3g | net carbs: 2g | fiber: 1g

Chili Lime Shrimp

Prep time: 5 minutes | Cook time: 5 minutes | Serves 4

1 pound (454 g) medium shrimp, peeled and deveined
1 tablespoon salted butter, melted
2 teaspoons chili powder
¼ teaspoon garlic powder
¼ teaspoon salt
¼ teaspoon ground black pepper
½ small lime, zested and juiced, divided

1. In a medium bowl, toss shrimp with butter, then sprinkle with chili powder, garlic powder, salt, pepper, and lime zest.
2. Place shrimp into ungreased air fryer basket. Adjust the temperature to 400°F (204°C) and air fry for 5 minutes. Shrimp will be firm and form a "C" shape when done.
3. Transfer shrimp to a large serving dish and drizzle with lime juice. Serve warm.

Per Serving
calories: 98 | fat: 4g | protein: 13g
carbs: 2g | net carbs: 1g | fiber: 1g

BBQ Shrimp with Creole Butter Sauce

Prep time: 10 minutes | Cook time: 12 to 15 minutes | Serves 4

6 tablespoons unsalted butter	1 teaspoon Creole seasoning
⅓ cup Worcestershire sauce	1½ pounds (680 g) large uncooked shrimp, peeled and deveined
3 cloves garlic, minced	
Juice of 1 lemon	2 tablespoons fresh parsley
1 teaspoon paprika	

1. Preheat the air fryer to 370ºF (188ºC).
2. In a large microwave-safe bowl, combine the butter, Worcestershire, and garlic. Microwave on high for 1 to 2 minutes until the butter is melted. Stir in the lemon juice, paprika, and Creole seasoning. Add the shrimp and toss until thoroughly coated.
3. Transfer the mixture to a casserole dish or pan that fits in your air fryer. Pausing halfway through the cooking time to turn the shrimp, air fry for 12 to 15 minutes, until the shrimp are cooked through. Top with the parsley just before serving.

Per Serving
calories: 300 | fat: 19g | protein: 24g
carbs: 8g | net carbs: 8g | fiber: 0g

Spanish Shrimp Kebabs

Prep time: 10 minutes | Cook time: 12 to 15 minutes | Serves 4

1½ pounds (680 g) large shrimp, peeled and deveined	paprika
	¾ teaspoon salt
1 large bell pepper, seeded and chopped into 1-inch pieces	3 cloves garlic, minced
	8 ounces (227 g) smoked chorizo, sliced into ½-inch rounds
2 tablespoons olive oil	
1 teaspoon smoked	

1. Preheat the air fryer to 400ºF (204ºC).
2. In a large bowl, combine the shrimp, bell pepper, olive oil, paprika, salt, and garlic. Toss gently until thoroughly coated.
3. Thread the shrimp, peppers, and sausage onto the skewers, alternating ingredients as you go.

4. Working in batches if necessary and pausing halfway through the cooking time to turn the skewers, air fry the skewers for 12 to 15 minutes, until the peppers are tender and the shrimp are cooked through.

Per Serving
calories: 450 | fat: 30g | protein: 38g
carbs: 6g | net carbs: 5g | fiber: 1g

Tuna Patties with Spicy Sriracha Sauce

Prep time: 10 minutes | Cook time: 10 minutes | Serves 4

2 (6-ounce / 170-g) cans tuna packed in oil, drained	mayonnaise
	1 teaspoon dried dill
3 tablespoons almond flour	½ teaspoon onion powder
2 tablespoons	Pinch of salt and pepper

Spicy Sriracha Sauce:

¼ cup mayonnaise	1 teaspoon garlic powder
1 tablespoon Sriracha sauce	

1. Preheat the air fryer to 380ºF (193ºC). Line the basket with parchment paper.
2. In a large bowl, combine the tuna, almond flour, mayonnaise, dill, and onion powder. Season to taste with salt and freshly ground black pepper. Use a fork to stir, mashing with the back of the fork as necessary, until thoroughly combined.
3. Use an ice cream scoop to form the tuna mixture patties. Place the patties in a single layer on the parchment paper in the air fryer basket. Press lightly with the bottom of the scoop to flatten into a circle about ½ inch thick. Pausing halfway through the cooking time to turn the patties, air fry for 10 minutes until lightly browned.
4. To make the Sriracha sauce: In a small bowl, combine the mayonnaise, Sriracha, and garlic powder. Serve the tuna patties topped with the Sriracha sauce.

Per Serving
calories: 390 | fat: 29g | protein: 29g
carbs: 2g | net carbs: 1g | fiber: 1g

Cucumber and Salmon Salad

Prep time: 10 minutes | Cook time: 8 to 10 minutes | Serves 2

1 pound (454 g) salmon fillet
1½ tablespoons olive oil, divided
1 tablespoon sherry vinegar
1 tablespoon capers, rinsed and drained
1 seedless cucumber, thinly sliced
¼ Vidalia onion, thinly sliced
2 tablespoons chopped fresh parsley
Salt and freshly ground black pepper, to taste

1. Preheat the air fryer to 400ºF (204ºC).
2. Lightly coat the salmon with ½ tablespoon of the olive oil. Place skin-side down in the air fryer basket and air fry for 8 to 10 minutes until the fish is opaque and flakes easily with a fork. Transfer the salmon to a plate and let cool to room temperature. Remove the skin and carefully flake the fish into bite-size chunks.
3. In a small bowl, whisk the remaining 1 tablespoon olive oil and the vinegar until thoroughly combined. Add the flaked fish, capers, cucumber, onion, and parsley. Season to taste with salt and freshly ground black pepper. Toss gently to coat. Serve immediately or cover and refrigerate for up to 4 hours.

Per Serving
calories: 440 | fat: 28g | protein: 39g
carbs: 7g | net carbs: 6g | fiber: 1g

Tuna Steaks with Olive Tapenade

Prep time: 10 minutes | Cook time: 10 minutes | Serves 4

4 (6-ounce / 170-g) ahi tuna steaks
1 tablespoon olive oil
Salt and freshly
Olive Tapenade:
½ cup pitted kalamata olives
1 tablespoon olive oil
1 tablespoon chopped fresh parsley
ground black pepper, to taste
½ lemon, sliced into 4 wedges

1 clove garlic
2 teaspoons red wine vinegar
1 teaspoon capers, drained

1. Preheat the air fryer to 400ºF (204ºC).
2. Drizzle the tuna steaks with the olive oil and sprinkle with salt and black pepper. Arrange the tuna steaks in a single layer in the air fryer basket. Pausing to turn the steaks halfway through the cooking time, air fry for 10 minutes until the fish is firm.
3. To make the tapenade: In a food processor fitted with a metal blade, combine the olives, olive oil, parsley, garlic, vinegar, and capers. Pulse until the mixture is finely chopped, pausing to scrape down the sides of the bowl if necessary. Spoon the tapenade over the top of the tuna steaks and serve with lemon wedges.

Per Serving
calories: 275 | fat: 14g | protein: 36g
carbs: 2g | net carbs: 1g | fiber: 1g

Scallops in Lemon-Butter Sauce

Prep time: 10 minutes | Cook time: 6 minutes | Serves 2

8 large dry sea scallops (about ¾ pound / 340 g)
Salt and freshly ground black pepper, to taste
2 tablespoons olive oil
2 tablespoons unsalted butter, melted
2 tablespoons chopped flat-leaf parsley
1 tablespoon fresh lemon juice
2 teaspoons capers, drained and chopped
1 teaspoon grated lemon zest
1 clove garlic, minced

1. Preheat the air fryer to 400ºF (204ºC).
2. Use a paper towel to pat the scallops dry. Sprinkle lightly with salt and pepper. Brush with the olive oil. Arrange the scallops in a single layer in the air fryer basket. Pausing halfway through the cooking time to turn the scallops, air fry for about 6 minutes until firm and opaque.
3. Meanwhile, in a small bowl, combine the oil, butter, parsley, lemon juice, capers, lemon zest, and garlic. Drizzle over the scallops just before serving.

Per Serving
calories: 170 | fat: 13g | protein: 11g
carbs: 4g | net carbs: 3g | fiber: 0g

Friday Night Fish Fry

Prep time: 10 minutes | Cook time: 10 minutes | Serves 4

1 large egg
½ cup powdered Parmesan cheese (about 1½ ounces / 43 g)
1 teaspoon smoked paprika
¼ teaspoon celery salt
¼ teaspoon ground black pepper
4 (4-ounce / 113-g) cod fillets
Chopped fresh oregano or parsley, for garnish (optional)
Lemon slices, for serving (optional)

1. Spray the air fryer basket with avocado oil. Preheat the air fryer to 400ºF (204ºC).
2. Crack the egg in a shallow bowl and beat it lightly with a fork. Combine the Parmesan cheese, paprika, celery salt, and pepper in a separate shallow bowl.
3. One at a time, dip the fillets into the egg, then dredge them in the Parmesan mixture. Using your hands, press the Parmesan onto the fillets to form a nice crust. As you finish, place the fish in the air fryer basket.
4. Air fry the fish in the air fryer for 10 minutes, or until it is cooked through and flakes easily with a fork. Garnish with fresh oregano or parsley and serve with lemon slices, if desired.
5. Store leftovers in an airtight container in the refrigerator for up to 3 days. Reheat in a preheated 400ºF (204ºC) air fryer for 5 minutes, or until warmed through.

Per Serving
calories: 164 | fat: 5g | protein: 26g
carbs: 1g | net carbs: 1g | fiber: 0g

Fish Fillets with Lemon-Dill Sauce

Prep time: 5 minutes | Cook time: 7 minutes | Serves 4

1 pound (454 g) snapper, grouper, or salmon fillets
Sea salt and freshly ground black pepper, to taste
1 tablespoon avocado oil
¼ cup sour cream
¼ cup sugar-free mayonnaise
2 tablespoons fresh dill, chopped, plus more for garnish
1 tablespoon freshly squeezed lemon juice
½ teaspoon grated lemon zest

1. Pat the fish dry with paper towels and season well with salt and pepper. Brush with the avocado oil.
2. Set the air fryer to 400ºF (204ºC). Place the fillets in the air fryer basket and air fry for 1 minute.
3. Lower the air fryer temperature to 325ºF (163ºC) and continue cooking for 5 minutes. Flip the fish and cook for 1 minute more or until an instant-read thermometer reads 145ºF (63ºC). (If using salmon, cook it to 125ºF / 52ºC for medium-rare.)
4. While the fish is cooking, make the sauce by combining the sour cream, mayonnaise, dill, lemon juice, and lemon zest in a medium bowl. Season with salt and pepper and stir until combined. Refrigerate until ready to serve.
5. Serve the fish with the sauce, garnished with the remaining dill.

Per Serving
calories: 304 | fat: 19g | protein: 30g
carbs: 2g | net carbs: 2g | fiber: 0g

Fish Taco Bowl

Prep time: 10 minutes | Cook time: 12 minutes | Serves 4

½ teaspoon salt
¼ teaspoon garlic powder
¼ teaspoon ground cumin
4 (4-ounce / 113-g) cod fillets
4 cups finely shredded green cabbage
⅓ cup mayonnaise
¼ teaspoon ground black pepper
¼ cup chopped pickled jalapeños

1. Sprinkle salt, garlic powder, and cumin over cod and place into ungreased air fryer basket. Adjust the temperature to 350ºF (177ºC) and air fry for 12 minutes, turning fillets halfway through cooking. Cod will flake easily and have an internal temperature of at least 145ºF (63ºC) when done.
2. In a large bowl, toss cabbage with mayonnaise, pepper, and jalapeños until fully coated. Serve cod warm over cabbage slaw on four medium plates.

Per Serving
calories: 221 | fat: 13g | protein: 18g
carbs: 4g | net carbs: 2g | fiber: 2g

Southern-Style Catfish

Prep time: 10 minutes | Cook time: 12 minutes | Serves 4

4 (7-ounce / 198-g) catfish fillets
⅓ cup heavy whipping cream
1 tablespoon lemon juice
1 cup blanched finely

ground almond flour
2 teaspoons Old Bay seasoning
½ teaspoon salt
¼ teaspoon ground black pepper

1. Place catfish fillets into a large bowl with cream and pour in lemon juice. Stir to coat.
2. In a separate large bowl, mix flour and Old Bay seasoning.
3. Remove each fillet and gently shake off excess cream. Sprinkle with salt and pepper. Press each fillet gently into flour mixture on both sides to coat.
4. Place fillets into ungreased air fryer basket. Adjust the temperature to 400°F (204°C) and air fry for 12 minutes, turning fillets halfway through cooking. Catfish will be golden brown and have an internal temperature of at least 145°F (63°C) when done. Serve warm.

Per Serving
calories: 284 | fat: 14g | protein: 32g
carbs: 1g | net carbs: 0g | fiber: 1g

Pecan-Crusted Catfish

Prep time: 5 minutes | Cook time: 12 minutes | Serves 4

½ cup pecan meal
1 teaspoon fine sea salt
¼ teaspoon ground
For Garnish (Optional):
Fresh oregano

black pepper
4 (4-ounce / 113-g) catfish fillets

Pecan halves

1. Spray the air fryer basket with avocado oil. Preheat the air fryer to 375°F (191°C).
2. In a large bowl, mix the pecan meal, salt, and pepper. One at a time, dredge the catfish fillets in the mixture, coating them well. Use your hands to press the pecan meal into the fillets. Spray the fish with avocado oil and place them in the air fryer basket.

3. Air fry the coated catfish for 12 minutes, or until it flakes easily and is no longer translucent in the center, flipping halfway through.
4. Garnish with oregano sprigs and pecan halves, if desired.
5. Store leftovers in an airtight container in the fridge for up to 3 days. Reheat in a preheated 350°F (177°C) air fryer for 4 minutes, or until heated through.

Per Serving
calories: 162 | fat: 11g | protein: 17g
carbs: 1g | net carbs: 0g | fiber: 1g

Sweet and Spicy Salmon

Prep time: 5 minutes | Cook time: 10 to 12 minutes | Serves 4

½ cup sugar-free mayonnaise
2 tablespoons Swerve
2 teaspoons Dijon mustard
1 canned chipotle chile in adobo sauce, diced

1 teaspoon adobo sauce (from the canned chipotle)
16 ounces (454 g) salmon fillets
Salt and freshly ground black pepper, to taste

1. In a small food processor, combine the mayonnaise, Swerve, Dijon mustard, chipotle pepper, and adobo sauce. Process for 1 minute until everything is combined and the Swerve is no longer granular.
2. Season the salmon with salt and pepper. Spread half of the sauce over the fish, and reserve the remainder of the sauce for serving.
3. Set the air fryer to 400°F (204°C). Place the salmon in the air fryer basket. Air fry for 5 minutes. Flip the salmon and cook for 5 to 7 minutes more, until an instant-read thermometer reads 125°F (52°C) (for medium-rare).
4. Serve warm with the remaining sauce.

Per Serving
calories: 326 | fat: 25g | protein: 23g
carbs: 1g | net carbs: 1g | fiber: 0g

Marinated Swordfish Skewers

Prep time: 10 minutes | Cook time: 6 to 8 minutes | Serves 4

1 pound (454 g) filleted swordfish	2 teaspoons Dijon mustard
¼ cup avocado oil	Sea salt and freshly ground black pepper, to taste
2 tablespoons freshly squeezed lemon juice	
1 tablespoon minced fresh parsley	3 ounces (85 g) cherry tomatoes

1. Cut the fish into 1½-inch chunks, picking out any remaining bones.
2. In a large bowl, whisk together the oil, lemon juice, parsley, and Dijon mustard. Season to taste with salt and pepper. Add the fish and toss to coat the pieces. Cover and marinate the fish chunks in the refrigerator for 30 minutes.
3. Remove the fish from the marinade. Thread the fish and cherry tomatoes on 4 skewers, alternating as you go.
4. Set the air fryer to 400ºF (204ºC). Place the skewers in the air fryer basket and air fry for 3 minutes. Flip the skewers and cook for 3 to 5 minutes longer, until the fish is cooked through and an instant-read thermometer reads 140ºF (60ºC).

Per Serving
calories: 315 | fat: 20g | protein: 29g
carbs: 2g | net carbs: 2g | fiber: 0g

Salmon Patties

Prep time: 5 minutes | Cook time: 8 minutes | Serves 4

12 ounces (340 g) pouched pink salmon	flour
3 tablespoons mayonnaise	½ teaspoon Cajun seasoning
⅓ cup blanched finely ground almond	1 medium avocado, peeled, pitted, and sliced

1. In a medium bowl, mix salmon, mayonnaise, flour, and Cajun seasoning. Form mixture into four patties.
2. Place patties into ungreased air fryer basket. Adjust the temperature to 400ºF (204ºC) and air fry for 8 minutes, turning patties halfway through cooking. Patties will be done when firm and golden brown.

3. Transfer patties to four medium plates and serve warm with avocado slices.

Per Serving
calories: 263 | fat: 18g | protein: 20g
carbs: 5g | net carbs: 2g | fiber: 3g

Tuna Melt Croquettes

Prep time: 10 minutes | Cook time: 8 minutes per batch | Makes 1 dozen croquettes

2 (5-ounce / 142-g) cans tuna, drained	2 teaspoons prepared yellow mustard
1 (8-ounce / 227-g) package cream cheese, softened	1 large egg
½ cup finely shredded Cheddar cheese	1½ cups pork dust or powdered Parmesan cheese
2 tablespoons diced onions	Fresh dill, for garnish (optional)

For Serving (Optional):

Cherry tomatoes	Yellow mustard
Mayonnaise	

1. Preheat the air fryer to 400ºF (204ºC).
2. Make the patties: In a large bowl, stir together the tuna, cream cheese, Cheddar cheese, onions, mustard, and egg until well combined.
3. Place the pork dust in a shallow bowl.
4. Form the tuna mixture into twelve 1½-inch balls. Roll the balls in the pork dust and use your hands to press it into a thick crust around each ball. Flatten the balls into ½-inch-thick patties.
5. Working in batches to avoid overcrowding, place the patties in the air fryer basket, leaving space between them. Air fry for 8 minutes, or until golden brown and crispy, flipping halfway through.
6. Garnish the croquettes with fresh dill, if desired, and serve with cherry tomatoes and dollops of mayo and mustard on the side.
7. Store leftovers in an airtight container in the refrigerator for up to 4 days. Reheat in a preheated 400ºF (204ºC) air fryer for about 3 minutes, until heated through.

Per Serving
calories: 528 | fat: 36g | protein: 48g
carbs: 2g | net carbs: 2g | fiber: 0g

Asian Marinated Salmon

Prep time: 5 minutes | Cook time: 6 minutes | Serves 2

Marinade:

¼ cup wheat-free tamari or coconut aminos
2 tablespoons lime or lemon juice
2 tablespoons sesame oil
2 tablespoons Swerve confectioners'-style sweetener, or a few drops liquid stevia

2 teaspoons grated fresh ginger
2 cloves garlic, minced
½ teaspoon ground black pepper
2 (4-ounce / 113-g) salmon fillets (about 1¼ inches thick)
Sliced green onions, for garnish

Sauce (Optional):

¼ cup beef broth
¼ cup wheat-free tamari
3 tablespoons Swerve confectioners'-style sweetener or equivalent amount of liquid or powdered sweetener

1 tablespoon tomato sauce
1 teaspoon stevia glycerite (optional)
⅛ teaspoon guar gum or xanthan gum (optional, for thickening)

1. Make the marinade: In a medium-sized shallow dish, stir together all the ingredients for the marinade until well combined. Place the salmon in the marinade. Cover and refrigerate for at least 2 hours or overnight.
2. Preheat the air fryer to 400ºF (204ºC).
3. Remove the salmon fillets from the marinade and place them in the air fryer, leaving space between them. Air fry for 6 minutes, or until the salmon is cooked through and flakes easily with a fork.
4. While the salmon cooks, make the sauce, if using: Place all the sauce ingredients except the guar gum in a medium-sized bowl and stir until well combined. Taste and adjust the sweetness to your liking. While whisking slowly, add the guar gum. Allow the sauce to thicken for 3 to 5 minutes. (The sauce can be made up to 3 days ahead and stored in an airtight container in the fridge.) Drizzle the sauce over the salmon before serving.
5. Garnish the salmon with sliced green onions before serving. Store leftovers in an airtight container in the fridge for up to 3 days. Reheat in a preheated 350ºF (177ºC) air fryer for 3 minutes, or until heated through.

Per Serving
calories: 311 | fat: 18g | protein: 31g
carbs: 9g | net carbs: 8g | fiber: 1g

Parmesan Lobster Tails

Prep time: 5 minutes | Cook time: 7 minutes | Serves 4

4 (4-ounce / 113-g) lobster tails
2 tablespoons salted butter, melted
1½ teaspoons Cajun seasoning, divided
¼ teaspoon salt

¼ teaspoon ground black pepper
¼ cup grated Parmesan cheese
½ ounce (14 g) plain pork rinds, finely crushed

1. Cut lobster tails open carefully with a pair of scissors and gently pull meat away from shells, resting meat on top of shells.
2. Brush lobster meat with butter and sprinkle with 1 teaspoon Cajun seasoning, ¼ teaspoon per tail.
3. In a small bowl, mix remaining Cajun seasoning, salt, pepper, Parmesan, and pork rinds. Gently press ¼ mixture onto meat on each lobster tail.
4. Carefully place tails into ungreased air fryer basket. Adjust the temperature to 400ºF (204ºC) and air fry for 7 minutes. Lobster tails will be crispy and golden on top and have an internal temperature of at least 145ºF (63ºC) when done. Serve warm.

Per Serving
calories: 184 | fat: 9g | protein: 23g
carbs: 1g | net carbs: 1g | fiber: 0g

Mouthwatering Cod over Creamy Leek Noodles

Prep time: 10 minutes | Cook time: 24 minutes | Serves 4

1 small leek, sliced into long thin noodles (about 2 cups)
½ cup heavy cream
2 cloves garlic, minced
1 teaspoon fine sea

salt, divided
4 (4-ounce / 113-g) cod fillets (about 1 inch thick)
½ teaspoon ground black pepper

Coating:

¼ cup grated Parmesan cheese
2 tablespoons mayonnaise
2 tablespoons unsalted butter,

softened
1 tablespoon chopped fresh thyme, or ½ teaspoon dried thyme leaves, plus more for garnish

1. Preheat the air fryer to 350°F (177°C).
2. Place the leek noodles in a casserole dish or a pan that will fit in your air fryer.
3. In a small bowl, stir together the cream, garlic, and ½ teaspoon of the salt. Pour the mixture over the leeks and cook in the air fryer for 10 minutes, or until the leeks are very tender.
4. Pat the fish dry and season with the remaining ½ teaspoon of salt and the pepper. When the leeks are ready, open the air fryer and place the fish fillets on top of the leeks. Air fry for 8 to 10 minutes, until the fish flakes easily with a fork (the thicker the fillets, the longer this will take).
5. While the fish cooks, make the coating: In a small bowl, combine the Parmesan, mayo, butter, and thyme.
6. When the fish is ready, remove it from the air fryer and increase the heat to 425°F (218°C) (or as high as your air fryer can go). Spread the fillets with a ½-inch-thick to ¾-inch-thick layer of the coating.
7. Place the fish back in the air fryer and air fry for 3 to 4 minutes, until the coating browns.

8. Garnish with fresh or dried thyme, if desired. Store leftovers in an airtight container in the refrigerator for up to 3 days. Reheat in a casserole dish in a preheated 350°F (177°C) air fryer for 6 minutes, or until heated through.

Per Serving

calories: 345 | fat: 25g | protein: 25g
carbs: 3g | net carbs: 2g | fiber: 1g

Tuna-Stuffed Tomatoes

Prep time: 5 minutes | Cook time: 5 minutes | Serves 2

2 medium beefsteak tomatoes, tops removed, seeded, membranes removed
2 (2.6-ounce / 74-g) pouches tuna packed in water, drained
1 medium stalk celery, trimmed and chopped

2 tablespoons mayonnaise
¼ teaspoon salt
¼ teaspoon ground black pepper
2 teaspoons coconut oil
¼ cup shredded mild Cheddar cheese

1. Scoop pulp out of each tomato, leaving ½-inch shell.
2. In a medium bowl, mix tuna, celery, mayonnaise, salt, and pepper. Drizzle with coconut oil. Spoon ½ mixture into each tomato and top each with 2 tablespoons Cheddar.
3. Place tomatoes into ungreased air fryer basket. Adjust the temperature to 320°F (160°C) and air fry for 5 minutes. Cheese will be melted when done. Serve warm.

Per Serving

calories: 219 | fat: 15g | protein: 18g
carbs: 4g | net carbs: 3g | fiber: 1g

Stuffed Flounder Florentine

Prep time: 10 minutes | Cook time: 25 minutes | Serves 4

¼ cup pine nuts
2 tablespoons olive oil
½ cup chopped tomatoes
1 (6-ounce / 170-g) bag spinach, coarsely chopped
2 cloves garlic, chopped
Salt and freshly ground black pepper,
to taste
2 tablespoons unsalted butter, divided
4 flounder fillets (about 1½ pounds / 680 g)
Dash of paprika
½ lemon, sliced into 4 wedges

1. Place the pine nuts in a 6-cup baking dish that fits in your air fryer. Set the air fryer to 400°F (204°C) and air fry for 4 minutes until the nuts are lightly browned and fragrant. Remove the baking dish from the air fryer, tip the nuts onto a plate to cool, and continue preheating the air fryer. When the nuts are cool enough to handle, chop them into fine pieces.
2. In the 6-cup baking dish, combine the oil, tomatoes, spinach, and garlic. Use tongs to toss until thoroughly combined. Air fry for 5 minutes until the tomatoes are softened and the spinach is wilted.
3. Transfer the vegetables to a bowl and stir in the toasted pine nuts. Season to taste with salt and freshly ground black pepper.
4. Place 1 tablespoon of the butter in the bottom of the baking dish. Lower the heat on the air fryer to 350°F (177°C).
5. Place the flounder on a clean work surface. Sprinkle both sides with salt and black pepper. Divide the vegetable mixture among the flounder fillets and carefully roll up, securing with toothpicks.
6. Working in batches if necessary, arrange the fillets seam-side down in the baking dish along with 1 tablespoon of water. Top the fillets with remaining 1 tablespoon butter and sprinkle with a dash of paprika. Cover loosely with foil and air fry for 10 to 15 minutes until the fish is opaque and flakes easily with a fork. Remove the toothpicks before serving with the lemon wedges.

Per Serving
calories: 390 | fat: 29g | protein: 29g
carbs: 4g | net carbs: 3g | fiber: 1g

Shrimp Caesar Salad

Prep time: 10 minutes | Cook time: 4 to 6 minutes | Serves 4

12 ounces (340 g) fresh large shrimp, peeled and deveined
1 tablespoon plus 1 teaspoon freshly squeezed lemon juice, divided
4 tablespoons olive oil or avocado oil, divided
2 garlic cloves, minced, divided
¼ teaspoon sea salt, plus additional to season the marinade
¼ teaspoon freshly ground black pepper, plus additional to season the marinade
⅓ cup sugar-free mayonnaise
2 tablespoons freshly grated Parmesan cheese
1 teaspoon Dijon mustard
1 tinned anchovy, mashed
12 ounces (340 g) romaine hearts, torn

1. Place the shrimp in a large bowl. Add 1 tablespoon of lemon juice, 1 tablespoon of olive oil, and 1 minced garlic clove. Season with salt and pepper. Toss well and refrigerate for 15 minutes.
2. While the shrimp marinates, make the dressing: In a blender, combine the mayonnaise, Parmesan cheese, Dijon mustard, the remaining 1 teaspoon of lemon juice, the anchovy, the remaining minced garlic clove, ¼ teaspoon of salt, and ¼ teaspoon of pepper. Process until smooth. With the blender running, slowly stream in the remaining 3 tablespoons of oil. Transfer the mixture to a jar; seal and refrigerate until ready to serve.
3. Remove the shrimp from its marinade and place it in the air fryer basket in a single layer. Set the air fryer to 400°F (204°C) and air fry for 2 minutes. Flip the shrimp and cook for 2 to 4 minutes more, until the flesh turns opaque.
4. Place the romaine in a large bowl and toss with the desired amount of dressing. Top with the shrimp and serve immediately.

Per Serving
calories: 329 | fat: 30g | protein: 16g
carbs: 4g | net carbs: 2g | fiber: 2g

Coconut Shrimp with Spicy Dipping Sauce

Prep time: 15 minutes | Cook time: 8 minutes | Serves 4

1 (2½-ounce / 71-g) bag pork rinds	powder
	2 eggs
¾ cup unsweetened shredded coconut flakes	1½ pounds (680 g) large shrimp, peeled and deveined
¾ cup coconut flour	½ teaspoon salt
1 teaspoon onion powder	¼ teaspoon freshly ground black pepper
1 teaspoon garlic	

Spicy Dipping Sauce:

½ cup mayonnaise	Zest and juice of ½ lime
2 tablespoons Sriracha	1 clove garlic, minced

1. Preheat the air fryer to 390ºF (199ºC).
2. In a food processor fitted with a metal blade, combine the pork rinds and coconut flakes. Pulse until the mixture resembles coarse crumbs. Transfer to a shallow bowl.
3. In another shallow bowl, combine the coconut flour, onion powder, and garlic powder; mix until thoroughly combined.
4. In a third shallow bowl, whisk the eggs until slightly frothy.
5. In a large bowl, season the shrimp with the salt and pepper, tossing gently to coat.
6. Working a few pieces at a time, dredge the shrimp in the flour mixture, followed by the eggs, and finishing with the pork rind crumb mixture. Arrange the shrimp on a baking sheet until ready to air fry.
7. Working in batches if necessary, arrange the shrimp in a single layer in the air fryer basket. Pausing halfway through the cooking time to turn the shrimp, air fry for 8 minutes until cooked through.
8. To make the sauce: In a small bowl, combine the mayonnaise, Sriracha, lime zest and juice, and garlic. Whisk until thoroughly combined. Serve alongside the shrimp.

Per Serving
calories: 580 | fat: 44g | protein: 39g
carbs: 8g | net carbs: 4g | fiber: 4g

Classic Fish Sticks with Tartar Sauce

Prep time: 10 minutes | Cook time: 12 to 15 minutes | Serves 4

1½ pounds (680 g) cod fillets, cut into 1-inch strips	ground black pepper
	2 eggs
1 teaspoon salt	¾ cup almond flour
½ teaspoon freshly	¼ cup grated Parmesan cheese

Tartar Sauce:

½ cup sour cream	drained and chopped
½ cup mayonnaise	½ teaspoon dried dill
3 tablespoons chopped dill pickle	1 tablespoon dill pickle liquid (optional)
2 tablespoons capers,	

1. Preheat the air fryer to 400ºF (204ºC).
2. Season the cod with the salt and black pepper; set aside.
3. In a shallow bowl, lightly beat the eggs. In a second shallow bowl, combine the almond flour and Parmesan cheese. Stir until thoroughly combined.
4. Working with a few pieces at a time, dip the fish into the egg mixture followed by the flour mixture. Press lightly to ensure an even coating.
5. Working in batches if necessary, arrange the fish in a single layer in the air fryer basket and spray lightly with olive oil. Pausing halfway through the cooking time to turn the fish, air fry for 12 to 15 minutes, until the fish flakes easily with a fork. Let sit in the basket for a few minutes before serving with the tartar sauce.
6. To make the tartar sauce: In a small bowl, combine the sour cream, mayonnaise, pickle, capers, and dill. If you prefer a thinner sauce, stir in the pickle liquid.

Per Serving
calories: 600 | fat: 42g | protein: g
carbs: 14g | net carbs: 12g | fiber: 2g

Chapter 10 Desserts

Coconut Flour Mug Cake

Prep time: 5 minutes | Cook time: 25 minutes | Serves 1

1 large egg
2 tablespoons coconut flour
2 tablespoons heavy whipping cream
2 tablespoons

granular erythritol
¼ teaspoon vanilla extract
¼ teaspoon baking powder

1. In a 4-inch ramekin, whisk egg, then add remaining ingredients. Stir until smooth. Place into the air fryer basket.
2. Adjust the temperature to 300°F (149°C) and bake for 25 minutes. When done a toothpick should come out clean. Enjoy right out of the ramekin with a spoon. Serve warm.

Per Serving
calories: 237 | fat: 16g | protein: 9g
carbs: 10g | net carbs: 5g | fiber: 5g

Crustless Peanut Butter Cheesecake

Prep time: 10 minutes | Cook time: 10 minutes | Serves 2

4 ounces (113 g) cream cheese, softened
2 tablespoons confectioners' erythritol

1 tablespoon all-natural, no-sugar-added peanut butter
½ teaspoon vanilla extract
1 large egg, whisked

1. In a medium bowl, mix cream cheese and erythritol until smooth. Add peanut butter and vanilla, mixing until smooth. Add egg and stir just until combined.
2. Spoon mixture into an ungreased springform pan and place into air fryer basket. Adjust the temperature to 300°F (149°C) and bake for 10 minutes. Edges will be firm, but center will be mostly set with only a small amount of jiggle when done.
3. Let pan cool at room temperature 30 minutes, cover with plastic wrap, then place into refrigerator at least 2 hours. Serve chilled.

Per Serving
calories: 282 | fat: 23g | protein: 9g
carbs: 13g | net carbs: 3g | fiber: 10g

Chocolate Lava Cakes

Prep time: 5 minutes | Cook time: 15 minutes | Serves 2

2 large eggs, whisked
¼ cup blanched finely ground almond flour
½ teaspoon vanilla

extract
2 ounces (57 g) low-carb chocolate chips, melted

1. In a medium bowl, mix eggs with flour and vanilla. Fold in chocolate until fully combined.
2. Pour batter into two ramekins greased with cooking spray. Place ramekins into air fryer basket. Adjust the temperature to 320°F (160°C) and bake for 15 minutes. Cakes will be set at the edges and firm in the center when done. Let cool 5 minutes before serving.

Per Serving
calories: 260 | fat: 21g | protein: 11g
carbs: 21g | net carbs: 11g | fiber: 10g

Strawberry Shortcake

Prep time: 10 minutes | Cook time: 25 minutes | Serves 6

2 tablespoons coconut oil
1 cup blanched finely ground almond flour
2 large eggs, whisked
½ cup granular erythritol
1 teaspoon baking

powder
1 teaspoon vanilla extract
2 cups sugar-free whipped cream
6 medium fresh strawberries, hulled and sliced

1. In a large bowl, combine coconut oil, flour, eggs, erythritol, baking powder, and vanilla. Pour batter into an ungreased round nonstick baking dish.
2. Place dish into air fryer basket. Adjust the temperature to 300°F (149°C) and bake for 25 minutes. When done, shortcake should be golden and a toothpick inserted in the middle will come out clean.
3. Remove dish from fryer and let cool 1 hour.
4. Once cooled, top cake with whipped cream and strawberries to serve.

Per Serving
calories: 235 | fat: 21g | protein: 6g
carbs: 5g | net carbs: 3g | fiber: 2g

Coconut Flour Cake

Prep time: 10 minutes | Cook time: 25 minutes | Serves 6

2 tablespoons salted butter, melted
1/3 cup coconut flour
2 large eggs, whisked
1/2 cup granular erythritol
1 teaspoon baking powder
1 teaspoon vanilla extract
1/2 cup sour cream

1. Mix all ingredients in a large bowl. Pour batter into an ungreased round nonstick baking dish.
2. Place baking dish into air fryer basket. Adjust the temperature to 300ºF (149ºC) and bake for 25 minutes. The cake will be dark golden on top, and a toothpick inserted in the center should come out clean when done.
3. Let cool in dish 15 minutes before slicing and serving.

Per Serving
calories: 123 | fat: 9g | protein: 4g
carbs: 5g | net carbs: 3g | fiber: 2g

Pecan Brownies

Prep time: 10 minutes | Cook time: 20 minutes | Serves 6

1/2 cup blanched finely ground almond flour
1/2 cup powdered erythritol
2 tablespoons unsweetened cocoa powder
1/2 teaspoon baking powder
1/4 cup unsalted butter, softened
1 large egg
1/4 cup chopped pecans
1/4 cup low-carb, sugar-free chocolate chips

1. In a large bowl, mix almond flour, erythritol, cocoa powder, and baking powder. Stir in butter and egg.
2. Fold in pecans and chocolate chips. Scoop mixture into a round baking pan. Place pan into the air fryer basket.
3. Adjust the temperature to 300ºF (149ºC) and bake for 20 minutes.
4. When fully cooked a toothpick inserted in center will come out clean. Allow 20 minutes to fully cool and firm up.

Per Serving
calories: 215 | fat: 19g | protein: 4g
carbs: 5g | net carbs: 3g | fiber: 2g

Mini Chocolate Chip Pan Cookie

Prep time: 10 minutes | Cook time: 7 minutes | Serves 4

1/2 cup blanched finely ground almond flour
1/4 cup powdered erythritol
2 tablespoons unsalted butter, softened
1 large egg
1/2 teaspoon
unflavored gelatin
1/2 teaspoon baking powder
1/2 teaspoon vanilla extract
2 tablespoons low-carb, sugar-free chocolate chips

1. In a large bowl, mix almond flour and erythritol. Stir in butter, egg, and gelatin until combined.
2. Stir in baking powder and vanilla and then fold in chocolate chips. Pour batter into a round baking pan. Place pan into the air fryer basket.
3. Adjust the temperature to 300ºF (149ºC) and bake for 7 minutes.
4. When fully cooked, the top will be golden brown and a toothpick inserted in center will come out clean. Let cool at least 10 minutes.

Per Serving
calories: 188 | fat: 16g | protein: 5g
carbs: 4g | net carbs: 2g | fiber: 2g

Pumpkin Spice Pecans

Prep time: 5 minutes | Cook time: 6 minutes | Serves 4

1 cup whole pecans
1/4 cup granular erythritol
1 large egg white
1/2 teaspoon ground
cinnamon
1/2 teaspoon pumpkin pie spice
1/2 teaspoon vanilla extract

1. Toss all ingredients in a large bowl until pecans are coated. Place into the air fryer basket.
2. Adjust the temperature to 300ºF (149ºC) and air fry for 6 minutes.
3. Toss two to three times during cooking.
4. Allow to cool completely. Store in an airtight container up to 3 days.

Per Serving
calories: 178 | fat: 17g | protein: 3g
carbs: 4g | net carbs: 3g | fiber: 1g

Olive Oil Cake

Prep time: 10 minutes | Cook time: 30 minutes | Serves 8

2 cups blanched finely ground almond flour
5 large eggs, whisked
¾ cup extra-virgin olive oil
⅓ cup granular erythritol
1 teaspoon vanilla extract
1 teaspoon baking powder

1. In a large bowl, mix all ingredients. Pour batter into an ungreased round nonstick baking dish.
2. Place dish into air fryer basket. Adjust the temperature to 300ºF (149ºC) and bake for 30 minutes. The cake will be golden on top and firm in the center when done.
3. Let cake cool in dish 30 minutes before slicing and serving.

Per Serving
calories: 395 | fat: 37g | protein: 10g
carbs: 13g | net carbs: 2g | fiber: 11g

Vanilla Pound Cake

Prep time: 10 minutes | Cook time: 25 minutes | Serves 6

1 cup blanched finely ground almond flour
¼ cup salted butter, melted
½ cup granular erythritol
1 teaspoon vanilla extract
1 teaspoon baking powder
½ cup full-fat sour cream
1 ounce (28 g) full-fat cream cheese, softened
2 large eggs

1. In a large bowl, mix almond flour, butter, and erythritol.
2. Add in vanilla, baking powder, sour cream, and cream cheese and mix until well combined. Add eggs and mix.
3. Pour batter into a round baking pan. Place pan into the air fryer basket.
4. Adjust the temperature to 300ºF (149ºC) and bake for 25 minutes.
5. When the cake is done, a toothpick inserted in center will come out clean. The center should not feel wet. Allow it to cool completely, or the cake will crumble when moved.

Per Serving
calories: 253 | fat: 23g | protein: 7g
carbs: 5g | net carbs: 3g | fiber: 2g

Lemon Poppy Seed Macaroons

Prep time: 10 minutes | Cook time: 14 minutes | Makes 1 dozen cookies

2 large egg whites, room temperature
⅓ cup Swerve confectioners'-style sweetener or equivalent amount of powdered sweetener
2 tablespoons grated lemon zest, plus more
Lemon Icing:
¼ cup Swerve confectioners'-style sweetener or equivalent amount of
for garnish if desired
2 teaspoons poppy seeds
1 teaspoon lemon extract
¼ teaspoon fine sea salt
2 cups unsweetened shredded coconut

powdered sweetener
1 tablespoon lemon juice

1. Preheat the air fryer to 325ºF (163ºC). Line a pie pan or a casserole dish that will fit inside your air fryer with parchment paper.
2. Place the egg whites in a medium-sized bowl and use a hand mixer on high to beat the whites until stiff peaks form. Add the sweetener, lemon zest, poppy seeds, lemon extract, and salt. Mix on low until combined. Gently fold in the coconut with a rubber spatula.
3. Use a 1-inch cookie scoop to place the cookies on the parchment, spacing them about ¼ inch apart. Place the pan in the air fryer and bake for 12 to 14 minutes, until the cookies are golden and a toothpick inserted into the center comes out clean.
4. While the cookies bake, make the lemon icing: Place the sweetener in a small bowl. Add the lemon juice and stir well. If the icing is too thin, add a little more sweetener. If the icing is too thick, add a little more lemon juice.
5. Remove the cookies from the air fryer and allow to cool for about 10 minutes, then drizzle with the icing. Garnish with lemon zest, if desired.
6. Store leftovers in an airtight container in the fridge for up to 5 days or in the freezer for up to a month.

Per Serving
calories: 71 | fat: 7g | protein: 1g
carbs: 3g | net carbs: 1g | fiber: 2g

Brownies for Two

Prep time: 5 minutes | Cook time: 15 minutes | Serves 2

½ cup blanched finely ground almond flour
3 tablespoons granular erythritol
3 tablespoons unsweetened cocoa powder

½ teaspoon baking powder
1 teaspoon vanilla extract
2 large eggs, whisked
2 tablespoons salted butter, melted

1. In a medium bowl, combine flour, erythritol, cocoa powder, and baking powder.
2. Add in vanilla, eggs, and butter, and stir until a thick batter forms.
3. Pour batter into two ramekins greased with cooking spray and place ramekins into air fryer basket. Adjust the temperature to 325ºF (163ºC) and bake for 15 minutes. Centers will be firm when done. Let ramekins cool 5 minutes before serving.

Per Serving
calories: 367 | fat: 32g | protein: 14g
carbs: 9g | net carbs: 5g | fiber: 4g

Pecan Clusters

Prep time: 10 minutes | Cook time: 8 minutes | Serves 8

3 ounces (85 g) whole shelled pecans
1 tablespoon salted butter, melted
2 teaspoons confectioners'

erythritol
½ teaspoon ground cinnamon
½ cup low-carb chocolate chips

1. In a medium bowl, toss pecans with butter, then sprinkle with erythritol and cinnamon.
2. Place pecans into ungreased air fryer basket. Adjust the temperature to 350ºF (177ºC) and air fry for 8 minutes, shaking the basket two times during cooking. They will feel soft initially but get crunchy as they cool.
3. Line a large baking sheet with parchment paper.

4. Place chocolate in a medium microwave-safe bowl. Microwave on high, heating in 20-second increments and stirring until melted. Place 1 teaspoon chocolate in a rounded mound on ungreased parchment-lined baking sheet, then press 1 pecan into top, repeating with remaining chocolate and pecans.
5. Place baking sheet into refrigerator to cool at least 30 minutes. Once cooled, store clusters in a large sealed container in refrigerator up to 5 days.

Per Serving
calories: 136 | fat: 13g | protein: 2g
carbs: 11g | net carbs: 2g | fiber: 9g

Cream Cheese Shortbread Cookies

Prep time: 10 minutes | Cook time: 20 minutes | Makes 12 cookies

¼ cup coconut oil, melted
2 ounces (57 g) cream cheese, softened
½ cup granular

erythritol
1 large egg, whisked
2 cups blanched finely ground almond flour
1 teaspoon almond extract

1. Combine all ingredients in a large bowl to form a firm ball.
2. Place dough on a sheet of plastic wrap and roll into a 12-inch-long log shape. Roll log in plastic wrap and place in refrigerator 30 minutes to chill.
3. Remove log from plastic and slice into twelve equal cookies. Cut two sheets of parchment paper to fit air fryer basket. Place six cookies on each ungreased sheet. Place one sheet with cookies into air fryer basket. Adjust the temperature to 320ºF (160ºC) and bake for 10 minutes, turning cookies halfway through cooking. They will be lightly golden when done. Repeat with remaining cookies.
4. Let cool 15 minutes before serving to avoid crumbling.

Per Serving (1 cookie)
calories: 175 | fat: 16g | protein: 5g
carbs: 4g | net carbs: 2g | fiber: 2g

Lime Bars

Prep time: 10 minutes | Cook time: 33 minutes | Makes 12 bars

1½ cups blanched finely ground almond flour, divided

¾ cup confectioners' erythritol, divided

4 tablespoons salted butter, melted

½ cup fresh lime juice

2 large eggs, whisked

1. In a medium bowl, mix together 1 cup flour, ¼ cup erythritol, and butter. Press mixture into bottom of an ungreased round nonstick cake pan.
2. Place pan into air fryer basket. Adjust the temperature to 300°F (149°C) and bake for 13 minutes. Crust will be brown and set in the middle when done.
3. Allow to cool in pan 10 minutes.
4. In a medium bowl, combine remaining flour, remaining erythritol, lime juice, and eggs. Pour mixture over cooled crust and return to air fryer for 20 minutes at 300°F (149°C). Top will be browned and firm when done.
5. Let cool completely in pan, about 30 minutes, then chill covered in the refrigerator 1 hour. Serve chilled.

Per Serving
calories: 133 | fat: 12g | protein: 4g
carbs: 3g | net carbs: 2g | fiber: 1g

Almond Butter Cookie Balls

Prep time: 5 minutes | Cook time: 10 minutes | Makes 10 balls

1 cup almond butter

1 large egg

1 teaspoon vanilla extract

¼ cup low-carb protein powder

¼ cup powdered erythritol

¼ cup shredded unsweetened coconut

¼ cup low-carb, sugar-free chocolate chips

½ teaspoon ground cinnamon

1. In a large bowl, mix almond butter and egg. Add in vanilla, protein powder, and erythritol.
2. Fold in coconut, chocolate chips, and cinnamon. Roll into 1-inch balls. Place balls into a round baking pan and put into the air fryer basket.

3. Adjust the temperature to 320°F (160°C) and bake for 10 minutes.
4. Allow to cool completely. Store in an airtight container in the refrigerator up to 4 days.

Per Serving
calories: 224 | fat: 16g | protein: 11g
carbs: 6g | net carbs: 2g | fiber: 4g

Fried Cheesecake Bites

Prep time: 5 minutes | Cook time: 2 minutes | Makes 16 bites

8 ounces (227 g) cream cheese, softened

½ cup plus 2 tablespoons Swerve, divided

4 tablespoons heavy cream, divided

½ teaspoon vanilla extract

½ cup almond flour

1. In a stand mixer fitted with a paddle attachment, beat the cream cheese, ½ cup of the Swerve, 2 tablespoons of the heavy cream, and the vanilla until smooth. Using a small ice-cream scoop, divide the mixture into 16 balls and arrange them on a rimmed baking sheet lined with parchment paper. Freeze for 45 minutes until firm.
2. Line the air fryer basket with parchment paper and preheat the air fryer to 350°F (177°C).
3. In a small shallow bowl, combine the almond flour with the remaining 2 tablespoons Swerve.
4. In another small shallow bowl, place the remaining 2 tablespoons cream.
5. One at a time, dip the frozen cheesecake balls into the cream and then roll in the almond flour mixture, pressing lightly to form an even coating. Arrange the balls in a single layer in the air fryer basket, leaving room between them. Air fry for 2 minutes until the coating is lightly browned.

Per Serving (4 balls)
calories: 330 | fat: 30g | protein: 8g
carbs: 8g | net carbs: 7g | fiber: 1g

Cream Cheese Danish

Prep time: 20 minutes | Cook time: 15 minutes | Serves 6

¾ cup blanched finely ground almond flour
1 cup shredded Mozzarella cheese
5 ounces (142 g) full-fat cream cheese,
divided
2 large egg yolks
¾ cup powdered erythritol, divided
2 teaspoons vanilla extract, divided

1. In a large microwave-safe bowl, add almond flour, Mozzarella, and 1 ounce (28 g) cream cheese. Mix and then microwave for 1 minute.
2. Stir and add egg yolks to the bowl. Continue stirring until soft dough forms. Add ½ cup erythritol to dough and 1 teaspoon vanilla.
3. Cut a piece of parchment to fit your air fryer basket. Wet your hands with warm water and press out the dough into a ¼-inch-thick rectangle.
4. In a medium bowl, mix remaining cream cheese, erythritol, and vanilla. Place this cream cheese mixture on the right half of the dough rectangle. Fold over the left side of the dough and press to seal. Place into the air fryer basket.
5. Adjust the temperature to 330ºF (166ºC) and bake for 15 minutes.
6. After 7 minutes, flip over the Danish.
7. When done, remove the Danish from parchment and allow to completely cool before cutting.

Per Serving
calories: 185 | fat: 14g | protein: 7g
carbs: 3g | net carbs: 2g | fiber: 1g

Protein Powder Doughnut Holes

Prep time: 25 minutes | Cook time: 6 minutes | Makes 12 holes

½ cup blanched finely ground almond flour
½ cup low-carb vanilla protein powder
½ cup granular erythritol
½ teaspoon baking
powder
1 large egg
5 tablespoons unsalted butter, melted
½ teaspoon vanilla extract

1. Mix all ingredients in a large bowl. Place into the freezer for 20 minutes.
2. Wet your hands with water and roll the dough into twelve balls.
3. Cut a piece of parchment to fit your air fryer basket. Working in batches as necessary, place doughnut holes into the air fryer basket on top of parchment.
4. Adjust the temperature to 380ºF (193ºC) and air fry for 6 minutes.
5. Flip doughnut holes halfway through the cooking time.
6. Let cool completely before serving.

Per Serving
calories: 221 | fat: 1g | protein: 20g
carbs: 4g | net carbs: 2g | fiber: 2g

Mini Cheesecake

Prep time: 10 minutes | Cook time: 15 minutes | Serves 2

½ cup walnuts
2 tablespoons salted butter
2 tablespoons granular erythritol
4 ounces (113 g) full-fat cream cheese,
softened
1 large egg
½ teaspoon vanilla extract
⅛ cup powdered erythritol

1. Place walnuts, butter, and granular erythritol in a food processor. Pulse until ingredients stick together and a dough forms.
2. Press dough into a springform pan then place the pan into the air fryer basket.
3. Adjust the temperature to 400ºF (204ºC) and bake for 5 minutes.
4. When done, remove the crust and let cool.
5. In a medium bowl, mix cream cheese with egg, vanilla extract, and powdered erythritol until smooth.
6. Spoon mixture on top of baked walnut crust and place into the air fryer basket.
7. Adjust the temperature to 300ºF (149ºC) and bake for 10 minutes.
8. Once done, chill for 2 hours before serving.

Per Serving
calories: 531 | fat: 48g | protein: 11g
carbs: 7g | net carbs: 5g | fiber: 2g

Chocolate Mayo Cake

Prep time: 10 minutes | Cook time: 25 minutes | Serves 6

1 cup blanched finely ground almond flour
¼ cup salted butter, melted
½ cup plus 1 tablespoon granular erythritol
1 teaspoon vanilla extract
¼ cup full-fat mayonnaise
¼ cup unsweetened cocoa powder
2 large eggs

1. In a large bowl, mix all ingredients until smooth.
2. Pour batter into a round baking pan. Place into the air fryer basket.
3. Adjust the temperature to 300ºF (149ºC) and bake for 25 minutes.
4. When done, a toothpick inserted in center will come out clean. Allow cake to cool completely, or it will crumble when moved.

Per Serving
calories: 270 | fat: 25g | protein: 7g
carbs: 6g | net carbs: 3g | fiber: 3g

Pumpkin Cookie with Cream Cheese Frosting

Prep time: 10 minutes | Cook time: 7 minutes | Serves 6

½ cup blanched finely ground almond flour
½ cup powdered erythritol, divided
2 tablespoons butter, softened
1 large egg
½ teaspoon unflavored gelatin
½ teaspoon baking powder
½ teaspoon vanilla extract
½ teaspoon pumpkin pie spice
2 tablespoons pure pumpkin purée
½ teaspoon ground cinnamon, divided
¼ cup low-carb, sugar-free chocolate chips
3 ounces (85 g) full-fat cream cheese, softened

1. In a large bowl, mix almond flour and ¼ cup erythritol. Stir in butter, egg, and gelatin until combined.
2. Stir in baking powder, vanilla, pumpkin pie spice, pumpkin purée, and ¼ teaspoon cinnamon, then fold in chocolate chips.

3. Pour batter into a round baking pan. Place pan into the air fryer basket.
4. Adjust the temperature to 300ºF (149ºC) and bake for 7 minutes.
5. When fully cooked, the top will be golden brown and a toothpick inserted in center will come out clean. Let cool at least 20 minutes.
6. To make the frosting: mix cream cheese, remaining ¼ teaspoon cinnamon, and remaining ¼ cup erythritol in a large bowl. Using an electric mixer, beat until it becomes fluffy. Spread onto the cooled cookie. Garnish with additional cinnamon if desired.

Per Serving
calories: 199 | fat: 16g | protein: 5g
carbs: 5g | net carbs: 3g | fiber: 2g

Double Chocolate Brownies

Prep time: 5 minutes | Cook time: 15 to 20 minutes | Serves 8

1 cup almond flour
½ cup unsweetened cocoa powder
½ teaspoon baking powder
¹/₃ cup Swerve
¼ teaspoon salt
½ cup unsalted
butter, melted and cooled
3 eggs
1 teaspoon vanilla extract
2 tablespoons mini semisweet chocolate chips

1. Preheat the air fryer to 350ºF (177ºC). Line a cake pan with parchment paper and brush with oil.
2. In a large bowl, combine the almond flour, cocoa powder, baking powder, Swerve, and salt. Add the butter, eggs, and vanilla. Stir until thoroughly combined. (The batter will be thick.) Spread the batter into the prepared pan and scatter the chocolate chips on top.
3. Air fry for 15 to 20 minutes until the edges are set. (The center should still appear slightly undercooked.) Let cool completely before slicing. To store, cover and refrigerate the brownies for up to 3 days.

Per Serving
calories: 230 | fat: 20g | protein: 8g
carbs: 10g | net carbs: 7g | fiber: 3g

Flourless Cream-Filled Mini Cakes

Prep time: 10 minutes | Cook time: 10 minutes | Makes 8 cakes

Cake:
½ cup (1 stick) unsalted butter (or coconut oil for dairy-free)

4 ounces (113 g) unsweetened chocolate, chopped

¾ cup Swerve confectioners'-style sweetener or equivalent amount of powdered sweetener

3 large eggs

Filling:
1 (8-ounce / 227-g) package cream cheese (or Kite Hill brand cream cheese style spread for dairy-free), softened

¼ cup Swerve confectioners'-style sweetener or equivalent amount of powdered or liquid sweetener

For Garnish (Optional):
Whipped cream

Raspberries

1. Preheat the air fryer to 375ºF (191ºC). Grease eight (4-ounce / 113-g) ramekins.
2. Make the cake batter: Heat the butter and chocolate in a saucepan over low heat, stirring often, until the chocolate is completely melted. Remove from the heat.
3. Add the sweetener and eggs and use a hand mixer on low to combine well. Set aside.
4. Make the cream filling: In a medium-sized bowl, mix together the cream cheese and sweetener until well combined. Taste and add more sweetener if desired.
5. Divide the chocolate mixture among the greased ramekins, filling each one halfway. Place 1 tablespoon of the filling on top of the chocolate mixture in each ramekin.
6. Place the ramekins in the air fryer and bake for 10 minutes, or until the outside is set and the inside is soft and warm. Allow to cool completely, then top with whipped cream, if desired, and garnish with raspberries, if desired.
7. Store without whipped cream in an airtight container in the refrigerator for up to 4 days or in the freezer for up to a month. Serve leftovers chilled or reheat in a preheated 350ºF (177ºC) air fryer for 5 minutes, or until heated through.

Per Serving
calories: 330 | fat: 30g | protein: 6g
carbs: 5g | net carbs: 3g | fiber: 2g

Chocolate Chip-Pecan Biscotti

Prep time: 15 minutes | Cook time: 20 to 22 minutes | Serves 10

1¼ cups finely ground blanched almond flour

¾ teaspoon baking powder

½ teaspoon xanthan gum

¼ teaspoon sea salt

3 tablespoons unsalted butter, at room temperature

⅓ cup Swerve

1 large egg, beaten

1 teaspoon pure vanilla extract

⅓ cup chopped pecans

¼ cup stevia-sweetened chocolate chips, such as Lily's Sweets brand

Melted stevia-sweetened chocolate chips and chopped pecans, for topping (optional)

1. In a large bowl, combine the almond flour, baking powder, xanthan gum, and salt.
2. Line a cake pan that fits inside your air fryer with parchment paper.
3. In the bowl of a stand mixer, beat together the butter and Swerve. Add the beaten egg and vanilla, and beat for about 3 minutes.
4. Add the almond flour mixture to the butter-and-egg mixture; beat until just combined.
5. Stir in the pecans and chocolate chips.
6. Transfer the dough to the prepared pan, and press it into the bottom.
7. Set the air fryer to 325ºF (163ºC) and bake for 12 minutes. Remove from the air fryer and let cool for 15 minutes. Using a sharp knife, cut the cookie into thin strips, then return the strips to the cake pan with the bottom sides facing up.
8. Set the air fryer to 300ºF (149ºC). Bake for 8 to 10 minutes.
9. Remove from the air fryer and let cool completely on a wire rack. If desired, dip one side of each biscotti piece into melted chocolate chips, and top with chopped pecans.

Per Serving
calories: 148 | fat: 14g | protein: 4g
carbs: 11g | net carbs: 9g | fiber: 2g

Mini Peanut Butter Tarts

Prep time: 25 minutes | Cook time: 12 to 15 minutes | Serves 8

1 cup pecans
1 cup finely ground blanched almond flour
2 tablespoons unsalted butter, at room temperature
½ cup plus 2 tablespoons Swerve, divided
½ cup heavy (whipping) cream
2 tablespoons mascarpone cheese
4 ounces (113 g) cream cheese
½ cup sugar-free peanut butter
1 teaspoon pure vanilla extract
⅛ teaspoon sea salt
½ cup stevia-sweetened chocolate chips
1 tablespoon coconut oil
¼ cup chopped peanuts or pecans

1. Place the pecans in the bowl of a food processor; process until they are finely ground.
2. Transfer the ground pecans to a medium bowl and stir in the almond flour. Add the butter and 2 tablespoons of Swerve, and stir until the mixture becomes wet and crumbly.
3. Divide the mixture among 8 silicone muffin cups, pressing the crust firmly with your fingers into the bottom and part way up the sides of each cup.
4. Arrange the muffin cups in the air fryer basket, working in batches if necessary. Set the air fryer to 300ºF (149ºC) and bake for 12 to 15 minutes, until the crusts begin to brown. Remove the cups from the air fryer and set them aside to cool.
5. In the bowl of a stand mixer, combine the heavy cream and mascarpone cheese. Beat until peaks form. Transfer to a large bowl.
6. In the same stand mixer bowl, combine the cream cheese, peanut butter, remaining ½ cup of Swerve, vanilla, and salt. Beat at medium-high speed until smooth.
7. Reduce the speed to low and add the heavy cream mixture back a spoonful at a time, beating after each addition.
8. Spoon the peanut butter mixture over the crusts, and freeze the tarts for 30 minutes.
9. Place the chocolate chips and coconut oil in the top of a double boiler over high heat. Stir until melted, then remove from the heat.
10. Drizzle the melted chocolate over the peanut butter tarts. Top with the chopped nuts and freeze the tarts for another 15 minutes, until set.
11. Store the peanut butter tarts in an airtight container in the refrigerator for up to 1 week or in the freezer for up to 1 month.

Per Serving
calories: 491 | fat: 46g | protein: 11g
carbs: 15g | net carbs: 8g | fiber: 7g

Luscious Coconut Pie

Prep time: 5 minutes | Cook time: 45 minutes | Serves 6

1 cup plus ¼ cup unsweetened shredded coconut, divided
2 eggs
1½ cups almond milk
½ cup granulated Swerve
½ cup coconut flour
¼ cup unsalted butter, melted
1½ teaspoons vanilla extract
¼ teaspoon salt
2 tablespoons powdered Swerve (optional)
½ cup sugar-free whipped topping (optional)

1. Spread ¼ cup of the coconut in the bottom of a pie plate and place in the air fryer basket. Set the air fryer to 350ºF (177ºC) and air fry the coconut while the air fryer preheats, about 5 minutes, until golden brown. Transfer the coconut to a small bowl and set aside for garnish. Brush the pie plate with oil and set aside.
2. In a large bowl, combine the remaining 1 cup shredded coconut, eggs, milk, granulated Swerve, coconut flour, butter, vanilla, and salt. Whisk until smooth. Pour the batter into the prepared pie plate and air fry for 40 to 45 minutes, or until a toothpick inserted into the center of the pie comes out clean. (Check halfway through the baking time and rotate the pan, if necessary, for even baking.)
3. Remove the pie from the air fryer and place on a baking rack to cool completely. Garnish with the reserved toasted coconut and the powdered Swerve or sugar-free whipped topping, if desired. Cover and refrigerate leftover pie for up to 3 days.

Per Serving
calories: 220 | fat: 3g | protein: 5g
carbs: 7g | net carbs: 4g | fiber: 3g

Cinnamon Cupcakes with Cream Cheese Frosting

Prep time: 10 minutes | Cook time: 20 to 25 minutes | Serves 6

½ cup plus 2 tablespoons almond flour
2 tablespoons low-carb vanilla protein powder
⅛ teaspoon salt
1 teaspoon baking powder
¼ teaspoon ground cinnamon
¼ cup unsalted butter
¼ cup Swerve
2 eggs
½ teaspoon vanilla extract

2 tablespoons heavy cream
Cream Cheese Frosting:
4 ounces (113 g) cream cheese, softened
2 tablespoons unsalted butter, softened
½ teaspoon vanilla extract
2 tablespoons powdered Swerve
1 to 2 tablespoons heavy cream

1. Preheat the air fryer to 320ºF (160ºC). Lightly coat 6 silicone muffin cups with oil and set aside.
2. In a medium bowl, combine the almond flour, protein powder, salt, baking powder, and cinnamon; set aside.
3. In a stand mixer fitted with a paddle attachment, beat the butter and Swerve until creamy. Add the eggs, vanilla, and heavy cream, and beat again until thoroughly combined. Add half the flour mixture at a time to the butter mixture, mixing after each addition, until you have a smooth, creamy batter.
4. Divide the batter evenly among the muffin cups, filling each one about three-fourths full. Arrange the muffin cups in the air fryer and air fry for 20 to 25 minutes, or until a toothpick inserted into the center of a cupcake comes out clean. Transfer the cupcakes to a rack and let cool completely.
5. To make the cream cheese frosting: In a stand mixer fitted with a paddle attachment, beat the cream cheese, butter, and vanilla until fluffy. Add the Swerve and mix again until thoroughly combined. With the mixer running, add the heavy cream a tablespoon at a time until the frosting is smooth and creamy. Frost the cupcakes as desired.

Per Serving
calories: 280 | fat: 25g | protein: 8g
carbs: 6g | net carbs: 5g | fiber: 1g

Chocolate Meringue Cookies

Prep time: 10 minutes | Cook time: 1 hour | Makes 16 cookies

3 large egg whites
¼ teaspoon cream of tartar
¼ cup Swerve confectioners'-style sweetener or

equivalent amount of powdered sweetener
2 tablespoons unsweetened cocoa powder

1. Preheat the air fryer to 225ºF (107ºC). Line a pie pan or a dish that will fit in your air fryer with parchment paper.
2. In a small bowl, use a hand mixer to beat the egg whites and cream of tartar until soft peaks form. With the mixer on low, slowly sprinkle in the sweetener and mix until it's completely incorporated. Continue to beat with the mixer until stiff peaks form.
3. Add the cocoa powder and gently fold until it's completely incorporated.
4. Spoon the mixture into a piping bag with a ¾-inch tip. (If you don't have a piping bag, snip the corner of a large resealable plastic bag to form a ¾-inch hole.) Pipe sixteen 1-inch meringue cookies onto the lined pie pan, spacing them about ¼ inch apart.
5. Place the pan in the air fryer and bake for 1 hour, until the cookies are crispy on the outside, then turn off the air fryer and let the cookies stand in the air fryer for another 20 minutes before removing and serving.

Per Serving
calories: 12 | fat: 0g | protein: 2g
carbs: 1g | net carbs: 1g | fiber: 0g

Lemon Curd Pavlova

Prep time: 10 minutes | Cook time: 1 hour | Serves 4

Shell:
3 large egg whites
¼ teaspoon cream of tartar
¾ cup Swerve confectioners'-style sweetener

or equivalent amount of powdered sweetener
1 teaspoon grated lemon zest
1 teaspoon lemon extract

Lemon Curd:
1 cup Swerve confectioners'-style sweetener
or equivalent amount of liquid or powdered
sweetener

½ cup lemon juice
4 large eggs
½ cup coconut oil

For Garnish (Optional):
Blueberries
Swerve confectioners'-style sweetener or equivalent amount of powdered sweetener

1. Preheat the air fryer to 275ºF (135ºC). Thoroughly grease a pie pan with butter or coconut oil.
2. Make the shell: In a small bowl, use a hand mixer to beat the egg whites and cream of tartar until soft peaks form. With the mixer on low, slowly sprinkle in the sweetener and mix until it's completely incorporated.
3. Add the lemon zest and lemon extract and continue to beat with the hand mixer until stiff peaks form.
4. Spoon the mixture into the greased pie pan, then smooth it across the bottom, up the sides, and onto the rim to form a shell. Bake for 1 hour, then turn off the air fryer and let the shell stand in the air fryer for 20 minutes. (The shell can be made up to 3 days ahead and stored in an airtight container in the refrigerator, if desired.)
5. While the shell bakes, make the lemon curd: In a medium-sized heavy-bottomed saucepan, whisk together the sweetener, lemon juice, and eggs. Add the coconut oil and place the pan on the stovetop over medium heat. Once the oil is melted, whisk constantly until the mixture thickens and thickly coats the back of a spoon, about 10 minutes. Do not allow the mixture to come to a boil.
6. Pour the lemon curd mixture through a fine-mesh strainer into a medium-sized bowl. Place the bowl inside a larger bowl filled with ice water and whisk occasionally until the curd is completely cool, about 15 minutes.
7. Place the lemon curd on top of the shell and garnish with blueberries and powdered sweetener, if desired. Store leftovers in the refrigerator for up to 4 days.

Per Serving
calories: 332 | fat: 33g | protein: 9g | carbs: 4g | net carbs: 3g | fiber: 1g

Halle Berries-and-Cream Cobbler

Prep time: 10 minutes | Cook time: 25 minutes | Serves 4

12 ounces (340 g) cream cheese (1½ cups), softened
1 large egg
¾ cup Swerve confectioners'-style sweetener

or equivalent amount of powdered sweetener
½ teaspoon vanilla extract
¼ teaspoon fine sea salt
1 cup sliced fresh raspberries or strawberries

Biscuits:
3 large egg whites
¾ cup blanched almond flour
1 teaspoon baking powder

2½ tablespoons very cold unsalted butter, cut into pieces
¼ teaspoon fine sea salt

Frosting:
2 ounces (57 g) cream cheese (¼ cup), softened
1 tablespoon Swerve confectioners'-style sweetener or equivalent amount of powdered

or liquid sweetener
1 tablespoon unsweetened, unflavored almond milk or heavy cream
Fresh raspberries or strawberries, for garnish

1. Preheat the air fryer to 400°F (204°C). Grease a pie pan.
2. In a large mixing bowl, use a hand mixer to combine the cream cheese, egg, and sweetener until smooth. Stir in the vanilla and salt. Gently fold in the raspberries with a rubber spatula. Pour the mixture into the prepared pan and set aside.
3. Make the biscuits: Place the egg whites in a medium-sized mixing bowl or the bowl of a stand mixer. Using a hand mixer or stand mixer, whip the egg whites until very fluffy and stiff.
4. In a separate medium-sized bowl, combine the almond flour and baking powder. Cut in the butter and add the salt, stirring gently to keep the butter pieces intact.
5. Gently fold the almond flour mixture into the egg whites. Use a large spoon or ice cream scooper to scoop out the dough and form it into a 2-inch-wide biscuit, making sure the butter stays in separate clumps. Place the biscuit on top of the raspberry mixture in the pan. Repeat with remaining dough to make 4 biscuits.
6. Place the pan in the air fryer and bake for 5 minutes, then lower the temperature to 325°F (163°C) and bake for another 17 to 20 minutes, until the biscuits are golden brown.
7. While the cobbler cooks, make the frosting: Place the cream cheese in a small bowl and stir to break it up. Add the sweetener and stir. Add the almond milk and stir until well combined. If you prefer a thinner frosting, add more almond milk.
8. Remove the cobbler from the air fryer and allow to cool slightly, then drizzle with the frosting. Garnish with fresh raspberries.
9. Store leftovers in an airtight container in the refrigerator for up to 3 days. Reheat the cobbler in a preheated 350°F (177°C) air fryer for 3 minutes, or until warmed through.

Per Serving
calories: 583 | fat: 51g | protein: 16g | carbs: 10g | net carbs: 7g | fiber: 3g

Chapter 11 Staples

Almond Glaze

Prep time: 5 minutes | Cook time: 0 minutes | Serves 8

½ cup Swerve
½ tablespoon unsalted butter, at room temperature
2 to 3 tablespoons heavy (whipping)

cream
¼ teaspoon almond extract
¼ teaspoon pure vanilla extract

1. Combine the Swerve, butter, 2 tablespoons of heavy cream, almond extract, and vanilla extract in a large bowl. Whisk until creamy, adding additional heavy cream as needed to achieve your preferred consistency.
2. Drizzle over cinnamon rolls, blueberry muffins, or cookies.

Per Serving
calories: 20 | fat: 2g | protein: 0g
carbs: 12g | net carbs: 12g | fiber: 0g

Avocado-Herb Compound Butter

Prep time: 25 minutes | Cook time: 0 minutes | Makes 2 cups

¼ cup butter, at room temperature
1 avocado, peeled, pitted, and cut into quarters
Juice of ½ lemon
2 teaspoons chopped cilantro

1 teaspoon chopped fresh basil
1 teaspoon minced garlic
Sea salt and freshly ground black pepper, to taste

1. Place the butter, avocado, lemon juice, cilantro, basil, and garlic in a food processor and process until smooth.
2. Season the butter with salt and pepper.
3. Transfer the mixture to a sheet of parchment paper and shape it into a log.
4. Place the parchment butter log in the refrigerator until it is firm, about 4 hours.
5. Serve slices of this butter with fish or chicken.
6. Store unused butter wrapped tightly in the freezer for up to 1 week.

Per Serving (1 tablespoon)
calories: 22 | fat: 2g | protein: 0g
carbs: 1g | net carbs: 1g | fiber: 0g

Creamy Sausage Gravy

Prep time: 10 minutes | Cook time: 13 minutes | Serves 8

1 tablespoon unsalted butter
12 ounces (340 g) breakfast sausage, casings removed
⅓ cup chopped onion
1 cup chicken broth
1 cup heavy (whipping) cream
8 ounces (227 g)

cream cheese, cut into cubes
¼ teaspoon xanthan gum
1½ teaspoons garlic powder
½ teaspoon sea salt
½ teaspoon freshly ground black pepper

1. Melt the butter in a large saucepan over medium-high heat. Add the sausage and cook, using a spoon to break up the meat, for about 6 minutes or until the sausage is no longer pink. Add the onion and cook for 2 minutes. Stir in the broth, heavy cream, cream cheese, and xanthan gum.
2. Bring the mixture to a simmer, whisking constantly. Reduce the heat to medium-low and cook until the mixture thickens, about 5 minutes.
3. Stir in the garlic powder, salt, and pepper; serve hot.

Per Serving
calories: 331 | fat: 32g | protein: 8g
carbs: 5g | net carbs: 5g | fiber: 0g

Air Fryer "Hard-Boiled" Eggs

Prep time: 2 minutes | Cook time: 18 minutes | Serves 4

4 large eggs   1 cup water

1. Place eggs into a 4-cup round baking-safe dish and pour water over eggs. Place dish into the air fryer basket.
2. Adjust the temperature to 300°F (149°C) and air fry for 18 minutes.
3. Store cooked eggs in the refrigerator until ready to use or peel and eat warm.

Per Serving
calories: 77 | fat: 4g | protein: 6g
carbs: 1g | net carbs: 1g | fiber: 0g

Green Basil Dressing

Prep time: 10 minutes | Cook time: 0 minutes | Makes 1 cup

1 avocado, peeled and pitted
¼ cup sour cream
¼ cup extra-virgin olive oil
¼ cup chopped fresh basil
1 tablespoon freshly squeezed lime juice
1 teaspoon minced garlic
Sea salt and freshly ground black pepper, to taste

1. Place the avocado, sour cream, olive oil, basil, lime juice, and garlic in a food processor and pulse until smooth, scraping down the sides of the bowl once during processing.
2. Season the dressing with salt and pepper.
3. Keep the dressing in an airtight container in the refrigerator for 1 to 2 weeks.

Per Serving (1 tablespoon)
calories: 173 | fat: 17g | protein: 5g
carbs: 1g | net carbs: 1g | fiber: 0g

Blue Cheese Dressing

Prep time: 5 minutes | Cook time: 0 minutes | Serves 12

¾ cup sugar-free mayonnaise
¼ cup sour cream
½ cup heavy (whipping) cream
1 teaspoon minced garlic
1 tablespoon freshly
squeezed lemon juice
1 tablespoon apple cider vinegar
1 teaspoon hot sauce
½ teaspoon sea salt
4 ounces (113 g) blue cheese, crumbled (about ¾ cup)

1. In a medium bowl, whisk together the mayonnaise, sour cream, and heavy cream.
2. Stir in the garlic, lemon juice, apple cider vinegar, hot sauce, and sea salt.
3. Add the blue cheese crumbles, and stir until well combined.
4. Transfer to an airtight container, and refrigerate for up to 1 week.

Per Serving
calories: 171 | fat: 18g | protein: 2g
carbs: 1g | net carbs: 1g | fiber: 0g

Creamy Mayonnaise

Prep time: 10 minutes | Cook time: 0 minutes | Makes 4 cups

2 large eggs
2 tablespoons Dijon mustard
1½ cups extra-virgin olive oil
¼ cup freshly squeezed lemon juice
Sea salt and freshly ground black pepper, to taste

1. Whisk the eggs and mustard together in a heavy, large bowl until very well combined, about 2 minutes.
2. Add the oil in a continuous thin stream, whisking constantly, until the mayonnaise is thick and completely emulsified.
3. Add the lemon juice and whisk until well blended.
4. Season with salt and pepper.

Per Serving (2 tablespoons)
calories: 61 | fat: 7g | protein: 0g
carbs: 0g | net carbs: 0g | fiber:0 g

Fathead Pizza Dough

Prep time: 10 minutes | Cook time: 0 minutes | Serves 8

6 ounces (170 g) low-moisture Mozzarella cheese, shredded (about 1½ cups)
2 ounces (57 g) cream cheese, diced
1 large egg
1 cup finely ground blanched almond flour
½ teaspoon sea salt
¼ teaspoon freshly ground black pepper

1. Combine the Mozzarella cheese and cream cheese in a medium saucepan over medium heat. Cook, stirring often, until the cheeses are melted.
2. Remove the pan from the heat and stir in the egg, almond flour, salt, and pepper.
3. Transfer the mixture to a sheet of parchment paper and knead the dough until it is well combined.
4. Place the dough between 2 sheets of parchment paper. Roll out the dough to your preferred thickness (or whatever thickness your recipe requires). Cook as directed to make pizza, calzones, or empanadas.

Per Serving
calories: 173 | fat: 15g | protein: 10g
carbs: 4g | net carbs: 2g | fiber: 2g

Tzatziki Sauce

Prep time: 15 minutes | Cook time: 0 minutes | Serves 6

½ cucumber, seeded and finely chopped
½ teaspoon sea salt, plus additional for seasoning
¾ cup sour cream

1 tablespoon freshly squeezed lemon juice
1 tablespoon chopped fresh dill
3 garlic cloves, minced

1. Place the cucumber in a colander set in the sink or over a bowl, and sprinkle it with salt. Let stand for 10 minutes, then transfer the cucumber to a clean dishcloth and wring it out, extracting as much liquid as you can.
2. In a medium bowl, stir together the cucumber, sour cream, lemon juice, dill, garlic, and ½ teaspoon of salt.
3. Store the sauce in an airtight container in the refrigerator for up to 4 days.

Per Serving
calories: 77 | fat: 6g | protein: 1g
carbs: 3g | net carbs: 3g | fiber: 0g

Herbed Balsamic Dressing

Prep time: 4 minutes | Cook time: 0 minutes | Makes 1 cup

1 cup extra-virgin olive oil
¼ cup balsamic vinegar
2 tablespoons chopped fresh oregano

1 teaspoon chopped fresh basil
1 teaspoon minced garlic
Sea salt and freshly ground black pepper, to taste

1. Whisk the olive oil and vinegar in a small bowl until emulsified, about 3 minutes.
2. Whisk in the oregano, basil, and garlic until well combined, about 1 minute.
3. Season the dressing with salt and pepper.
4. Transfer the dressing to an airtight container, and store it in the refrigerator for up to 1 week. Give the dressing a vigorous shake before using it.

Per Serving (1 tablespoon)
calories: 83 | fat: 9g | protein: 0g
carbs: 0g | net carbs: 0g | fiber: 0g

Elevated Tartar Sauce

Prep time: 5 minutes | Cook time: 0 minutes | Serves 8

½ cup sugar-free mayonnaise
¼ cup diced dill pickles
1 shallot, diced
2 tablespoons drained capers, rinsed and chopped
2 teaspoons Swerve

2 teaspoons dill pickle juice
1 teaspoon dried dill
½ teaspoon sea salt
½ teaspoon freshly ground black pepper
⅛ teaspoon cayenne pepper

1. In a medium bowl, mix together the mayonnaise, pickles, shallot, capers, Swerve, pickle juice, dill, salt, pepper, and cayenne pepper until thoroughly combined.
2. Cover and refrigerate until ready to serve.

Per Serving
calories: 93 | fat: 11g | protein: 0g
carbs: 2g | net carbs: 1g | fiber: 1g

Taco Seasoning

Prep time: 5 minutes | Cook time: 0 minutes | Serves 8

3 tablespoons chili powder
1½ tablespoons ground cumin
1½ tablespoons garlic powder
1 tablespoon sea salt
2 teaspoons onion powder

2 teaspoons smoked paprika
2 teaspoons dried oregano
1 teaspoon freshly ground black pepper
¼ teaspoon cayenne pepper

1. In a small bowl, combine the chili powder, cumin, garlic powder, salt, onion powder, smoked paprika, oregano, black pepper, and cayenne pepper.
2. Transfer to a small, airtight jar, seal, and store in your pantry.

Per Serving
calories: 23 | fat: 1g | protein: 1g
carbs: 4g | net carbs: 2g | fiber: 2g

Garlic Ranch Dressing

Prep time: 10 minutes | Cook time: 0 minutes | Serves 12

¼ cup heavy (whipping) cream
1 teaspoon apple cider vinegar
½ cup sugar-free mayonnaise
½ cup sour cream
1 tablespoon minced garlic
1 teaspoon dried

oregano
1 teaspoon onion powder
1 teaspoon sea salt
½ teaspoon dried dill
½ teaspoon freshly ground black pepper
Additional heavy cream or bone broth, for thinning

1. Whisk together the heavy cream and apple cider vinegar in a medium bowl until combined. Let the mixture rest for 10 minutes, then whisk in the mayonnaise, sour cream, garlic, oregano, onion powder, salt, dill, and pepper.
2. Thin the dressing to your desired consistency, using more heavy cream or bone broth (it will no longer be vegetarian if you use bone broth).
3. Transfer to an airtight container, and refrigerate for up to 1 week.

Per Serving
calories: 103 | fat: 11g | protein: 1g
carbs: 2g | net carbs: 2g | fiber: 0g

Traditional Caesar Dressing

Prep time: 10 minutes | Cook time: 5 minutes | Makes 1½ cups

2 teaspoons minced garlic
4 large egg yolks
¼ cup wine vinegar
½ teaspoon dry mustard
Dash Worcestershire sauce

1 cup extra-virgin olive oil
¼ cup freshly squeezed lemon juice
Sea salt and freshly ground black pepper, to taste

1. To a small saucepan, add the garlic, egg yolks, vinegar, mustard, and Worcestershire sauce and place over low heat.
2. Whisking constantly, cook the mixture until it thickens and is a little bubbly, about 5 minutes.

3. Remove from saucepan from the heat and let it stand for about 10 minutes to cool.
4. Transfer the egg mixture to a large stainless steel bowl. Whisking constantly, add the olive oil in a thin stream.
5. Whisk in the lemon juice and season the dressing with salt and pepper.
6. Transfer the dressing to an airtight container and keep in the refrigerator for up to 3 days.

Per Serving (2 tablespoons)
calories: 180 | fat: 20g | protein: 1g
carbs: 1g | net carbs: 1g | fiber: 0g

Strawberry Butter

Prep time: 25 minutes | Cook time: 0 minutes | Makes 3 cups

2 cups shredded unsweetened coconut
1 tablespoon coconut oil
¾ cup fresh strawberries

½ tablespoon freshly squeezed lemon juice
1 teaspoon alcohol-free pure vanilla extract

1. Put the coconut in a food processor and purée it until it is buttery and smooth, about 15 minutes.
2. Add the coconut oil, strawberries, lemon juice, and vanilla to the coconut butter and process until very smooth, scraping down the sides of the bowl.
3. Pass the butter through a fine sieve to remove the strawberry seeds, using the back of a spoon to press the butter through.
4. Store the strawberry butter in an airtight container in the refrigerator for up to 2 weeks.
5. Serve chicken or fish with a spoon of this butter on top.

Per Serving (1 tablespoon)
calories: 23 | fat: 2g | protein: 0g
carbs: 1g | net carbs: 1g | fiber: 0g

Appendix 1: Measurement Conversion Chart

VOLUME EQUIVALENTS(DRY)

US STANDARD	METRIC (APPROXIMATE)
1/8 teaspoon	0.5 mL
1/4 teaspoon	1 mL
1/2 teaspoon	2 mL
3/4 teaspoon	4 mL
1 teaspoon	5 mL
1 tablespoon	15 mL
1/4 cup	59 mL
1/2 cup	118 mL
3/4 cup	177 mL
1 cup	235 mL
2 cups	475 mL
3 cups	700 mL
4 cups	1 L

VOLUME EQUIVALENTS(LIQUID)

US STANDARD	US STANDARD (OUNCES)	METRIC (APPROXIMATE)
2 tablespoons	1 fl.oz.	30 mL
1/4 cup	2 fl.oz.	60 mL
1/2 cup	4 fl.oz.	120 mL
1 cup	8 fl.oz.	240 mL
1 1/2 cup	12 fl.oz.	355 mL
2 cups or 1 pint	16 fl.oz.	475 mL
4 cups or 1 quart	32 fl.oz.	1 L
1 gallon	128 fl.oz.	4 L

TEMPERATURES EQUIVALENTS

FAHRENHEIT(F)	CELSIUS(C) (APPROXIMATE)
225 °F	107 °C
250 °F	120 °C
275 °F	135 °C
300 °F	150 °C
325 °F	160 °C
350 °F	180 °C
375 °F	190 °C
400 °F	205 °C
425 °F	220 °C
450 °F	235 °C
475 °F	245 °C
500 °F	260 °C

WEIGHT EQUIVALENTS

US STANDARD	METRIC (APPROXIMATE)
1 ounce	28 g
2 ounces	57 g
5 ounces	142 g
10 ounces	284 g
15 ounces	425 g
16 ounces (1 pound)	455 g
1.5 pounds	680 g
2 pounds	907 g

Appendix 2: Air Fryer Cooking Chart

Beef

Item	Temp (°F)	Time (mins)	Item	Temp (°F)	Time (mins)
Beef Eye Round Roast (4 lbs.)	400 °F	45 to 55	Meatballs (1-inch)	370 °F	7
Burger Patty (4 oz.)	370 °F	16 to 20	Meatballs (3-inch)	380 °F	10
Filet Mignon (8 oz.)	400 °F	18	Ribeye, bone-in (1-inch, 8 oz)	400 °F	10 to 15
Flank Steak (1.5 lbs.)	400 °F	12	Sirloin steaks (1-inch, 12 oz)	400 °F	9 to 14
Flank Steak (2 lbs.)	400 °F	20 to 28			

Chicken

Item	Temp (°F)	Time (mins)	Item	Temp (°F)	Time (mins)
Breasts, bone in (1 ¼ lb.)	370 °F	25	Legs, bone-in (1 ¾ lb.)	380 °F	30
Breasts, boneless (4 oz)	380 °F	12	Thighs, boneless (1 ½ lb.)	380 °F	18 to 20
Drumsticks (2 ½ lb.)	370 °F	20	Wings (2 lb.)	400 °F	12
Game Hen (halved 2 lb.)	390 °F	20	Whole Chicken	360 °F	75
Thighs, bone-in (2 lb.)	380 °F	22	Tenders	360 °F	8 to 10

Pork & Lamb

Item	Temp (°F)	Time (mins)	Item	Temp (°F)	Time (mins)
Bacon (regular)	400 °F	5 to 7	Pork Tenderloin	370 °F	15
Bacon (thick cut)	400 °F	6 to 10	Sausages	380 °F	15
Pork Loin (2 lb.)	360 °F	55	Lamb Loin Chops (1-inch thick)	400 °F	8 to 12
Pork Chops, bone in (1-inch, 6.5 oz)	400 °F	12	Rack of Lamb (1.5 – 2 lb.)	380 °F	22

Fish & Seafood

Item	Temp (°F)	Time (mins)	Item	Temp (°F)	Time (mins)
Calamari (8 oz)	400 °F	4	Tuna Steak	400 °F	7 to 10
Fish Fillet (1-inch, 8 oz)	400 °F	10	Scallops	400 °F	5 to 7
Salmon, fillet (6 oz)	380 °F	12	Shrimp	400 °F	5
Swordfish steak	400 °F	10			

Vegetables

INGREDIENT	AMOUNT	PREPARATION	OIL	TEMP	COOK TIME
Asparagus	2 bunches	Cut in half, trim stems	2 Tbsp	420°F	12-15 mins
Beets	1½ lbs	Peel, cut in ½-inch cubes	1Tbsp	390°F	28-30 mins
Bell peppers (for roasting)	4 peppers	Cut in quarters, remove seeds	1Tbsp	400°F	15-20 mins
Broccoli	1 large head	Cut in 1-2-inch florets	1Tbsp	400°F	15-20 mins
Brussels sprouts	1lb	Cut in half, remove stems	1Tbsp	425°F	15-20 mins
Carrots	1lb	Peel, cut in ¼-inch rounds	1 Tbsp	425°F	10-15 mins
Cauliflower	1 head	Cut in 1-2-inch florets	2 Tbsp	400°F	20-22 mins
Corn on the cob	7 ears	Whole ears, remove husks	1 Tbps	400°F	14-17 mins
Green beans	1 bag (12 oz)	Trim	1 Tbps	420°F	18-20 mins
Kale (for chips)	4 oz	Tear into pieces, remove stems	None	325°F	5-8 mins
Mushrooms	16 oz	Rinse, slice thinly	1 Tbps	390°F	25-30 mins
Potatoes, russet	1½ lbs	Cut in 1-inch wedges	1 Tbps	390°F	25-30 mins
Potatoes, russet	1lb	Hand-cut fries, soak 30 mins in cold water, then pat dry	½ -3 Tbps	400°F	25-28 mins
Potatoes, sweet	1lb	Hand-cut fries, soak 30 mins in cold water, then pat dry	1 Tbps	400°F	25-28 mins
Zucchini	1lb	Cut in eighths lengthwise, then cut in half	1 Tbps	400°F	15-20 mins

Appendix 3: Recipe Index

A

Ahi Tuna Steaks 118
Air Fryer "Hard-Boiled" Eggs 144
Air-Fried Okra 48
Almond Butter Cookie Balls 135
Almond Glaze 144
Almond-Cauliflower Gnocchi 57
Almond-Crusted Chicken 66
Asian Marinated Salmon 126
Avocado Fries 38
Avocado-Herb Compound Butter 144

B

Baby Back Ribs 88
Bacon and Cheese Quiche 11
Bacon and Cheese Stuffed Pork Chops 88
Bacon and Egg Bites 35
Bacon and Spinach Egg Muffins 13
Bacon Guacamole Burgers 108
Bacon Lovers' Stuffed Chicken 74
Bacon Wedge Salad 90
Bacon-and-Eggs Avocado 21
Bacon-Pickle Bites 36
Bacon-Wrapped Asparagus 42
Bacon-Wrapped Brie 26
Bacon-Wrapped Cabbage Bites 36
Bacon-Wrapped Jalapeño Poppers 27
Bacon-Wrapped Scallops 119
Bacon-Wrapped Vegetable Kebabs 92
Bacon, Cheese, and Avocado Melt 10
Bacon, Egg, and Cheese Roll Ups 17
Baked Jalapeño and Cheese Cauliflower Mash 49
Basic Spaghetti Squash 53
BBQ Shrimp with Creole Butter Sauce 121
Beef and Broccoli Stir-Fry 92
Beef Empanadas 109
Beefy Poppers 108
Blackened Cajun Chicken Tenders 68
Blackened Steak Nuggets 95
BLT Breakfast Wrap 24
Blue Cheese Dressing 145
Blue Cheese Steak Salad 113
Blueberry Muffins 13
Bone-in Pork Chops 94
Breaded Shrimp Tacos 120
Breakfast Calzone 22
Breakfast Cobbler 24

Breakfast Meatballs 12
Breakfast Pizza 14
Breakfast Sammies 20
Broccoli and Cheese Stuffed Chicken 72
Broccoli Crust Pizza 56
Broccoli-Cheese Fritters 60
Broccoli-Mushroom Frittata 18
Brownies for Two 134
Brussels Sprouts with Bacon 44
Brussels Sprouts with Pecans and Gorgonzola 46
Buffalo Cauliflower 41
Buffalo Cauliflower Bites with Blue Cheese 63
Buffalo Cauliflower Wings 50
Buffalo Chicken Breakfast Muffins 14
Buffalo Chicken Cheese Sticks 65
Buffalo Chicken Dip 26
Buffalo Chicken Tenders 71
Buffalo Chicken Wings 78
Buffalo Egg Cups 9
Bunless Breakfast Turkey Burgers 16
Burger Bun for One 43
Butter and Bacon Chicken 74
Buttery Green Beans 41
Buttery Mushrooms 40
Buttery Pork Chops 88

C-D

Cabbage Wedges with Caraway Butter 44
Cajun Breakfast Sausage 18
Cajun Salmon 115
Cajun-Breaded Chicken Bites 79
Cajun-Spiced Kale Chips 38
Calamari Rings 33
Caprese Eggplant Stacks 53
Cauliflower Rice Balls 50
Cauliflower Rice-Stuffed Peppers 54
Cauliflower Steak with Gremolata 56
Cheddar Soufflés 11
Cheese Crisps 37
Cheeseburger Casserole 109
Cheesy Bell Pepper Eggs 10
Cheesy Cauliflower "Hash Browns" 16
Cheesy Cauliflower Pizza Crust 60
Cheesy Loaded Broccoli 40
Chicken and Broccoli Casserole 83
Chicken Cordon Bleu Casserole 68
Chicken Enchiladas 69

Chicken Fried Steak with Cream Gravy 112
Chicken Kiev 80
Chicken Nuggets 78
Chicken Paillard 81
Chicken Parmesan 86
Chicken Patties 72
Chicken Pesto Parmigiana 82
Chicken Pesto Pizzas 77
Chicken Strips with Satay Sauce 82
Chili Lime Shrimp 120
Chipotle Aioli Wings 75
Chipotle Drumsticks 70
Chipotle Taco Pizzas 110
Chocolate Chip-Pecan Biscotti 138
Chocolate Lava Cakes 131
Chocolate Mayo Cake 137
Chocolate Meringue Cookies 140
Chorizo and Beef Burger 88
Cilantro Lime Baked Salmon 118
Cilantro Lime Chicken Thighs 70
Cinnamon Cupcakes with Cream Cheese Frosting 140
Cinnamon Rolls 18
Classic Fish Sticks with Tartar Sauce 129
Cobb Salad 75
Coconut Flour Cake 132
Coconut Flour Mug Cake 131
Coconut Shrimp 115
Coconut Shrimp with Spicy Dipping Sauce 129
Crab Cakes 116
Crab Legs 116
Crab-Stuffed Avocado Boats 119
Cream Cheese Danish 136
Cream Cheese Shortbread Cookies 134
Creamy Mayonnaise 145
Creamy Sausage Gravy 144
Crispy Cabbage Steaks 61
Crispy Eggplant Rounds 56
Crispy Fish Sticks 116
Crispy Tofu 58
Crustless Peanut Butter Cheesecake 131
Crustless Spinach Cheese Pie 54
Cucumber and Salmon Salad 122
Curry Roasted Cauliflower 47
Deconstructed Chicago Dogs 95
Denver Omelet 19
Deviled Eggs 31
Dijon Roast Cabbage 43
Dinner Rolls 45
Doro Wat Wings 28
Double Chocolate Brownies 137

Double-Dipped Mini Cinnamon Biscuits 19
Dry Rub Chicken Wings 30

E-F

Egg White Cups 11
Eggplant Lasagna 62
Eggplant Parmesan 58
Elevated Tartar Sauce 146
Everything Bagels 23
Everything Kale Chips 26
Fajita Meatball Lettuce Wraps 99
Fajita-Stuffed Chicken Breast 69
Fathead Pizza Dough 145
"Faux-Tato" Hash 43
Fish Fillets with Lemon-Dill Sauce 123
Fish Taco Bowl 123
Flatbread 42
Flourless Cream-Filled Mini Cakes 138
Foil-Packet Lobster Tail 117
Friday Night Fish Fry 123
Fried Cheesecake Bites 135
Fried Chicken Breasts 79
Fried Green Tomatoes 42
Fried Pickles 30
Fried Zucchini Salad 47

G

Garlic Cheese Bread 26
Garlic Dill Wings 65
Garlic Lemon Scallops 117
Garlic Parmesan Drumsticks 73
Garlic Parmesan-Roasted Cauliflower 41
Garlic Ranch Dressing 147
Garlic Roasted Broccoli 42
Garlic White Zucchini Rolls 63
Garlic-Marinated Flank Steak 98
Garlic-Parmesan Jícama Fries 45
Ginger Turmeric Chicken Thighs 76
Goat Cheese-Stuffed Flank Steak 98
Greek Beef Kebabs with Tzatziki 90
Greek Chicken Stir-Fry 65
Greek Stuffed Eggplant 59
Greek Stuffed Tenderloin 111
Green Basil Dressing 145
Green Bean Casserole 49
Green Eggs and Ham 17
Green Tomato Salad 47
Grilled Steaks with Horseradish Cream 103
Ground Beef Taco Rolls 107
Gyro Breakfast Patties with Tzatziki 21

H-I

Halle Berries-and-Cream Cobbler 142
Herb-Crusted Lamb Chops 111

Herbed Balsamic Dressing 146
Home-Style Rotisserie Chicken 67
Italian Baked Cod 119
Italian Baked Egg and Veggies 59
Italian Chicken Thighs 65
Italian Sausages with Peppers and Onions 104
Italian-Style Pork Chops 97

J-K

Jalapeño and Bacon Breakfast Pizza 11
Jalapeño Popper Chicken 72
Jalapeño Popper Egg Cups 10
Jalapeño Popper Hasselback Chicken 69
Jalapeño Popper Pork Chops 94
Jerk Chicken Kebabs 76
Jerk Chicken Thighs 67
Keto Quiche 22
Kielbasa and Cabbage 98
Kohlrabi Fries 50

L

Lemon Chicken 67
Lemon Curd Pavlova 141
Lemon Garlic Shrimp 115
Lemon Pepper Drumsticks 71
Lemon Poppy Seed Macaroons 133
Lemon Thyme Roasted Chicken 71
Lemon-Blueberry Muffins 15
Lemon-Dijon Boneless Chicken 80
Lemon-Garlic Mushrooms 44
Lemon-Thyme Asparagus 40
Lime Bars 135
Loaded Cauliflower Steak 52
London Broil with Herb Butter 105
Luscious Coconut Pie 139

M-N

Marinated Steak Tips with Mushrooms 92
Marinated Swordfish Skewers 125
Mediterranean Pan Pizza 52
Mediterranean Stuffed Chicken Breasts 85
Mediterranean Zucchini Boats 43
Mediterranean-Style Cod 117
Meritage Eggs 14
Mexican Shakshuka 9
Mexican-Style Shredded Beef 89
Mini Cheesecake 136
Mini Chocolate Chip Pan Cookie 132
Mini Greek Meatballs 31
Mini Peanut Butter Tarts 139
Mojito Lamb Chops 104
Mouthwatering Cod over Creamy Leek
Noodles 127
Mozzarella Sticks 33

Mozzarella-Stuffed Meatballs 28
Mustard Herb Pork Tenderloin 91
Nashville Hot Chicken 86
Nutty Granola 16

O-P

Olive Oil Cake 133
Onion Rings 29
Pancake for Two 12
Parmesan Artichokes 53
Parmesan Herb Focaccia Bread 48
Parmesan Lobster Tails 126
Parmesan-Crusted Pork Chops 89
Parmesan-Crusted Steak 113
Parmesan-Rosemary Radishes 40
Pecan Brownies 132
Pecan Clusters 134
Pecan-Crusted Catfish 124
Pecan-Crusted Chicken Tenders 74
Peppercorn-Crusted Beef Tenderloin 89
Pepperoni Chips 32
Pepperoni Rolls 31
Personal Cauliflower Pizzas 84
Pesto Spinach Flatbread 57
Pesto Vegetable Skewers 55
Pigs in a Blanket 93
Pizza Eggs 12
Pizza Rolls 34
Poblano Pepper Cheeseburgers 105
Porchetta-Style Chicken Breasts 81
Pork Meatballs 89
Pork Milanese 101
Pork Rind Fried Chicken 77
Pork Spare Ribs 94
Pork Taco Bowls 95
Pork Tenderloin with Avocado Lime Sauce 101
Portobello Eggs Benedict 20
Portobello Mini Pizzas 61
Prosciutto Pierogi 35
Prosciutto-Wrapped Guacamole Rings 34
Protein Powder Doughnut Holes 136
Pumpkin Cookie with Cream Cheese Frosting 137
Pumpkin Spice Muffins 17
Pumpkin Spice Pecans 132

Q-R

Quiche-Stuffed Peppers 54
Quick Chicken Fajitas 66
Radish Chips 45
Rainbow Salmon Kebabs 120
Ranch Roasted Almonds 28
Reuben Egg Rolls 32
Ricotta and Sausage Pizzas 97

Roast Beef with Horseradish Cream 100
Roasted Broccoli Salad 52
Roasted Garlic 41
Roasted Salsa 46
Roasted Veggie Bowl 59
Rosemary Roast Beef 96

S

Salami Roll-Ups 37
Salmon Patties 125
Salt and Vinegar Pork Belly Chips 29
Sausage and Cauliflower Arancini 102
Sausage and Cheese Balls 9
Sausage and Pork Meatballs 96
Sausage and Spinach Calzones 91
Sausage and Zucchini Lasagna 99
Sausage-Cheddar Bites 36
Sausage-Stuffed Mushrooms 37
Sausage-Stuffed Peppers 90
Savory Ranch Chicken Bites 38
Savory Sausage Cobbler 100
Scallops in Lemon-Butter Sauce 122
Scotch Eggs 93
Sesame Beef Lettuce Tacos 110
Sesame-Crusted Tuna Steak 116
Short Ribs with Chimichurri 106
Shrimp Caesar Salad 128
Shrimp Kebabs 119
Shrimp Scampi 118
Simple Buttery Cod 117
Simply Terrific Turkey Meatballs 73
Smoky Chicken Leg Quarters 77
Smoky Pork Tenderloin 91
Smoky Sausage Patties 13
Smoky Zucchini Chips 27
Snow Crab Legs 115
Southern-Style Catfish 124
Southwestern Breakfast Taco 15
Southwestern Ham Egg Cups 10
Spaghetti Squash Alfredo 61
Spaghetti Zoodles and Meatballs 112
Spanish Shrimp Kebabs 121
Spice-Rubbed Chicken Thighs 75
Spice-Rubbed Pork Loin 96
Spice-Rubbed Turkey Breast 79
Spicy Cheese-Stuffed Mushrooms 29
Spicy Roasted Bok Choy 49
Spicy Turkey Meatballs 37
Spinach and Feta Egg Bake 15
Spinach and Feta-Stuffed Chicken Breast 73
Spinach and Provolone Steak Rolls 93
Spinach and Sweet Pepper Poppers 48

Spinach Omelet 12
Spinach-Artichoke Stuffed Mushrooms 55
Steak Gyro Platter 107
Steaks with Walnut-Blue Cheese Butter 102
Strawberry Butter 147
Strawberry Shortcake 131
Stuffed Chicken Florentine 68
Stuffed Flounder Florentine 128
Stuffed Portobellos 57
Swedish Meatloaf 103
Sweet and Spicy Beef Jerky 30
Sweet and Spicy Pecans 27
Sweet and Spicy Salmon 124
Sweet Pepper Nachos 53

T

Taco Chicken 85
Taco Seasoning 146
Tandoori Chicken 78
Tenderloin with Crispy Shallots 97
Tex-Mex Chicken Roll-Ups 84
Thai Tacos with Peanut Sauce 83
Thanksgiving Turkey Breast 66
Three Cheese Dip 32
Three-Cheese Zucchini Boats 55
Tomato and Bacon Zoodles 106
Traditional Caesar Dressing 147
Tuna Cakes 118
Tuna Melt Croquettes 125
Tuna Patties with Spicy Sriracha Sauce 121
Tuna Steaks with Olive Tapenade 122
Tuna-Stuffed Tomatoes 127
Turkey Meatloaf 76
Turkey Pot Pie 70
Turkey Sausage Breakfast Pizza 23
Tzatziki Sauce 146

V-W

Vanilla Pound Cake 133
Vegetable Burgers 54
Veggie Frittata 9
White Cheddar and Mushroom Soufflés 58
Whole Roasted Lemon Cauliflower 60

Z

Zucchini Cauliflower Fritters 52
Zucchini Fritters 46
Zucchini-Ricotta Tart 62

Made in the USA
Columbia, SC
11 April 2021

35978305R00089